The Politics of Linkage

Brian Bow

The Politics of Linkage
Power, Interdependence, and Ideas
in Canada-US Relations

UBCPress · Vancouver · Toronto

20 19 18 17 16 15 14 13 12 11 10 09   5 4 3 2 1

Printed in Canada on FSC-certified ancient-forest-free paper (100% post-consumer recycled) that is processed chlorine- and acid-free.

Library and Archives Canada Cataloguing in Publication

Bow, Brian J.
    The politics of linkage : power, interdependence, and ideas in Canada-US relations / Brian Bow.

Includes bibliographical references and index.
ISBN 978-0-7748-1695-3 (bound); ISBN 978-0-7748-1696-0 (pbk.);
ISBN 978-0-7748-1697-7 (e-book)

    1. Canada – Foreign relations – United States. 2. United States – Foreign relations – Canada. 3. Canada – Foreign relations – 1945-. 4. United States – Foreign relations – 20th century. 5. United States – Foreign relations – 21st century. I. Title.

FC249.B695 2009   327.7107309'045   C2009-905201-6

Canada

UBC Press gratefully acknowledges the financial support for our publishing program of the Government of Canada through the Book Publishing Industry Development Program (BPIDP), and of the Canada Council for the Arts, and the British Columbia Arts Council.

This book has been published with the help of a grant from the Canadian Federation for the Humanities and Social Sciences, through the Aid to Scholarly Publications Programme, using funds provided by the Social Sciences and Humanities Research Council of Canada.

UBC Press
The University of British Columbia
2029 West Mall
Vancouver, BC V6T 1Z2
604-822-5959 / Fax: 604-822-6083
www.ubcpress.ca

For Jacquie, for everything, forever

Contents

Acknowledgments

This book has taken a very long time to come together, and the list of people and organizations to thank for their help and support is a fairly long one. First, many thanks to Matthew Evangelista, Jonathan Kirshner, Chris Way, and especially Peter Katzenstein, a great mentor and friend. Thanks also to all my classmates at Cornell University, particularly Jason Lyall and Kevin Strompf, for their advice and support.

My sincere thanks to all of the academic colleagues who helped out with advice and criticism related to various parts of this project, at various stages (some so long ago that they might not even remember it): David Biette, David Black, Stephen Clarkson, David Dewitt, Paul Dibb, Greg Donaghy, Charles Doran, Michael Hart, Frank Harvey, Brian Job, John Kirton, Philippe Lagassé, Patrick Lennox, John McDougall, Dan Middlemiss, Maureen Molot, Don Munton, Kim Richard Nossal, John Odell, Robert Pastor, Louis Pauly, Chris Sands, Duncan Snidal, Denis Stairs, Brian Tomlin, and Gil Winham.

My gratitude and best wishes to all of the current and former government officials in Canada and the United States who shared their time and insights with me as part of the research for this book. Special thanks to the former officials who made time for extended interviews, particularly Terry Breese, Ken Calder, Allan Gotlieb, Basil Robinson, Vladimir Toumanoff, Peter Towe, and the late Ivan Head, Simon Reisman, and Mitchell Sharp.

My thanks also to the staffs of the national archives in Ottawa and in Washington and to the various institutions that hosted me or helped in some way with practicalities during the research: the Cornell-in-Washington Program, the BMW Center for German and European Studies at Georgetown University, the School of International Service at American University, the Norman Paterson School of International Affairs at Carleton University, and the Research School of Pacific and Asian Studies at Australian National University.

I would also like to acknowledge and express my gratitude to the various agencies that have contributed to the research at various stages: the Social

Sciences and Humanities Research Council of Canada; the John F. Kennedy Presidential Library; the Mario Einaudi Center for International Studies and the Walter J. Carpenter Chair at Cornell University; and the Centre for Foreign Policy Studies at Dalhousie University.

Thanks also to Daniel Watt and Andrew Law for research assistance that contributed to later revisions and to Sean Clark for his work on the index. And thanks to all of my students over the last few years, at Cornell, at the University of British Columbia, and at Dalhousie.

My sincere appreciation to Emily Andrew, Randy Schmidt, and the staff of UBC Press. My thanks also to the two anonymous reviewers arranged by the Press. Their suggestions greatly improved the overall clarity and flow of this book.

I am grateful for the advice and support that I have had from others, but of course I accept responsibility for any errors or omissions in the result.

Last, but certainly not least, my love and profound gratitude to my wife and two daughters, for inspiration and understanding.

Abbreviations

AWPPA	Arctic Waters Pollution Prevention Act
BMD	ballistic missile defence
CUSFTA	Canada-US Free Trade Agreement
DPSA	Defence Production Sharing Agreement
EMR	Energy, Mines and Resources Canada
FIRA	Foreign Investment Review Agency
GATT	General Agreement on Tariffs and Trade
ICJ	International Court of Justice
ICSC	International Commission for Supervision and Control
IEA	International Energy Agency
IMCO	International Marine Consultative Organization
ISAF	International Security Assistance Force
ITC	International Trade Commission
MOIP	Mandatory Oil Import Program
NAC	National Archives of Canada
NAFTA	North American Free Trade Agreement
NARA	National Archives and Records Administration
NATO	North Atlantic Treaty Organization
NDP	New Democratic Party
NEP	National Energy Program
NORAD	North American Aerospace Defence Command (formerly North American Air Defence Command)
OAPEC	Organization of Arab Petroleum Exporting Countries
OECD	Organisation for Economic Co-operation and Development

OPEC	Organization of Petroleum Exporting Countries
PIP	Petroleum Incentive Program
PJBD	Permanent Joint Board on Defence
PMO	Prime Minister's Office
TEA	United States Trade Expansion Act of 1962
USSR	Union of Soviet Socialist Republics
US NORTHCOM	United States Northern Command
USTR	Office of the United States Trade Representative
WTO	World Trade Organization

The Politics of Linkage

1

The Social Foundations of the Special Relationship

Policy-makers and pundits often say that there is – or at least that there once was – a "special relationship" between Canada and the United States. There are of course a number of other countries (e.g., Britain, Australia, Israel, Japan) that have claimed to have their own special relationship with the US. But "some special relationships are [apparently] more special than others,"[1] and Canadians have traditionally believed that their relations with the US were genuinely exceptional, not only in the sense that the two countries share common interests and values but also in the sense that the US has given Canada special attention and consideration. Those who study the bilateral relationship closely know that American policy-makers do not spend a lot of time thinking about Canada, but they often do seem to treat Canada differently from other countries.

More skeptical observers have argued that the special relationship is a myth – a story about friendship that coincides with, and conceals, the stark calculations of national interest that really drive Canada-US relations. The relationship seems special because the two countries' interests happen to overlap most of the time; the real tests of the relationship are those rare occasions when national interests clearly diverge, and there the US has tended to be just as tough with Canada as with anyone else. Perhaps even tougher. Rather than a genuine friendship, the skeptics might say, the relationship between the US and Canada is like the classical Greek story of the crocodile and the trochilus ("crocodile bird"). The crocodile opens its mouth to let the little bird pick bits of food from between its teeth, and both benefit. The crocodile resists the urge to try to take a second lunch, because it knows it will need to have its teeth cleaned again tomorrow. But if the bird pecks a little too hard in a sensitive spot, then there will be a loud snap, and one less trochilus on the riverbank. This kind of symbiotic relationship is special in the sense that it is different from what we might normally expect (i.e., it doesn't look like the law of the jungle), but it is not special in the sense that there is any meaningful connection. There may be mutual restraint from day to day, but there is no real sense of mutual obligation, without which there can be no assurance of restraint in those times when it is most needed.

The overarching argument of this book is that there was a time – in the early Cold War decades – when the Canada-US relationship *was* genuinely special, in that it was governed by a distinctive diplomatic culture that shaped the way policy-makers on both sides thought about what their interests were and how bilateral disputes could be resolved. Conflicts of interest could therefore be resolved "between friends," even when the stakes were high and when personal relationships between political leaders were not particularly friendly. Since the 1970s, however, the nature of the relationship has changed; if it is still special today, it is only so in the crocodile-and-trochilus sense. There are still policy-makers on both sides of the border who are committed to a special way of doing things, but the people who think that way are no longer consistently able to direct the bilateral relationship accordingly.

The postwar diplomatic culture was a way of thinking about how the bilateral relationship ought to be "managed," which was shared within a network of high- and mid-level officials in Ottawa and Washington. For members of this transgovernmental network, "conflicts of interest ... [were] essentially 'problems' to be solved rather than ... confrontations to be won."[2] Over time, Canadian and American officials developed a set of specific – but still mostly tacit – bargaining norms, which former Canadian ambassador to Washington Allan Gotlieb once referred to as the "rules of the game" for Canada-US relations: grievances were to be raised behind closed doors, disagreements would always be resolved "on their merits," through technical arguments, and – perhaps most important of all – neither side would try to force a favourable resolution of an issue by making coercive linkages to other, unrelated issues.[3]

These rules were developed through a process of informal signalling, reinforced by normative arguments about mutual obligation, and maintained through interpersonal contacts within the transgovernmental network that they defined. There were moments where the rules were explicitly called on or openly challenged, but for the most part they existed as a set of tacit understandings. It was not until just a few years before they began to lose their grip – ironically – that the core principles of the postwar diplomatic culture were spelled out as such, in a 1965 report by former ambassadors Arnold Heeney and Livingston Merchant, titled *Principles for Partnership*.[4]

Beginning in the early 1970s, the proponents of the postwar diplomatic culture were increasingly marginalized by new actors and new decision-making procedures, especially on the American side. With the displacement of the postwar transgovernmental network and its distinctive bargaining norms, broader structural features associated with interdependence – and, later, formal institutional structures – came to the fore. The fragmentation of foreign-policy decision-making created space for various bureaucratic and societal interest groups to drive US responses to provocative Canadian policies, either by putting pressure on government to pursue linkages or by politically opposing specific linkage scenarios.

In advancing a social interpretation of Canada-US relations, I mean to directly challenge more thoroughly structural accounts of the relationship – that is, those that focus on the overall asymmetry of power and the configuration of basic interests.[5] I do not mean to argue that structural features are not important, however. In fact, the social aspect of the relationship I describe was originally enabled by, and ultimately proved dependent on, favourable structural conditions: the Cold War alliance, extensive economic interdependence, and relatively centralized domestic political institutions. Yet I will show that the pattern of Canada-US relations cannot be explained in terms of structure alone. Only by understanding the distinctive diplomatic culture that governed the relationship during this period can we account for the process and outcomes of bilateral bargaining in some crucial episodes and the broader pattern over time.

Nor, in making the argument that the Canada-US relationship has at times been governed by informal bargaining norms, do I mean to dismiss the importance of power. International relations theorists (particularly in the US) tend to ignore Canada-US relations because they are supposedly characterized by an "indifference to power," and are thus the great exception to the rule in international politics.[6] Some Canadian foreign-policy specialists, on the other hand, tend to see power everywhere in Canada-US relations, with little or no room for Canada to pursue a genuinely autonomous foreign policy.[7] The truth is somewhere in between. Power *is* in play when Canadian and American diplomats sit down at the bargaining table. But it is power exercised within certain limits, and therefore takes a different form than we might expect – a subtler and more complex form, which may be more characteristic of the relations between advanced industrial states than any simple theoretical model of international relations can convey.

The Question of Linkage

The focus in this book is on one specific element of the larger postwar diplomatic culture: the shared norm against resort to coercive issue linkages. Linkages, to be clear, are efforts to break an impasse or otherwise improve one's bargaining position on a particular issue by tying it to another, unrelated issue. Linkages can be cooperative or coercive, and they can be prospective (promises, threats) or retrospective (rewards, retaliation). Most government officials and many academic observers have argued that the virtual absence of coercive linkages is one of the most distinctive features of Canada-US relations, and for many it is the key to the special relationship.[8] Others have argued that linkages do in fact play an important role in Canada-US relations, although it is usually through the *anticipation* of American linkages and the profound self-restraint it induces in Canadian policy-makers.[9]

The question of linkage is a crucial one for Canada-US relations, and for Canadian foreign policy more generally. If the US is willing and able to use coercive linkages to force changes to Canadian policies, then Canada faces some tough choices. It can find ways to limit vulnerability by restraining or even rolling back interdependence between the two societies, which would involve severe – perhaps even catastrophic – economic costs for Canada. It can try to find ways to set limits on the exercise of American power, which apparently can be purchased only through reciprocal cessions of Canadian sovereignty, or perhaps not at all. Or it can find ways to live with profound vulnerability, which would ultimately amount to accepting strict limits on Canada's autonomy in both foreign and domestic policy.

If, on the other hand, the US is *not* willing and/or not able to make linkages in disputes with Canada, then the overall asymmetry of the relationship matters less, and the limits of what Canada can "get away with" depend on the specific bargaining context within particular issue areas. The diplomatic agenda would be that much more complex, but the scope of Canada's autonomy would be that much greater.

I make four main arguments. First, the US historically has not used direct, coercive linkages to force Canada to change its policies. American self-restraint has increased the space for Canada to pursue policies at odds with the US, and to exercise greater autonomy than the overall asymmetry of the relationship might lead us to expect. The expectation in Canada that the US might resort to linkages grew rapidly during the 1970s, however, and Canadian policy-makers have generally been much more cautious ever since, and more inclined to pursue previously unthinkable strategies (such as integration) as a way to set new limits on the exercise of American power.

Second, the reasons for American self-restraint have changed since the 1970s. In the early Cold War decades, the bilateral relationship was effectively governed by the broad diplomatic culture described here, and relevant US officials were committed to the norm against direct, coercive linkages. Their adherence to the norm was so reflexive, in fact, that American policy-makers tended not to see linkage options as options at all, even in high-stakes bilateral disputes. In the 1970s, a new cohort of policy-makers, who knew and cared little about Canada, began to make their presence felt, and the established transgovernmental network had to work hard to keep US bargaining strategies in line with the postwar diplomatic culture. The traditional foreign-policy bureaucracy's claim to "manage" the bilateral relationship broke down under pressure from a newly assertive Congress and increasingly overbearing "domestic" agencies. Canada-watchers in the State Department and other agencies continued to subscribe to the postwar diplomatic culture, but their ideas were far less influential in identifying and selecting foreign-policy priorities and diplomatic strategies.

Once the transgovernmental network had been effectively displaced, the degree to which the US would be prepared to bargain aggressively with Canada – up to and including resort to coercive linkages – depended mainly on shifting configurations of bureaucratic and societal interests within the United States. There was no sudden outbreak of coercive linkages in the 1970s, but – as I will explain below – that was mostly because of American officials' growing appreciation for the *domestic* political consequences of linkages, not because of broad adherence to a norm against them.

Third, the virtual foreclosure of these "hard" linkages as bargaining options for the US increased the importance of what we might call "soft" linkages. In what we normally think of as coercive linkage – what Wynne Plumptre once referred to as "tit for tat" retaliation[10] – the aggrieved party makes a threat, or actually lashes out, in a way that is immediate, direct, and unambiguous. But American policy-makers can also have other kinds of reactions to provocative Canadian policies, which may be less dramatic but have just as great an impact on Canadian interests. They can hold grudges against a particular Canadian government, or even against Canada more generally, and therefore refuse to expend political capital in issues that are more important to Ottawa. Whereas hard linkages generally involve an active change of policy, with actual or potential effects on the target that are readily observed and unmistakably negative, these soft linkages usually take the form of a malign passivity, and the relevant linkages between issues are often indirect and diffuse.

The Canada-US relationship requires perpetual care from bureaucratic managers and occasional attention from the political leadership, in order to prevent mobilized bureaucratic and societal interests from attacking and destabilizing the vast and complex latticework of bilateral agreements and informal trade-offs. The absence of this kind of care and attention can hurt the interests of both countries but it usually hurts Canada much more, so the US is in a position to signal its unhappiness with Canada, and even inflict harm on it, just by neglecting it.[11] At least in part because American officials have not seen hard linkages as real options vis-à-vis Canada, soft linkages have been much more important to the process and outcomes of Canada-US bargaining. Elsewhere I have offered a more general argument about how soft linkages play a role in the resolution of Canada-US disputes.[12] The primary concern of this book is hard linkages – or rather, the absence of hard linkages – and the implications for the process and outcomes of Canada-US bargaining. In exploring hard-linkage scenarios in the chapters that follow, I will also look for soft linkages and try to relate them to American officials' thinking about what bargaining strategies are available, and which are appropriate, in each of the four historical cases. Ultimately, as I will argue in the concluding chapter, the US tendency to limit itself to soft linkages has ambiguous implications for the management of the bilateral relationship and for Canadian autonomy.

Fourth, the mechanics of issue linkage in the Canada-US relationship, and their evolution over time, have important implications for the management of the bilateral agenda, and for Canadian foreign policy more generally. By understanding what was special about the special relationship during the early Cold War years, we can develop a better understanding of the choices that have been made since (e.g., the free trade agreements, defence integration/interoperability) and of some of the fundamental challenges for Canadian and American policy-makers today.

The Origins and Function of the Postwar Diplomatic Culture

The story of America's special relationship with Canada begins with the historic rapprochement between the US and Great Britain in the early and mid-nineteenth century. Before that, of course, the relationship was anything but special, with the US nervous about the prospect that Canada might be used as a staging area for Britain's anticipated attempt to reconquer the colonies, and at the same time coveting the land and resources of the north as part of broader aspirations to continental expansion ("manifest destiny").

As tensions between the US and Britain cooled in the nineteenth century, it became possible to negotiate the demilitarization of the US-Canada border, and to consider a more cooperative relationship with the new Canadian confederation.[13] An important by-product of the Anglo-American rapprochement, which supported the new view of Canada, was the popularization in the United States of a new sense of shared values and history within the family of "English-speaking" nations – "mother" England and her far-flung "daughters" (the United States, Canada, Australia, and New Zealand). Americans found their dealings with Canada easy and straightforward, and tended to see the interests of the two societies as naturally convergent. Many believed that some kind of political integration of the two societies was natural and inevitable, though perhaps not in the near future.

While relations generally improved through the late nineteenth and early twentieth centuries, the calm was broken by a number of relatively severe diplomatic confrontations, and the process and outcomes of these disputes tended to reaffirm our usual expectations about international politics, particularly where one country is much stronger than another. In the Alaska boundary dispute, in subsequent trade disputes such as those over lumber and fish, and in disputes over border issues such as the Chicago water diversion and Trail Smelter cases, the US bargained very aggressively with Canada

– often with Britain's acquiescence – and repeatedly forced Canada to back down.[14]

The nineteenth century's vague ideas about common values and shared destinies gave way in the middle of the twentieth century to a powerful sense of common purpose, which made possible a genuinely extraordinary sort of closeness between the two governments during the Second World War and the early decades of the Cold War. There had been extensive policy coordination and pooling of resources between the two countries during the First World War,[15] but this paled beside the breadth and depth of co-operation during the Second World War and the early years of the Cold War. In 1940, with the US not yet at war and Britain in serious jeopardy, Canada and the US negotiated a number of bilateral agreements that provided for very close coordination of defence and economic policies, and the US relied on Canada as a go-between with Britain. After Pearl Harbor, American commanders preferred to share the council table with Britain only, and Canadian diplomats and military officers were frozen out of allied strategic planning.[16] Yet close coordination of day-to-day preparations for war and management of the two increasingly intertwined economies quietly continued.

In fact, the two governments collaborated so extensively and so intimately on these more mundane issues during the later years of the war that it was sometimes difficult to tell where one left off and the other began.[17] The most prominent bilateral forum during the war was the Permanent Joint Board on Defence (PJBD), but more important connections were made at the working level between bureaucrats and military officers who mixed together on a day-to-day basis, to coordinate marshalling and transport of troops and war materiel, infrastructure building, and the ironing out of trade and monetary policy disputes. This collaboration was managed through a set of functional committees (e.g., Materials Coordinating, Joint Economic, Joint Agricultural), but the institutional format was less important than the approach, which emphasized personal relationships, pragmatism, and common purposes. The two governments certainly were not equal partners, but there was a strong sense on both sides that the urgency of wartime challenges and the spirit of partnership must override considerations of relative power. Even the usual state preoccupations with national sovereignty and legal precedent were relaxed, with resources pooled, laws and regulations set aside as necessary, and chains of political and military authority allowed to overlap and merge together.

Canadian officials were often frustrated that the US seemed inattentive to Canadian advice and concerns, and took access to Canadian territory and resources too much for granted; on a few occasions, they even complained that the US was "bullying" or being "imperialistic."[18] But their American counterparts, understandably preoccupied with other things, tended not to make much of these frictions, and the impression that wartime cooperation left on them was overwhelmingly positive. Most Americans – in Washington and elsewhere – knew little of Canada and its concerns, and blithely assumed that Canada's interests and values converged naturally with those of the US. Those who had worked most closely with Canadians during the war understood that the latter had special sensitivities about national sovereignty and their relationship with Britain, and could sometimes be prickly about these things, but they also generally held the popular perception that Canadians were fundamentally "like us," easy to work with, and owed a certain courtesy and goodwill.

Close relationships between government officials (i.e., transgovernmental networks) that might have evaporated after the war were sustained, and even extended, by two main postwar developments. First, the intensification of the Cold War drove the US to accept a more "permanent" global leadership role, and to seek out reliable allies and partners. With Western Europe in ruins, Canada stood out as an important diplomatic and strategic partner. It had a thriving economy, stores of strategic resources, and even a relatively substantial military force; its vast territory, recognized as important to American defence even during the war, took on a new strategic dimension in the 1950s, as US military planners worried about the prospect of a Soviet bomber attack.[19] Second, Canadian policy-makers were increasingly inclined after the war to think about fuelling the country's economic growth through greater access to US markets and greater reliance on US investment, as opposed to their traditional reliance on Britain. Canadian and American officials were thus brought together again on a day-to-day basis, seeking ways to encourage and channel the increasingly powerful tides of north-south commercial flows in ways that maximized joint gain and minimized political "complications."[20]

Like their British counterparts, Canadian officials tried to build up their profile and influence in Washington by appealing to the imagery and norms of the English-speaking family of nations – what some now refer to as the "Anglosphere."[21] These arguments resonated in Washington during the early postwar years, just as they had during the war, and American policy-makers embraced a sense of familiarity and common purpose with the UK, Canada, Australia, and New Zealand, as manifested in their close diplomatic partnership within military alliances and international organizations, and their close collaboration on intelligence gathering and analysis. Beyond sharing in democratic traditions and common opposition to Soviet expansionism (as with, say, France or Germany), these English-speaking countries were seen to be joined to the United States by a shared cultural heritage and a natural sense of mutual responsibility.[22] Thus, American policy-makers felt an obligation to grant these special allies exceptional access and special treatment, and in turn expected them to be reliably supportive and flexible on matters relating to national sovereignty (such as military bases). In this context, they worked out a distinctive set of bargaining norms to govern relations "among friends," emphasizing routine consultation, deference, and quiet diplomacy, and an obligation to resolve conflicts according to established principles, without resort to overt coercion.

This broader diplomatic culture took a specific, distinctive form in the context of the Canada-US bilateral relationship. Because American policy-makers' sense of the special relationship with Canada was predicated on their experience with informal collaboration, and because Canadian officials were determined to take relative power out of the equation, the dominant theme in the Canada-US relationship during the early Cold War decades was "partnership."[23] The underlying premise was that the interests of the two countries were essentially compatible (if not necessarily identical), and the ongoing challenge for policy-makers was to manage the bilateral relationship effectively. Domestic pressures and institutional obstacles meant that the sources of problems were always "political," but the mindset was to approach them as "technical" problems – in the sense that bilateral negotiation would amount to a search for the formula by which these cross-cutting pressures could be reconciled (or at least deflected) and mutual gains could be realized. In the language of bargaining theory, the two sides would always be attentive to "distributive" concerns, but ultimately they were committed to an "integrative" approach to bilateral bargaining.[24]

In keeping with this general aversion to "politicization," policy-makers in both countries were generally inclined to think that most issues ought to be handled by bureaucrats, not politicians. Negotiators on both sides were ultimately prepared to call on the political leadership when they reached a diplomatic impasse, but they were extraordinarily reluctant to do so, and tried to strictly minimize their reliance on bilateral summitry. They also preferred to avoid formal institution building and to manage issues on an ad hoc basis, through direct, personal contacts.[25] In fact, there was little effort by either side to plan for the long term or to think systematically about priorities or trade-offs across issues. Edelgard Mahant and Graeme Mount have argued that this indicates that the United States had "no policy" toward Canada,[26] but an informal, ad hoc approach to problem-solving is not necessarily the same as no approach at all.

The centrepiece in the distinctive set of bargaining norms governing Canada-US relations during this period was a shared understanding that conflicts must be resolved without making linkages between unrelated issues. Diplomats everywhere generally shy away from making coercive linkages when they can, because resorting to overt linkages means giving up on resolving a dispute "on its merits," brings the exercise of power into view, and runs the risk of setting off a spiral that might ultimately leave both sides worse off. But the avoidance of coercive issue linkages in the Canada-US relationship went beyond simple prudence; it was a norm deeply embedded in the policy communities of both countries, which – as I will show in the chapters that follow – had powerful effects on the process and outcomes of bilateral bargaining, even in severe and protracted disputes.

Canadian officials obviously had practical reasons to support a principle that would set limits on the exercise of American power. "The Yanks," as Allan Gotlieb has bluntly put it, "can out-link [Canada] any day of the week."[27] But the diplomatic record makes it clear that Canadian policy-makers' embrace of the norm was also rooted in moral convictions. When, for example, US negotiators at a March 1970 bilateral meeting hinted that their position on continental energy trade might be affected by Canada's attitude toward sovereignty over the Northwest Passage, the Canadians erupted in surprise and indignation, demanding clarification and pressing for explicit reaffirmation of the norm against linkage. (This episode is described in some detail in Chapter 4.)

US policy-makers' reasons for subscribing to the norm are more complex, and more interesting. Americans have always thought about their role and purposes as an international actor in "exceptionalist" terms, and have thus often been inhibited in the overt exercise of their country's enormous power.[28] But the history of US foreign policy makes it clear that, when the stakes are high, the US has been both willing and able to pursue coercive linkages. During the early Cold War years, for example, the US frequently used the threat to scale back foreign aid transfers as a lever for influencing the domestic and international policies of developing states. One of the most brutally direct examples in recent years unfolded during the lead-up to the Persian Gulf War. When the government of Yemen voted against the 1991 United Nations resolution authorizing the use of force against Iraq, Secretary of State James Baker reportedly declared it would be "the most expensive vote [they] ever cast," and Yemen's US$24 million aid allocation was abruptly terminated.[29]

The US has also been prepared, from time to time, to pursue coercive linkages even against some of its closest allies and economic partners. The Eisenhower administration, for example, used the threat to destabilize the pound to force Britain to back down in the Suez crisis.[30] The Nixon administration quietly threatened to block the reversion of Okinawa to Japan, to force that country to accept "voluntary" restrictions on textile exports.[31] And various administrations have tried to use border restrictions and trade leverage to try to compel Mexico to strengthen its efforts against drug trafficking.[32]

American officials' reservations about the use of coercive linkages have been deeper and more reflexive when it comes to Canada, because they have seen the relationship with Canada differently. On one hand, as outlined above, Americans had, over the preceding decades, come to see Canada as a close friend and junior partner, and so were inclined to see "principled" relations with Canada as an important measure of America's foreign-policy virtues.[33] This tendency was further reinforced in the early postwar years, as US policy-makers saw more and more of their foreign-policy choices through the prism of the Cold War struggle to win "hearts and minds" abroad. During the late 1940s and early 1950s, State and Defense Department officials often referred to the need to demonstrate, through friendly relations with Canada, that the US – unlike its communist rival – was not the kind of power that bullied its neighbours.[34]

These impulses encouraged American officials to exercise self-restraint in bilateral relations with Canada, but they didn't specify what kind of self-restraint. That was something learned through day-to-day engagement with Canadian counterparts. US officials who worked on Canadian issues after the war came to understand that coercive linkage had a special meaning north of the border, because of the depth and the asymmetry of interdependence between the two societies. The pursuit of overt, direct linkages, they understood, would trigger Canadians' latent impulse to reduce their vulnerability by breaking away, even at the risk of mutually damaging dislocations.[35]

The postwar diplomatic culture was something that emerged gradually through a process of mutual socialization, as government officials and military officers from the two countries learned to work with one another. They formed an informal transgovernmental network, held together by common interest in the health of "the relationship" and adherence to the postwar diplomatic culture described above. The American component of the network was anchored in the State Department – particularly in the Bureau of European and Canadian Affairs and the embassy in Ottawa – but it reached out into many other departments, where mid- and upper-level career bureaucrats had sustained experience in working closely with their Canadian counterparts, such as Defense, Transportation, and Treasury. Leading members of the network in the US included a number of prominent and influential policy-makers, including Livingston Merchant, Willis Armstrong, Philip Trezise, Julius Katz, and Rufus Z. Smith. But there were also dozens of lesser-known officials, who were involved in bilateral affairs at a lower level and/or for a shorter time but who were still plugged in to the network's way of managing the relationship and who carried that way of thinking into new agencies and assignments.

This network – and thus the reach of the postwar diplomatic culture – did not penetrate all parts of the US foreign-policy establishment. Thus, even at the peak of the network's influence in the late 1950s and mid-1960s, network-connected officials were sometimes compelled to take action to deflect proposals for coercive linkage initiated by "outsiders" – usually political appointees, or representatives of other departments – by making normative and practical arguments to the political leadership and/or by suffocating these options through lack of information.

In spite of these efforts, there were still some episodes where US officials sent signals (or were seen to have done so by their Canadian counterparts) about their willingness to pursue coercive linkages. One of these apparent exceptions was the "package deal" dispute of 1955, when the American representative to the UN told his Canadian counterpart that pushing ahead with the Canadian plan to break through the membership stalemate by setting aside the question of Taiwan was sure to provoke some kind of economic retaliation.[36] In this case, though – as in the other apparent violations of the norm during this period – the evidence suggests that the threat was not authorized by anyone in Washington or supported by any kind of assessment or planning.[37] Episodes like this are best understood as flashes of raw frustration – which might be reflective of underlying seriousness or resolve – not as calculated bargaining moves.

Some accounts have argued (or at least implied) that the norm against linkage – and other facets of the larger diplomatic culture – came into play only in low-stakes disputes, where it was much easier for like-minded bureaucrats to prevent "politicization."[38] The transgovernmental network's capacity to influence the bargaining agenda was certainly sorely tested in high-stakes disputes. During the early Cold War decades, however, it was nonetheless generally able to effectively derail or deflect pressures for coercive linkages, even in severe and protracted confrontations. This is not to say that US officials put Canadian interests ahead of American ones, or that Canada-US relations were always harmonious. US negotiators were often adversarial in bargaining with Canada, and some disputes became very acrimonious. The point here is that this competition played out within certain boundaries, and that those boundaries took a particular form. In fact, it is the *form* that is important here; special meaning was not attached to specific issue linkages, but rather to *(hard) linkages per se.*

It is important, moreover, to be clear that even among the most self-consciously committed members of the network, the norm against linkage was not absolute or unconditional. It was recognized on both sides that – at least hypothetically – there were actions that Canada might take that would constitute such an egregious threat to American interests that the US could not let them pass, and Canadian officials were constantly attentive to that threshold. "There were some buttons we could not push," remembers one former Canadian official. "[Our American counterparts] were usually not shy about telling us which ones they were."[39] There was, for example, a fairly robust consensus in Ottawa through most of the 1950s and 1960s in favour of diplomatic recognition of the People's Republic of China, but it was not acted on until the US started to move in this direction in 1970. Prior to that time, it was clear to successive Canadian governments that there was no prospect for changing the American position on this issue, and that it was simply not important enough to Canada to justify a direct diplomatic confrontation.[40] Every norm – from driving on the right side of the road to the laws against homicide – has its exceptions and its limitations, and this doesn't necessarily diminish the power of the norm itself. The norm against coercive linkage in Canada-US relations was important because it ruled out a wide array of bargaining options within the context of "normal" diplomatic give-and-take, raised the bar for identifying a provocation so grievous that it might justify making an exception, and shifted the burden of proof onto those that might support more aggressive strategies.

The Breakdown of the Postwar Diplomatic Culture

The transgovernmental network's capacity to shape the bargaining agenda according to its defining principles depended on its being insulated against pressure from bureaucratic rivals and mobilized societal actors, which in turn depended on the relative cohesion of the US foreign-policy making process during the early Cold War decades. When these institutional foundations were demolished, the network was disrupted, and the salience of the norm deteriorated.

The displacement of the transgovernmental network went through two main steps. The initial disruption came with the arrival of the Nixon administration in 1968, as foreign-policy decision-making was gathered into the hands of a small number of powerful cabinet figures, particularly President Richard Nixon himself, National Security Adviser Henry Kissinger, and Treasury Secretary John Connally. Secretary of State William Rogers was not one of these figures, and the State Department found itself isolated and ignored through most of the Nixon administration. The State Department had been battered and bruised by bureaucratic rivals ever since the "loss" of China and the McCarthy witchhunts, but now it was being second-guessed and supplanted even on day-to-day diplomatic "housekeeping."

The US-Canada network still retained some influence during this period, however, and, although it was unable to prevent some severe bilateral conflicts, it was able to deflect pressures for linkages against Canada. Given Nixon and Kissinger's well-known inclination toward issue linkage as a bargaining tool, and their lack of interest in the bilateral relationship, it was probably only a matter of time before the administration turned toward linkages with Canada. The line was finally crossed in August 1971, when Nixon supported Connally's decision to include Canada in a much larger linkage campaign: the abrupt suspension of the convertibility of gold and imposition of import surcharges as a means of forcing major commercial partners to pay the adjustment costs for the US balance of payments crisis.[41]

The decision to reject Canada's request for an exemption from the "Nixon shock" measures was an important moment, but it was not necessarily a turning point. The linkage cat had been let out of the bag, so to speak, but it was not clear at this point that it could not be put back. Even after Nixon's 1972 address to the Canadian Parliament, declaring an end to the "special relationship" and calling for a more "mature" partnership, many believed that old habits would be restored after Nixon had passed from the scene. There *was* a normalization of bilateral relations under Presidents Gerald Ford and Jimmy Carter, but this superficial restoration obscured a more permanent displacement of the network and its way of doing things.[42]

The driving force behind this shift was a change in the domestic political structure in the United States. Although direct presidential control over foreign-policy decision-making was loosened after Nixon left office, the White House retained – and continued to build on – its Nixon-era capacity for collecting information, identifying options, and generally containing or short-circuiting bureaucratic decision-making – and thus transgovernmental relations as well. At the same time, the weakening of the State Department under Nixon accelerated the encroachment of various domestic agencies on the traditional foreign-policy bureaucracy's turf, which had begun back in the 1950s. Finally, and most importantly, the Vietnam War and Watergate catalyzed a new Congressional assertiveness in all areas of foreign policy, and the creation of a number of new institutional mechanisms by which embattled domestic interests could pressure the executive to take action against other governments.[43]

It is important to be clear about the nature of the change: the declining salience of the norm against linkage after the early 1970s was not caused by the same old people coming to new ideas, but rather by a change in *whose* ideas were most influential within the agenda-setting process. The sense of community and shared purpose within the transgovernmental network was shaken by the bilateral conflicts of the late 1960s, and by broad demographic shifts within the American foreign-policy elite (e.g., generational turnover, replacement of northeasterners by southerners).[44] But the network continued to reproduce itself by socializing new officials to the old way of doing things, and interviews with former officials make it clear that Canada-watchers in the State Department continued to subscribe to similar ideas about what makes the bilateral relationship unique and how it ought to be managed. One former State Department official reflected: "From the first day, I was told all about the whole Livingston Merchant thing – that way of doing business ... and it seemed right to me, while I was there [on the Canada desk, in the early 1970s] ... It was the right way [to manage relations with Canada], obviously, as a set of principles, but in practice ... How could we actually do that?"[45]

As US foreign-policy decision-making became more fragmented, the members of the transgovernmental network were increasingly drowned out, or pushed out of the way, by other actors, many of whom knew little and cared little about Canada and had little or no professional interest in the overall health of the bilateral relationship. More and more of these new voices were inclined to advocate linkages as a way of forcing changes to Canadian policies, partly because they were not bound by the same normative commitments and partly because they cared less about the diplomatic consequences.

Advocates of "getting tough" with Canada have often been frustrated, however, in their attempts to identify issue linkages that would actually work, both diplomatically and politically. The extensive interdependence between the two societies has been a major factor in Canadian policy-making since the beginning of the twentieth century, if not earlier, but it has had a profound effect on the range of bargaining options for the US only since the late 1960s. Three main developments have raised the domestic political costs for US policy-makers considering linkages against Canada, each one reinforcing those that came before.

The US economy was in theory a generally "open" one since the end of the Second World War, but in practice it was mostly self-contained, and only a small share of its exports and imports were with Canada. Economic interdependence between the US and Canada was not really substantial in the US, in commercial or political terms, until sometime in the 1960s, or perhaps the 1970s. As I will explain in Chapter 2, the growing number of US firms and communities in the US that would be hurt by a disruption of established connections with Canada created new domestic political obstacles to linkage.

The increasing importance of potential domestic political opposition to linkage was reinforced by the same fragmentation of power that disrupted the postwar transgovernmental network. As international developments began to have greater and greater impacts on their functional domains and political constituencies, domestic agencies became increasingly disinclined to defer to the State Department, and even the White House, on foreign-policy issues from trade and investment to environmental cooperation. At the same time, the growing assertiveness of Congress after the early 1970s meant that various interest groups had new information about how bilateral relations affected their interests, and new avenues for putting pressure on the executive branch. Those mechanisms became increasingly formalized after the mid-1960s, as the US government created a variety of legal and quasi-judicial policy review institutions (such as the International Trade Commission), which became focal points for disgruntled American interest groups working in tacit transnational alliance with Canadian firms or government.

The US was also increasingly held back by international institutional commitments, particularly after the signing of the Canada-US Free Trade Agreement (CUSFTA) in 1987. The General Agreement on Tariffs and Trade (GATT) had always served as an attractive alternative to unilateral arm-twisting, at least on trade issues, and as a potential limit on US resort to linkages, because it gave weight to normative proscriptions against certain kinds of retaliation (e.g., tariffs and certain nontariff barriers). The much more substantial CUSFTA and World Trade Organization (WTO) regimes discourage linkages even more effectively, because they cover a wider range of policy instruments (e.g., trade-related subsidies, regulation, taxes, etc.), and they have more robust mechanisms for detecting and imposing costs on rule breakers.

Thus, while one kind of constraint on US power – the postwar diplomatic culture and the transgovernmental network that carried it – has unravelled, another set of constraints – interdependence and institutions – has emerged to take its place. One might argue that not much has changed, since coercive linkages are still not a feature of Canada-US relations, and Canada is still in a position to press its issue-specific bargaining advantages. As I will argue in Chapter 7, however, this historic transition from one kind of bilateral bargaining relationship to another does have important implications for diplomatic practice, specific political outcomes, and ongoing debates about the nature and limits of Canadian autonomy.

Theoretical Implications

Beyond offering a new – or rather, renewed – interpretation of Canada-US relations, this book aspires to provoke a rethinking of the role of norms in noncooperative bargaining. This is an important area of research in a field that has tended to put a high priority on simplifying very complex relationships, and has in the process tended to overlook the social aspects of international bargaining. The history of Canada-US relations is an ideal setting in which to identify and evaluate the effects of bargaining norms on the process and outcomes of international negotiation. The richness and accessibility of the historical records (particularly on the Canadian side) and the depth of the relevant policy research give us a rare opportunity to look closely at the process leading up to particular diplomatic choices, and to put what we know about the bargaining over particular issues into a broader, multi-issue context.

Over the last twenty years, there has been growing interest in the dynamics and effects of norms within the larger literature on international cooperation and conflict, but there have been few efforts to try to connect insights from this general work to the puzzles and premises of bargaining theory, particularly with respect to coercive bargaining. It seems clear, however, that real-world negotiators are constantly engaged in sending and receiving signals, not only about their capabilities, intentions, and resolve but also about which kinds of bargaining moves they understand to be legitimate or illegitimate in the context of particular relationships. Because these bargaining norms are established, challenged, and reproduced through the process of arguing over procedures and formulas for negotiation, they may vary widely between different sets of bargainers and/or across different issue areas, and they may change over time.

Because the key bargaining norm governing Canada-US relations in the early Cold War years was a general proscription against coercive linkages, this book has special relevance for the branch of bargaining theory that is concerned with the calculus of issue linkage. The focus in that more specialized literature has mostly been on cooperative linkages – "issue trading" to expand the range of mutually acceptable settlements – but some attention has also been paid to the special dynamics of threats, retaliation, and other forms of coercive diplomacy.[46] Most of this work has been driven by abstract modelling of expected-utility calculations, often with attention to complications introduced by asymmetrical information and signalling problems.[47] What is missing from this literature is sustained attention to the possibility that bargainers might rule out particular types of linkages, or even linkages per se, on normative grounds.

It is important to recognize that the norm against issue linkage that is the focus of this book was part of a larger bundle of understandings about how the bargaining game was to be played within the Canada-US bilateral relationship – that is, a diplomatic culture. There has been some important work over the last few years on mapping out distinctive styles of bargaining within various international groupings, including the community of democracies, Arab states, and the members of the Association of Southeast Asian Nations.[48] This book's effort to trace the workings and effects of the distinctive diplomatic culture that governed Canada-US relations during the early Cold War years is intended to highlight the value of this avenue for theory and research, and to inductively identify key features that may be useful in designing future comparative studies.

The focus on identity and norms brings this study into the line of fire between rationalist-materialist and constructivist approaches to the study of institutions, which has emerged as one of the central lines of contemporary meta-theoretical debate in the study of international politics.[49] My main purpose here is to show that "norms matter" in a given context, and matter in a way that cannot simply be subsumed within prominent rational choice interpretations of Canada-US relations. The mere fact that norms matter, however, is not necessarily a serious problem for rational choice approaches generally, and the point here is not to try to knock down rational choice itself.[50] Rather, it is to show that the things that rational choice approaches focus our attention on – i.e., strategic choice, given a set of prior preferences and beliefs – are not always the most interesting parts of the story. In the Canada-US experience, the unexpected pattern of dispute outcomes is best explained not by something unexpected about the way the bargaining context shaped negotiators' strategic choices but by something unexpected about the way that certain kinds of choices were ruled out in advance, because they held a certain meaning for decision-makers – a meaning that was in turn rooted in particular ideas about the respective states' priorities and purposes within the relationship.

Testing the Argument: A Preview

Arguments about the power of ideas are often dismissed for failing to meet the methodological standards set by more conventional approaches. Moravcsik, for example, argues that most constructivist accounts of European integration have failed to formulate their arguments in a way that could be empirically falsified, or to weigh them against credible rationalist-materialist alternatives.[51] This book was conceived with these complaints very much in mind, and it is designed to test my argument head to head against the most compelling rival interpretations. The deductive arguments and empirical expectations for these alternative accounts are outlined in detail in Chapter 2. Starting from Keohane and Nye's classic *Power and Interdependence*,[52] I develop a realist interpretation emphasizing alliance politics and strategic restraint, and two different arguments about the implications of interdependence, to set against my own diplomatic-culture interpretation. Keohane and Nye's argument about interdependence ("blocking coalitions") is undercut by the apparent deterioration of Canada's bargaining position in the 1970s, but the strategic restraint argument and the other version of the interdependence argument ("triggering coalitions") can account for this broad pattern of dispute outcomes, just as my diplomatic-culture interpretation can.

Because the strategic restraint, triggering coalitions, and diplomatic-culture interpretations all have very similar expectations about the broad pattern of dispute outcomes over time, it is necessary to look more closely at specific cases. Again, the details are given in Chapter 2, but the basic logic behind the selection of cases is as follows.

The dispute over nuclear weapons, considered in Chapter 3, is a crucial case for the diplomatic-culture interpretation. All of the other most prominent arguments about what drives the relationship lead us to expect the Kennedy administration to have been prepared to make overt, direct linkages in order to force the Diefenbaker government to accept and deploy nuclear weapons. Prime Minister John Diefenbaker's dissembling and delay on the issue was seen to undercut the bases for continental defence cooperation, and to create dangerous "demonstration" effects that challenged Washington's leadership on NATO nuclear policy. The nature of the issue meant that US debates about how to handle relations with Canada were kept within the executive branch, and mobilized societal interests had little to do with it. The governing parties had very different priorities, and the prime minister and president disliked and distrusted each another. Diplomatic engagements between the two governments became highly charged, and some established bargaining norms (such as quiet diplomacy) were clearly violated. Yet, in spite of the fact that a number of viable linkage scenarios were within reach, the US never actually pursued hard linkages, and Canada did not accept nuclear weapons until after Diefenbaker was replaced by Lester Pearson, two years after the dispute began. The US did make soft linkages, however, and Canadian interests suffered in a number of other issue areas.

The showdown over Canada's claim to sovereignty over Arctic waters, explored in Chapter 4, also supports the argument that the relationship was governed by a norm against linkages, but it can also help us see the early signs of the diplomatic culture's displacement. Again, Canada's position directly challenged core US national security priorities (in this case, their strategic and commercial interest in freedom of the seas), and set precedents that might be followed by other states. Again the governing parties had very different priorities, and again the prime minister and president did not get along. But, just as in the nuclear weapons dispute, US negotiators chose not to pursue coercive linkages, in spite of the fact that a number of viable linkage options were available to them. What is different here is that, whereas in the nuclear weapons dispute American policy-makers did not even recognize linkages as an option, in the Arctic waters dispute they actively debated specific linkage scenarios. At the end of the day, members of the transgovernmental network won the argument and linkages were rejected on normative grounds, but it was clear that the diplomatic landscape had changed. In this case as well, the foreclosure of hard linkages seems to have stirred up soft linkages, and the Nixon administration clearly held grudges that affected subsequent bilateral outcomes.

The Reagan administration's reaction to the announcement of the National Energy Program (NEP), the subject of Chapter 5, gives a sense of the way bilateral bargaining changed after the disruptions of the 1970s. The stakes for the US in this case were fairly high, in the sense that politically powerful multinational oil companies were pressing the US government to force Canada to roll back its new investment policies, and the Reagan administration was committed to protecting the principle of "national treatment" internationally. Canada's new oil and gas policies did not directly challenge core US national security concerns, however, and the likely effects on the US economy were marginal. Yet, in stark contrast to the way the US responded to Canada's challenges in the nuclear weapons and Arctic waters cases, here the Reagan administration was quick to consider coercive linkages in order to force Canada to back down. And Canada did back down, at least part of the way, by retracting some of the provisions of the NEP that the US objected to most strenuously. Nevertheless, it is striking how much difficulty the administration had in trying to identify and pursue a linkage scenario that would impose severe costs on Canada without provoking a sharp reaction from affected interests in the US. It seems that the US was again held back from pursuing effective hard linkages, but now it was held back by practical political obstacles rather than normative ones.

The situation was roughly similar in the 2002-4 dispute over war in Iraq, reviewed in Chapter 6, except that in this case Canada's position had very clear and direct national security implications for the United States. This was a case in which speculation about issue linkage was rampant in the media and in Canadian political debates, the Bush administration was clearly prepared to challenge traditional diplomatic practices, and there was not much trust and goodwill between the two governments. But the US ultimately did not mount an effective issue linkage in this case either. The reasons for US restraint are varied, including short time horizons and uncertainty about the Canadian position, "offsetting" Canadian contributions in Afghanistan and elsewhere, and domestic political obstacles facing all of the most prominent linkage scenarios. Again, it appears that US policy-makers were not held back by normative commitments, but rather by the constraining effects of interdependence and institutions.

In order to make the case that US negotiators were or were not held back by the absence or presence of viable linkage options, it is necessary to look beyond the core dispute in each case. I therefore consider at least three of the most widely talked about or most likely linkage scenarios in each of the four cases, to assess whether the executive branch was in a position to make its decision on those issues conditional on the resolution of the core dispute, and to assess the balance of domestic political pressures supporting or opposing these linkage scenarios. In addition, since the argument advanced in this book is mostly about the *reasons* why the United States chooses one bargaining strategy over another, it is important to look beyond the outcomes of disputes and explore the process by which strategy choices were made. The second half of Chapter 2 outlines the criteria for identifying and evaluating specific linkage scenarios, and for matching up the rival theoretical arguments' expectations about the process leading to a decision on the bargaining strategy to be pursued in each dispute.

Implications for Canada-US Relations

It is important to get these cases right, for at least three reasons. First, each of these four episodes is controversial in its own right, as historians have argued about whether and how linkages were made, and how this might have influenced the outcomes of the disputes. The research for this study draws on new materials, including recently released archival materials and interviews with key decision-makers in Ottawa and Washington, and provides new insight into the perceptions, priorities, and politics behind government decisions in each of these high-stakes disputes.

Second, close study of these cases is the best way to resolve theoretical debates about how to understand the broad pattern of Canada-US bargaining over time. Because several of the key theoretical arguments have similar expectations about this broad pattern, we can properly assess these rival interpretations only by looking more closely at the inner workings of particular cases. But we don't want to look at just any handful of cases. In addition to having been extensively studied and debated, and so offering us more of the close-range information we need, the four cases reviewed here are drawn from different phases of the history of the bilateral relationship, giving us not only a way to test the before-and-after expectations of the rival theories but also snapshots of crucial turning-point moments in Canada-US relations. More importantly, these cases are valuable because they represent "hard cases," in which the expectations of the diplomatic-culture interpretation are diametrically opposed to those of the leading alternatives, and therefore address the complaints of Moravcsik and others about constructivists' collective failure to properly engage with their materialist rivals.

Third, and equally important, the resolution of this debate about what drove Canada-US relations in the past has important implications for the present and the future. The breakdown of the postwar network and norms has had profound effects on the way that the two countries engage with one another. Some of the more disruptive tendencies have been reinforced by the inflated expectations created by the grander "special relationship" mythology that sprouted up around the much more modest postwar diplomatic culture, and by the same fragmentation of power that undercut that diplomatic culture. These implications are more fully developed in Chapter 7, but I will highlight three of them here to give the reader a sense of what is at stake.

To begin with, there is – and there has been since the 1970s – a widespread belief among pundits and the general public that the quality of Canada-US diplomacy has deteriorated because the quality of Canadian and American diplomats has declined.[53] There may be an element of truth in this, in the sense that the foreign-policy bureaucracy today tends to create and reward administrative competence rather than diplomatic dexterity. But if the quality of Canada-US diplomacy has declined over the last thirty years or so, it is primarily because of the changing nature of the political context for bilateral relations, not the quality of the diplomats themselves.

The fragmentation of power in both countries has made it harder for senior foreign-policy bureaucrats to "manage" the bilateral agenda, and the subsequent raising of the political stakes has given the political leadership powerful incentives to intervene in the process, further muddying the waters and polarizing bilateral disputes. The net result is that neither government can be as clear and consistent as it once was about what its basic negotiating position is, what compromises it would be willing to accept, or what measures it would be willing to take in order to get its own way. Although – as I will illustrate in Chapters 5 and 6 – impulses to pursue coercive linkages are still held in check by a variety of political and practical constraints, impulses to talk tough – and even to make unsupported linkage threats – are not. We have therefore seen more frequent and more intense outbreaks of speculation about possible arm-twisting and retaliation, more aggressive grandstanding and tit-for-tat escalation, and frequent deterioration of the tone of the bilateral relationship, even in times when presidents and prime ministers have generally compatible agendas and are personally committed to improving the bilateral relationship.

Careful thinking about what was distinctive about the relationship in the early Cold War decades, and the developments that disrupted the old order, can also help us see why we cannot go back to the kind of close relationship the two countires enjoyed in the past. Some have argued recently that Canada can restore its damaged ties with the US by seeking stronger personal relationships between prime minister and president, and/or by being a more loyal and useful diplomatic and military supporter. But the case studies reviewed here raise serious questions about these arguments. The nuclear weapons and Arctic waters cases suggest that US self-restraint during the early Cold War years was not strictly conditional on positive personal relationships between leaders or on strong diplomatic and military support. And the various frustrations of the Mulroney government in the 1980s (e.g., acid rain, South Africa) and the Harper government more recently (e.g., lumber trade, border security measures) suggest that neither strong personal relationships nor strong defence ties necessarily guarantee favourable treatment in Washington.

The rise and fall of the postwar diplomatic culture can also help us better understand Canada's historic turn toward regional integration in the 1980s. Much as we usually think of Canada as a dedicated advocate of multilateral institution building, when it came to primarily continental issues, successive Canadian governments generally preferred, during the 1950s and 1960s, to keep things strictly bilateral and as informal as possible. This was partly a reflection of the reflexive commitment of members of the transgovernmental network to keep things "technical" and avoid politicization, but it was also a reflection of the way that the special circumstances of the early Cold War allowed them to effectively manage the bilateral agenda as they saw fit, and the strength of US commitment to the postwar diplomatic culture gave

Canadian policy-makers confidence that the US would continue to exercise deference and self-restraint. After the fragmentation of power in the 1970s, amid growing uncertainty in Canada about whether the US would continue to abide by the norms of the postwar diplomatic culture, Canadian policy-makers became convinced that they would need to find new ways to contain the exercise of American power.[54] Mulroney's "leap of faith" to free trade was driven by anxiety about Congressional protectionism and the prime minister's own desire to "lock in" market reforms in Canada, but it also reflected the bureaucracy's determination to find ways to restrain what was seen to be an increasingly parochial, confrontational, and unpredictable US government.

There were of course frustrations and regrets in Canada-US relations during the early Cold War decades, but there is also reason to look back with nostalgia on the 1950s and 1960s as a diplomatic "golden age."[55] Policy-makers on both sides of the border were able to manage the bilateral agenda according to a set of shared principles and priorities, engineering a series of formal and informal understandings that served mutual interests and avoided domestic political trouble – the Defence Production Sharing Agreement, the Auto Pact, the oil import quota exemption, and so on. What is most striking, from the point of view of international relations theory, is how many of these outcomes favoured the interests and priorities of the weaker power. On the whole, however, American policy-makers also had reasons to be satisfied with the way the relationship worked during the 1950s and 1960s, in spite of their exasperation over nuclear weapons, commodity trade disputes, and the war in Vietnam. Adhering to the postwar diplomatic culture reassured Canadians about the implications of growing interdependence, defused potentially serious political conflicts in the US, and reinforced Americans' sense of their country's role and purposes in the world.

The social and structural underpinnings of the postwar special relationship came undone in the 1970s, and Canada has had no choice but to seek out new ways to manage its all-important relationship with the United States. The effort to engage directly with Congress and the various domestic bureaucracies, pioneered by Allan Gotlieb's embassy in the 1980s, is an important coping strategy, but – as Gotlieb himself has argued – it is "not enough by itself." Hope springs eternal for renewal through stronger personal relationships between political leaders, but, while showing off access to the White House may boost the prime minister's profile and credibility, it rarely seems to lead to tangible influence or special treatment on the important issues. Lacking other promising options, Canadian policy-makers have (more or less reluctantly) turned to bilateral and regional integration, through formal agreements such as the CUSFTA and the North American Free Trade Agreement (NAFTA), or through informal policy coordination.

These arrangements do set up additional political and international-legal constraints on the United States, by fostering interdependence or by creating new institutional checks on US resort to policy levers such as countervailing and anti-dumping legislation. It is important to be clear, however, that they come at a cost, as Canada must give up some of its own policy levers in exchange. Some in Canada have been perfectly happy with this arrangement, with the idea that these levers do little more than create inefficiencies and distortions anyway, but the current global economic turmoil and the other major economies' ready resort to previously disavowed forms of state intervention suggest that we may want to hold on to some of these policy instruments after all. The formal constraints on US policy-making secured through integration may seem much more substantial than the informal understandings that governed bilateral relations in the early Cold War years, but Canada's disappointing experience with softwood lumber in the NAFTA dispute resolution process suggests that even the most ambitious formal institutional constraints may not be enough to tie down American power and parochialism.

2
Power, Interdependence, and Ideas

The most focused and systematic study of the question of issue linkage in the Canada-US context that we have so far is actually a relatively minor part of a much broader theoretical work on international cooperation: Robert Keohane and Joseph Nye's classic *Power and Interdependence,* published a little over thirty years ago.[1] The core argument there was that the extraordinary breadth and depth of interdependence between Canada and the United States in the early Cold War years made it possible for the two countries to move into a different kind of international relationship, in which the outcomes of bilateral bargaining were not driven by raw aggregate power but rather by the complex interplay of international regimes and domestic politics. Extensive interdependence, they argued, generated new transnational and transgovernmental coalitions, which would intervene to block issue linkages that might hurt both countries' interests. Policy-makers on both sides of the border soon came to recognize these political obstacles to coercive diplomacy, moreover, and turned necessity into a virtue by embracing a shared norm against coercive linkages. With linkages off the table, Canada was able to push ahead on issues where it had an advantage, and thus did far better in bilateral disputes with the United States than the overall asymmetry of the relationship would lead us to expect.

Keohane and Nye's interpretation provides great insight into what is distinctive about the Canada-US relationship, and its implications for broader theories of international relations. As an analysis of linkage politics in the Canada-US context, however, it is flawed in at least four ways: (1) Its expectations about the long-term pattern of dispute outcomes are not borne out by subsequent events; (2) it does not give its main theoretical rival, the realist perspective on international relations, a fair shake; (3) it conflates two different kinds of explanations for US self-restraint; and (4) it is predicated on too narrow a conception of what issue linkages might look like, and therefore misses out on the main way in which linkage politics have actually played out in the Canada-US context. By working through these four problems, we can identify some of the main themes in the existing literature on Canada-US bargaining, and set the stage for the alternative interpretation offered in this book.

The most striking problem with Keohane and Nye's account is one that we can see only with the benefit of thirty years of hindsight. Their argument was predicated on a time-series comparison of Canada-US bargaining outcomes in the 1920s and 1930s with those from the 1950s and 1960s (supplemented by a cross-sectional comparison with Australia-US bargaining outcomes in the same time periods). They argued that the exceptional breadth and depth of interdependence between Canada and the US, which took shape mostly after the Second World War, created the conditions in which it was possible for Canada to have its way in more than half of the bilateral disputes in the 1950s and 1960s. If the bases for Canada's bargaining leverage vis-à-vis the US were that simple, presumably things could only get better for Canada in the decades that followed, because social and economic interconnections between the two countries continued to multiply – indeed, they accelerated markedly – after 1970. But a review of the diplomatic record since then suggests that Canada's bargaining position has not improved, and actually may have deteriorated.

Keohane and Nye found support for their interpretation in a long list of bilateral disputes from the 1950s and 1960s in which Canadian negotiators got more of what they wanted than their American counterparts did. Canada suffered diplomatic setbacks on issues such as magazine taxes and the deployment of nuclear weapons, but it also enjoyed a fairly long list of striking successes, including the independent positions taken on the United Nations membership issue and the Quemoy and Matsu crisis, the avoidance of import restrictions on Canadian oil and lumber, and the favourable resolution of the auto production dispute. When we look at the process and outcomes of bilateral disputes since the early 1970s, on the other hand, two patterns stand out: more of the disputes between the two countries have been initiated by the US, and more of them have been resolved (or not resolved) on terms favouring the US.[2] Among the major diplomatic defeats of the 1980s and 1990s were successive setbacks on softwood lumber trade; trade restrictions on steel, beef, and wheat; and long, painful delays and unsatisfying resolutions on fisheries, water pollution, and acid rain.

Whereas in the early Cold War decades there had been a rough parity between disputes over "high politics" issues (those pertaining to strategy and diplomacy) and "low politics" issues (those related to trade, investment, or regulation), the balance tipped decisively to the latter after the early 1970s. This is probably a reflection not only of the greater political salience of these low politics issues in the context of US integration into the world economy, but also of the increasing importance of local bread-and-butter issues as Congress and various domestic agencies became more assertive on foreign-policy issues. Canada has not done nearly as well with these types of issues, as the US has been prepared to bargain more aggressively and Canadian diplomats have found few reliable levers for influence on American policy outcomes.

The main way in which we see an apparent change in the Canada-US relationship, however, is not in the disputes that did break out, but rather in the ones that did not. Whereas in the 1960s, Canada was prepared to challenge the US on a variety of "high politics" issues, both important and unimportant, since the early 1970s it has broken with the US on only a few very high-profile issues, each of which seemed to reflect genuinely exceptional domestic political circumstances.[3] Canada's aggressive advocacy of the Mine Ban Treaty was driven mostly by the policy leadership of Lloyd Axworthy, and its intransigence on missile defence and the war in Iraq seem to have been driven by the perceived need to take diplomatic risks in order to appease domestic political challenges. Canadian attempts to challenge the US on "low politics" issues have been similarly unsuccessful since the early 1970s, as seen in Canada's backing down from investment restrictions on oil and gas, broadcasting, and publishing. When the US has challenged Canada on low politics issues, on the other hand, Canadian negotiators have not been able to get the US to change course, as we have seen in the disputes over US restrictions on Canadian lumber, wheat, pork, beer, asbestos, and steel.

Power: Alliance Politics and Strategic Restraint
One possible explanation for both the exceptional pattern of the early Cold War decades and the apparent change after the 1970s is the theory that Keohane and Nye set out to knock down: realism. As the authors themselves later acknowledged, the counter-argument that *Power and Independence* presented, and quickly knocked down, was a straw-man version of the realist perspective.[4] A more sophisticated version of the theory, focusing on alliance politics, presents a real challenge to their interpretation.

Keohane and Nye's starting point was the argument that, since Canada actually got more of what it wanted in some of its disputes with the US, realism's "overall power model" was flatly contradicted, and thus there must be something going on that only interdependence could explain. It is true that realists tend to think about power as the ultimate means and end in international politics. But realists understand that power is more complicated than the overall power model allows, and that many different kinds of circumstances can get in the way of translating raw power into political influence.[5] It is not hard to think of episodes where domestic politics, for example, have clearly interfered with American efforts at coercive diplomacy. But we should be cautious about inferring from this that the US doesn't bargain aggressively with Canada because it *cannot* do so, particularly when we can think of reasons why it might make a deliberate choice to hold back.

Realists expect states to put security ahead of other foreign-policy goals, and most therefore recognize that more powerful states might sometimes be inclined to let smaller allies go their own way on less important low politics issues, in order to secure their ready compliance on more important high politics issues.[6] There is no question that this was a central feature of the American approach to managing relations with Western Europe and Japan during the early Cold War decades, and many have argued that it was crucial to US relations with Canada as well. To the extent that this is so, it suggests that the Canada-US relationship was a "special" one in the sense that it was favourable to Canadian autonomy (at least on some issues), but not in the sense that it was distinctive or unique.

In the immediate aftermath of the Second World War, Canada was an important ally to the United States because its territory was essential to the strategic defence of the continent and it was a substantial, secure source of supply for strategic resources such as oil and uranium. With most of the major powers in ruins, Canada's military and industrial base in 1945 was among the world's largest, and its "oversized" wartime and early postwar contributions echoed through the early Cold War decades. Canada was also seen by American policy-makers as an important diplomatic supporter in this period, undertaking a variety of important tasks such as intermediation, multilateral problem-solving, and – beginning with the Suez crisis in 1956 – peacekeeping.

Beginning in the 1960s, however, Canada's value as a strategic and diplomatic supporter went into steep decline, both relative to those of other allies and in absolute terms. The development of intercontinental ballistic missiles made the threat of a Soviet bomber attack far less relevant, and therefore did the same to the United States' need for access to Canadian territory. Canadian oil and uranium were still of vital strategic importance to the US, but Canada's less cooperative approach to these resources in the 1960s encouraged the US to look for alternative sources of supply. Canada was still seen as a valuable diplomatic supporter, but US confidence in its reliability had begun to erode, particularly after frictions over the war in Vietnam. And of course Canadian defence spending, expressed as a percentage of GNP, has fallen steadily – and sometimes dramatically – since the 1950s. Andrew Cohen, among others, has argued that these trends are reflective of Canada's declining importance as an international actor more generally, and John Noble has warned of a long-term "drift towards irrelevance."[7] As Canada's capacity to make itself useful to the United States has deteriorated, it has been argued, so has the basis for US self-restraint in the face of provocative Canadian policies.

This "strategic restraint" argument can account for the broad pattern of Canada-US bargaining since 1945.[8] Canada's value to the US as a strategic and diplomatic supporter was greatest in the 1950s and 1960s, when Canada was most inclined to pursue policies at odds with the US, and most likely to get away with doing so. At the same time, the onset of détente and the emergence of superpower bilateralism made all allies less important to the US. These developments started to take hold in the early 1960s, but they were not widely appreciated in Washington until the end of that decade. The recognition of Canada's declining value thus fits quite neatly with the pattern of Canada-US bargaining. Since the late 1960s, the US has been increasingly inclined to bargain aggressively with Canada, and this has been reflected in both the tone and the outcomes of bilateral disputes. Canadian governments, on the other hand, vacillated between extremes in confrontation (John Diefenbaker) and cooperation (Lester Pearson) during the 1960s, struggling to adapt to the new American attitude and the evolving global strategic context. By the mid-1970s, a new pattern had emerged, in which most bilateral conflicts were triggered by the US, Canada was not so inclined to provoke the US through demonstrations of its autonomy, and most bilateral confrontations were resolved in ways that generally favoured the US.

Strategic restraint is undoubtedly an important part of the story, but there are reasons to think that it is not the whole story. To begin with, there have been a number of episodes in which changing international circumstances and/or deliberate policy choices increased Canada's value to the US, but this did not necessarily translate into an appreciable improvement in Canada's bargaining position. During the mid-1980s, for example, the Cold War confrontation had intensified, and the Mulroney government boosted defence spending[9] and took a more collaborative approach to international diplomacy, increasing Canada's profile in Washington and earning a great deal of goodwill from the Reagan administration. But Mulroney was frustrated to find that this goodwill could not be readily converted into diplomatic influence on issues that were most important to Canada, such as acid rain.[10]

More importantly, there have been a number of episodes – both in the early Cold War decades and afterward – in which Canada pursued policies that directly challenged important national security priorities of the United States, without paying a price in terms of direct, coercive linkages. Given that the core premise in the strategic restraint account is that the US puts security ahead of all other foreign-policy goals, then – as much as it might be generally inclined to be forbearing with Canada – the US ought to be prepared to bargain aggressively in order to prevent Canada from going ahead with policies that have a direct, negative impact on US national security. And it should be prepared to do so even where more aggressive bargaining moves might entail significant costs in other areas (i.e., economic disruptions or domestic political opposition). In each of the four case studies reviewed in the chapters that follow, Canada pursued policies that were clearly out of step with the US national security agenda, not only within the bilateral context but also – and perhaps more importantly – in terms of broader international priorities and precedents. American self-restraint in these cases raises serious questions about the value of the strategic restraint interpretation, and a realist take on Canada-US relations more generally.

Interdependence: Blocking and Triggering Coalitions

The third problem with Keohane and Nye's explanation for US restraint in bilateral bargaining with Canada is that it is really two different explanations. The exceptional breadth and depth of interdependence between the two societies, they argue, generated an array of policy frictions that needed to be managed, and thus fostered the formation of an array of transnational and transgovernmental networks with a stake in keeping the relationship running smoothly. These new network actors would be conservative in their approach to the bilateral agenda, putting long-term stability ahead of potential short-term gains, and would therefore naturally recognize a mutual interest in disavowing potentially disruptive issue linkages. This is essentially a functionalist argument about a particular bargaining norm's being brought about by the need for such a norm. But we know intuitively – and the historical literature on international negotiation confirms – that cooperative bargaining norms don't necessarily appear, or persist, just because there is a need for them.[11] Keohane and Nye's argument about independence and their argument about bargaining norms are therefore theoretically and logically independent, and we ought to assess them accordingly.

The crucial layer, from Keohane and Nye's point of view, is evidently the argument about interdependence and its implications. Because linkages are predicated on the disruption of some aspect of the bilateral relationship, they argue, every linkage scenario creates costs for some established interests in both countries. If, for example, American negotiators were to demand a change to Canadian defence policy, and back up that demand by threatening to impose new restrictions on imports of Canadian lumber, that threat would set up costs not only for lumber producers in Canada but also for homebuilders in the US, who could be expected to mobilize to prevent their interests from being sacrificed to some larger diplomatic agenda. As interdependence expanded and intensified, Keohane and Nye argued, there was a steady proliferation of these blocking coalitions, until the pursuit of coercive linkages became virtually impossible.

This is closely related to a much broader argument about interdependence: the old cliché that the interpenetration of the two societies has made it impossible for the United States to punish Canada without having it "bounce back" and hurt the US as well. What is different in Keohane and Nye's version is that they have also identified and explained the political mechanism that would identify and correct potentially self-destructive acts of retaliation. It is a compelling argument, at least in the abstract, and it is also an important part of the story, but – as with the realist's strategic restraint account outlined above – it is not the whole story. The main problem, as noted above, is that interdependence between the two countries has intensified since the end of Keohane and Nye's study period, but the Canadian bargaining position has not improved. In fact, there are signs – as noted above – that it has actually weakened.

It could be, on the other hand, that growing interdependence has actually made the US *more* inclined to pursue coercive linkages. It is true that interdependence generates domestic and transnational coalitions with an interest in blocking linkages that hurt their interests. But interdependence can also generate coalitions with an acute sense of grievance that put pressure on their government to get tough with cross-border rivals, which might push government officials toward issue linkages as a way to break a deadlock and secure tangible results. The softwood lumber dispute, briefly mentioned above, is a useful example. Since the early 1960s, expanded transport links, differing regulatory regimes, and shifting exchange rates have helped Canadian producers capture larger shares of the US lumber market. In each subsequent round of the never-ending dispute, the growing sense of grievance among American producers set up the potential for coercive linkages, both in the sense that the US lumber lobby might demand them as part of a general push for more aggressive bargaining tactics, and in the sense that other interest groups (e.g., oil importers, automakers, farmers) might recognize Canada's political vulnerability on the lumber issue and call for a more aggressive stance on lumber in order to force concessions on "their" issues. And in fact this sort of thing has happened on a number of occasions.

It was easy for the United States to be relatively tolerant of other countries' efforts to take advantage of it, particularly on economic issues, during the early Cold War decades. It was of course threatened by the Soviet Union, but it had the advantage in terms of the overall strategic balance, and it could draw on the support of a wide network of allies and clients. Until the mid-1960s, moreover, the US was far beyond its nearest competitors in terms of economic productivity and technological dynamism, and its cultural exports were popular and profitable in virtually every corner of the globe. Whereas the world economy depended on the United States, the US did not really depend on the world economy. The American market was still a relatively self-contained one, and exports accounted for only about 5 percent of GDP. This was true also of America's commercial and financial relationships with Canada. The two economies had become deeply interpenetrated by the mid-1960s, but, whereas just over 65 percent of Canada's exports went to the US, the equivalent figure for the US was less than 4 percent.[12]

Deep interdependence between Canada and the United States came about gradually through the postwar era, but American sensitivity to interdependence came about relatively abruptly, in the late 1960s and early 1970s. The US balance of payments, which deteriorated steadily through the 1960s, compelled successive administrations to take increasingly aggressive steps to try to force the costs of adjustment onto others, culminating in the "Nixon shocks" of August 1971. The rough unilateralism reflected in Nixon's approach was consistent with a growing impatience in the US with free-riding by traditional allies and trade partners. Domestic political turmoil and the war in Vietnam had created a sense of weakness and vulnerability in the United States, and Americans were less inclined to be generous with others or to pay the costs of international leadership.[13]

Canada-US relations in the 1950s and 1960s were characterized by what has been called "the politics of exceptionalism."[14] As part of a larger tendency to think in terms of common interests and purposes, American policy-makers signed a number of favourable bilateral deals with Canada (e.g., North American Air Defence Agreement, Defence Production Sharing Agreement, Auto Pact) and gave Canada a series of ad hoc special exemptions from general policies (e.g., balance of payments measures of 1963 and 1968, "overland exemption" to oil import restrictions). It was of course in the interest of the United States to have a strong and prosperous ally to the north, but these agreements were seen by most at the time to be disproportionately favourable to Canada, and many believed that, while cancelling these deals would have devastating effects on Canada, it would probably not do much harm to the US. These arrangements therefore created a reservoir of "unexploited bargaining power" for the US, and thus also an array of credible coercive linkage options.[15] Canada's only partially successful struggle to win an exemption from the "Nixon shock" policies signalled that the age of sweetheart deals and special exemptions was basically over. Since then, the US has watered down or withdrawn most of these postwar special arrangements, and has generally refused – for practical and principled reasons – to make new ones. This has been bad news for Canada in the sense that it finds it harder to get something for nothing, but it can also be seen as good news, in the sense that the most promising vehicles for potential coercive linkages have been taken out of play.

Interdependence has cross-cutting implications when it comes to the overall pattern of Canada-US bilateral bargaining outcomes. It means that policy choices made in Canada are now more likely to have a significant negative effect on the interests of at least some groups in the US, and therefore to trigger domestic political pressures for coercive linkages. But it also means that there are more domestic interest groups in the US with a stake in the overall relationship, who are likely to intervene politically to block potential linkages that might hurt their interests. These trends are an important part of the story as well, but we will need to look more closely at specific episodes and issues in order to understand how interdependence plays into the process and outcomes of bargaining, and to see how it relates to other factors, such as strategic restraint.

Ideas: A Distinctive Diplomatic Culture

This brings us to the other layer of Keohane and Nye's account: bargaining norms. We cannot really understand the way that the structural features described above bounded Canada-US bargaining without looking more closely at the *process* of bargaining, and more specifically at the way officials on both sides came to accept a shared norm against direct, coercive linkages. Keohane and Nye see the emergence of conflict-defusing bargaining norms – and the norm against linkage specifically – as a natural outgrowth of deep interdependence between the two countries. The pattern of dispute outcomes I have described above suggests, however, that interdependence is not a sufficient condition for this kind of cooperative relationship; one might make the argument that it is not a necessary condition either, although there is no way to test this in the context of the Canada-US relationship.

Keohane and Nye were quite right in pointing to the importance of a shared norm against coercive linkages in explaining what was different about the process and outcomes of bilateral bargaining between Canada and the US. But their shallow, functionalist account cannot really explain why the norm had so much weight in US relations with Canada but not with other important partners like Britain or Japan, nor can it explain the norm's declining salience after the early 1970s. It is only with reference to the social origins of this distinctive diplomatic culture that we can understand the former, and it is only with reference to the permissive domestic political context of the early Cold War years (and its unravelling) that we can really understand the latter.

It is interesting to note that some other culturally similar and extensively interpenetrated societies – Sweden and Norway, for example – also fostered the emergence of similarly intimate transgovernmental connections and similarly rich diplomatic cultures in the middle part of the twentieth century.[16] The specific content of the bargaining norms that governed the Sweden-Norway relationship was subtly but importantly different, however. The guiding theme there was "coherence," strongly emphasizing close consultation in policy design and extensive practical collaboration in policy implementation. Most of the norms governing that bilateral relationship had to do with who should share what information with whom and under what circumstances, and what principles should guide joint policy-making.

Canadian and American policy-makers, on the other hand, tended to think and talk more about "partnership," and to put more emphasis on safeguarding autonomy, coping with frictions stemming from policies developed independently, and working together to avoid domestic political trouble. The partnership metaphor tended to echo the imagery and language of military alliance, which is consistent with the diplomatic culture's crystallization in the crucible of the Second World War and the early years of the Cold War. The emphasis on safeguarding autonomy reflected Canada's sensitivity to the overall asymmetry of power, and the focus on minimizing policy frictions – or at least containing the domestic political flare-ups that went with them – reflected concerns that were shared by both sets of officials but more acutely felt in the United States.

The diplomatic culture that evolved within the Canada-US relationship was shaped by a process of signalling and response, through day-to-day cooperation between government officials. Canadian officials made it clear that they were prepared to be flexible and responsive in serving as a strategic and diplomatic ally and in managing the gradual integration of the two economies, but they expected to have continuous reassurances from the United States that it would not try to manipulate the asymmetry of interdependence to compromise Canada's sovereignty and basic policy autonomy. The American policy-makers who worked most closely with Canada recognized and accepted these expectations, but made it clear that they expected Canada to be "reasonable" and reliable. There was a tacit recognition on both sides that there was a quid pro quo in play,[17] but each side tended to frame its expectations of the other in terms of moral absolutes, following from the special obligations that came with partnership.

During the early Cold War decades, the members of the network were empowered to manage the bilateral relationship, and did so according to the norms and practices of the diplomatic culture. While the network was most deeply rooted, and the diplomatic culture therefore most salient – in the 1950s and 1960s – US policy-makers were not inclined to pursue, or even think about, coercive linkages vis-à-vis Canada. This meant that successive Canadian governments were in a position to be assertive in their bilateral dealings with the US, pressing issue-specific advantages to get much more of what they wanted than the overall asymmetry of the bilateral relationship would lead us to expect. Even the most committed members of the network recognized that there were limits to US self-restraint, but those limits were remarkably expansive, and could be tested with some confidence, because they were structured around a normative rejection of linkages per se.

The other part of the argument advanced here – and the way in which it diverges most clearly from Keohane and Nye's interpretation – is the explanation for the diplomatic culture's declining salience after the early 1970s. Economic interdependence between the two countries continued to get broader and deeper through the 1970s and 1980s, and accelerated markedly after the signing of the CUSFTA in 1987, but transgovernmental connections broke down, the salience of the norm against coercive linkages faded, and the process and outcomes of bilateral bargaining changed.

The coherence and salience of the postwar diplomatic culture was a product of the special institutional context that emerged in the early Cold War decades, and could not hold together after that arrangement had broken down. When we are comparing political systems, we usually think of the United States as having an especially society-dominated domestic political structure, with fragmented and decentralized political institutions.[18] But when the US foreign-policy process is compared across different time periods, what stands out is the way that American institutions were *relatively* state-dominated and centralized during the early Cold War decades, not only in high politics issues but also in areas such as trade and investment.

Three main developments in the US drove the displacement of the transgovernmental network: the increased intrusiveness of the White House and its interagency committees (such as the National Security Council) in micromanaging politically sensitive issues; the new assertiveness of Congress after the Vietnam War and Watergate, in both high and low politics issues; and the aggressiveness of other departments' poaching on the State Department's traditional turf, as the internationalization of policy blurred the line between domestic and foreign-policy issues. Similar developments were taking place in Canada at the same time, except that the primary challenge to centralized policy-making was federal-provincial rather than between executive and legislature. The changes in the Canadian system affected the tone of bilateral bargaining, particularly in the 1970s, but it was the changing domestic political structure in the United States that was pivotal to the larger transformation of the bilateral relationship.

A number of scholars and diplomats have lamented the way that the fragmentation of US decision-making has complicated the relationship with Canada, but only a few have tied it to the breakdown of postwar bargaining norms.[19] Both parts of the equation are important. The larger pattern of Canada-US relations cannot be accounted for by a straightforward story about bargaining norms, because the declining salience of the norm can be explained only in terms of domestic structural change. Nor can it be accounted for in terms of domestic politics alone, because the depth and consistency of US restraint in the early Cold War years can be accounted for only by the norm's proscription of coercive linkage (as opposed to other kinds of limits on the exercise of US power).

Four Crises in Canada-US Relations

Keohane and Nye's argument about growing interdependence and the pro-liferation of blocking coalitions is seriously undercut by the broad pattern of dispute outcomes over time. Interdependence has grown over time, yet the Canadian bargaining position does not seem to have improved – indeed, it may have deteriorated since the 1970s. Yet blocking coalitions do seem to be important to the way that the US approaches negotiation with Canada, and my research suggests that interdependence has had some of the effects that Keohane and Nye had in mind, if not necessarily in the same way. The other three general interpretations outlined above – strategic restraint, inter-dependence as a source of triggering coalitions, and diplomatic culture – can account for the basic pattern of dispute outcomes posited here: each leads us to expect the US to have exercised greater self-restraint during the 1950s and 1960s, and to be more inclined to pursue hard linkages afterward. Each therefore expects Canada to have initiated more challenges and to have walked away with more of what it hoped to achieve in the 1950s and 1960s, and to be more cautious and more often frustrated afterward.

Given that the basic expectations of these three interpretations are very similar for the broad pattern of dispute outcomes over time, the only way to break the impasse is to look more closely at some specific disputes. The chapters that follow offer detailed case studies of four of the highest-profile, highest-stakes bilateral disputes of the postwar era: the Diefenbaker-Kennedy confrontation over nuclear weapons (1959-63), the Trudeau-Nixon dispute over Canada's maritime claims in the Arctic (1969-71), the Trudeau-Reagan showdown over the National Energy Program (NEP) (1980-83), and the Chrétien-Bush tensions over the recent US-led intervention in Iraq (2002-4).

The nuclear weapons and Arctic waters disputes took place during the time when the norm against coercive linkages was still firmly rooted (the latter after the supporting transgovernmental network had begun to fray), and the NEP and Iraq cases took place after it had been uprooted. Each case is therefore a test in itself, and the four cases taken together give us a way to assess the larger before-and-after argument.

It is not easy to make a compelling general argument based on a handful of historical cases. In their account of Canada-US relations, in fact, Keohane and Nye specifically warned against the tendency for those with differing interpretations of the relationship to rely on "well-chosen anecdote[s]."[20] The four cases here have been carefully chosen, but in a different sort of way. Rather than looking for episodes to "illustrate" or "confirm" the argu-ment advanced here, I have deliberately chosen the kinds of cases that are *least* likely to support it – that is, cases for which the strategic restraint and interdependence interpretations would expect the US to have done some-thing very different from what the diplomatic-culture interpretation expects.

In addition to testing each of the main alternatives outlined above, moreover, these cases also enable us to rule out other prominent arguments about when and how linkage comes into play in Canada-US relations.

All four cases involve bilateral disputes where the stakes for the United States were high. Thus we can set aside the fairly common argument that the main reason the US has not pursued hard linkages against Canada is simply that Canada has never pursued policies that are sufficiently provocative.[21] That argument has always verged on tautology, since the only "evidence" given to support the proposition that Canada has not pushed too hard is the fact that the US has not retaliated. In each of our four cases, American officials believed that failure to change Canadian policy would have significant, negative effects on the interests of the United States, they were clearly (and often publicly) intensely frustrated by the Canadian position, and they invested substantial time and resources into looking for ways to get Canada to back down. This last point is an important one: it was not that the US did nothing to respond to Canadian policies, but rather that it chose to pursue options other than coercive issue linkages, even in some cases where linkages might have been the most promising option in strict cost/benefit terms.

Moreover, the issues at stake were not only important ones: in all four of the cases – particularly the two earlier disputes – Canadian policy initiatives were seen by American officials to have a direct, negative impact on core US national security priorities. Realism, as outlined above, expects powerful states to be tolerant of challenges by allies on low politics issues, in order to reinforce their leadership on more important high politics issues. Based on the realist argument about strategic restraint, we might say that it is not necessarily surprising that the US deferred to Canada on the Chicago water diversion disputes of the 1950s, or that it let Canada have most of what it wanted in the Auto Pact negotiations in the early 1960s. To the extent that American policy-makers really do follow a stable hierarchy of issues, however, with national security always at the top, they should be expected to be more assertive in disputes over important high politics issues, and to take whatever means may be necessary to prevent small allies like Canada from compromising US national security or directly challenging America's international leadership.

Presumably this sensitivity to security issues, and the impulse to maintain control, will be even more intense when global strategic tensions are most acute, as they were for the United States in the Cold War in the 1950s and early 1960s (prior to the onset of détente), during the renewal of Cold War tensions in the early 1980s, and after the terrorist attacks of 11 September 2001. Three of the four cases here clearly fall into these periods when strategic challenges for the US were most pressing, and one could argue that the Arctic waters case might be seen in this light as well, given American sensitivity to diplomatic challenges in the final years of the Vietnam War.

Furthermore, realists should expect powerful states to be particularly inclined to bargain aggressively with smaller allies when they pursue policies that set unwelcome international precedents or set up dangerous "demonstration effects" for other allies or clients. It is one thing for the US to look the other way when Canada pursues provocative policies within the narrow bilateral context, or for the US to resolve bilateral conflicts by making special exemptions to US policies. It is quite another for American policy-makers to permit Canada to follow through on policies that challenge America's international leadership within a multilateral regime, or set dangerous precedents that might be followed by other allies or clients.

Because the stakes were high in each of these four disputes, they all moved quickly up the political ladder from bureaucratic managers to the political leadership. These cases therefore also directly confront the common argument that Canadian bargaining successes are often attributable to asymmetries of attention, where Canada does well simply because it can afford to assign higher-ranking, more experienced officials to the relevant file.[22] They are thus hard cases for the diplomatic-culture interpretation in another sense, since it will naturally be more difficult for the US members of the transgovernmental network to influence the process and outcome of a dispute after it has become "politicized."

Another bit of conventional wisdom on linkage politics in Canada-US relations is that conflict is more likely when political leaderships with "mismatched" values and priorities are in power.[23] Today we usually expect conflict to be most intense when a Liberal prime minister is lined up against a Republican president. But it has really been this way only since 1968. Prior to that, the Progressive Conservative party generally sought greater distance from the US, and the Liberal party was more inclined toward what is sometimes disparagingly called "continentalism." The Democratic party is usually seen to be more multilateralist and more in tune with Canadian priorities, yet it also represents the interests of organized labour in the US, and therefore triggers Canadian fears of US protectionism. Nevertheless, it is possible to work out basic expectations based on this "political compatibility" theory, and they are reasonably well supported by the pattern of bilateral disputes over the last sixty years. The periods we usually think of as most conflictual, and where the US has been seen to have bargained most aggressively with Canada – the early 1960s, the late 1960s and early 1970s, and the early 1980s – are ones with mismatching parties in power.

But that still leaves unanswered the question of why Canada was able to get away with so many provocative policies in these periods, particularly in the early and very late 1960s, and why Canada had so many diplomatic setbacks in the matching-party periods of the 1980s and 1990s. This is explored in greater detail in the chapters that follow, as all four of the cases feature mismatched parties in power: in each pair of cases (the two earlier cases and the two later cases), we have a Conservative prime minister facing off against a Democratic president and a Liberal prime minister facing off against a Republican president.

It was not only political parties that were mismatched in these episodes, as the political leaders in each of the first three disputes – Diefenbaker and Kennedy, Trudeau and Nixon, Trudeau and Reagan, and Chrétien and Bush – had very different political priorities and negotiating styles, and their personal relationships were characterized by misperception, mistrust, and confrontation. We are therefore also in a position to test another folk theory about linkage politics: the argument that linkages come into play when the prime minister and the president don't get along personally.[24]

The dispute over nuclear weapons in the early 1960s (Chapter 3) is the most difficult case for the diplomatic-culture interpretation, because Diefenbaker's obstructionism and his questionable public statements about NATO nuclear policy directly challenged core US national security concerns, because the negotiations eventually became thoroughly "politicized," and because the personal relationship between Diefenbaker and Kennedy was characterized by mutual contempt and mistrust. US self-restraint is particularly striking in this case, given the Kennedy administration's ready resort to hard linkages in the concurrent nuclear weapons dispute with France. Soft linkages, on the other hand, did have important effects on the bilateral agenda during the early 1960s, as Kennedy's frustration with Diefenbaker seems to have affected the executive branch's management of other, concurrent issues, such as the US Interest Equalization Tax and import restrictions on Canadian lumber, oil, and strategic minerals.

The confrontation over Canada's unilateral claim to jurisdiction over the waters of the Arctic archipelago in 1970 (Chapter 4) is also a hard case for the diplomatic-culture interpretation. Again, Canada pursued a policy that directly threatened important elements of the US national security agenda, in this case America's enduring interest in maintaining unrestricted naval and commercial access to strategic straits and waterways. And US self-restraint with Canada is that much more remarkable given the Nixon administration's inclination to pursue linkages in a similar, concurrent dispute with another country – in this case, Indonesia, over its subsequent claim to the Strait of Malacca. Just as in the nuclear weapons dispute, the foreclosure of hard linkage options in the Canada-US context seems to have intensified US frustration, and may have contributed to subsequent soft linkages, as reflected in the Nixon administration's foot-dragging on Great Lakes water pollution regulations, the breakdown of talks on the development of a continental energy market, and even the decision to include Canada on the list of target countries for the August 1971 "Nixon shocks."

The Arctic waters case is particularly important to the larger purposes of this study, because it erupted in the middle of the transition between the two main phases of the history of the bilateral relationship. It is therefore useful both in pinpointing the timing of the shift and in helping to reveal some aspects of the processes that drove it.

The tensions surrounding the NEP in the early 1980s (Chapter 5) represent a different kind of case, which plays a different part within the research design. Here the puzzle is not why the US was so reserved in a high-stakes dispute over high politics, but rather why it was so inclined to pursue linkage in a dispute over a low politics issue (investment regulation) in an area with some indirect national security implications. Oil and gas issues are always important within the Canada-US context, and substantial investments and profits were certainly at issue, but – in terms of the broader national interests of the United States – the stakes in the NEP dispute were just not as high as they had been in the nuclear weapons and Arctic waters disputes. Yet Reagan administration officials jumped very quickly to consideration of hard linkages, and seemed to go out of their way to signal this to their Canadian counterparts. Ultimately, robust linkage commitments were not made, but that had more to do with domestic political obstacles rather than any enduring commitment to postwar bargaining norms.

The diplomatic tensions surrounding Canada's repudiation of the "Coalition of the Willing" in Iraq in 2003 (Chapter 6) belong to a different kind of episode from the first three – one that revolved around the American reaction to a Canadian decision *not* to do something. In that sense at least, it might have been easier for the US to look the other way. But here the decision not to cooperate had important diplomatic implications, as the Bush administration's primary interest in Canadian support was not based on the value of Canadian military contributions but rather on the importance of Canada's diplomatic endorsement, in terms of both international political legitimacy and US domestic political support. Again, as in the NEP dispute, the stakes for the US were substantial, but they were not nearly as extensive and immediate as those in the earlier disputes. And in another parallel with the NEP dispute, the evidence we have so far suggests that American policy-makers were inclined to look seriously at linkage options, but chose not to pursue them based on issue-by-issue, instrumental cost/benefit calculations, and not because of any kind of normative reservations. Soft linkages again played a major role in shaping the bilateral agenda during this period, as the grudges that the Bush administration held over Iraq undercut its interest in working out a deal with Canada on trade in lumber and beef, or in going to bat for Canada against Congressional pressures for tightened border security (i.e., Canada's inclusion in the Western Hemisphere Travel Initiative).

Outcome and Process

The basic outcomes of these four bilateral disputes are consistent with the expectations of the diplomatic-culture interpretation advanced here, and inconsistent here and there with those of the main alternatives. It is important to go beyond this basic pattern matching, however, and try to confirm that we have arrived at the right results for the right reasons. Three additional tests are therefore performed in each of the case study chapters that follow.[25] For each episode, I identify the most prominent hard linkage options for the US at the climax of the dispute, and assess their political "availability" and diplomatic viability based on a simple set of rational choice criteria. The construction and evaluation of these counterfactual scenarios is an important part of the argument, because a decision (or non-decision) not to pursue linkages is interesting only if it plays out where viable linkage options are clearly within reach. Next, I check the "activation" of various executive branch players in the US, to see whether there is evidence of the transgovernmental network at work. And finally, where possible, I look at the reasons that relevant policy-makers gave for their choices, based on archival records in the older cases and on interviews in the more recent ones.

Because in each of these four episodes there was a great deal of speculation in news reports and parliamentary debate about possible US strong-arm tactics, it is easy to identify specific linkage scenarios. It is also possible to put together a set of basic expected-utility criteria for evaluating the various scenarios, distilled from the extensive theoretical literature on issue linkage.

The theory, model building, and case study research in the broader bargaining literature shows that decisions about whether or not to pursue coercive linkages are enormously complex; nevertheless, it is possible to identify five basic expected-utility criteria to assess the viability of a linkage scenario:[26]

1   The risk/cost imposed on the target state (Canada) by the linkage must be greater than that for backing down – or at least seen to be so – or the target state will simply accept the linkage as the price to be paid for its challenge.[27] These costs may be understood in terms of generalized damage to national interests, or in terms of political danger to the governing party from mobilized domestic interests.

2   The risk/cost involved in going ahead with the linkage commitment cannot be (seen to be) greater than that for other options (e.g., doing nothing, offering incentives, etc.).[28] These considerations must include the risk that the linkage might drive the target state to make other

unwelcome policy adjustments, or push it to try to reduce its vulnerability to further pressure, even at the risk of setting off a spiral of
mutually damaging linkages.[29]

3   The state making the linkage must be able to credibly indicate that it
    could actually follow through with its threat. The linked policy should
    therefore be something under the immediate administrative control of
    the executive branch, which could be carried out in a timely way.

4   The state making the linkage must be able to credibly signal that it *would*
    follow through on the linkage, through its reputation for resolve and/
    or costly signals.[30]

5   Finally, the linkage must be (seen to be) "limited," in the sense that the
    pressure could be released if the other state changed its policy.

With this set of basic criteria, structured arguments can be made about
whether the US *would have been* likely to pursue a particular linkage option,
given the assumptions about US decision-making processes and priorities
entailed in each of the alternative interpretations of Canada-US bargaining.
Applications of the counterfactual criteria indicate that promising linkage
options were readily available to the respective administrations in the nuclear
weapons and Arctic waters cases, but not in the NEP and Iraq cases.

The main finding in the chapters that follow is that the political and institutional barriers to pursuing hard linkages to concurrent issues in the
nuclear weapons and Arctic waters disputes were not high enough to explain
US restraint, so there must have been other factors at work. In the NEP and
Iraq cases, on the other hand, the costs for the US in letting Canada have
its own way were considerably less than in those earlier disputes, so it is
striking that American policy-makers were clearly much more inclined to
think and talk about using hard linkages to pressure Canada into changing
its policies. Ultimately, however, none of the most prominent linkage scenarios was very promising in cost/benefit terms in these two later cases, and
the US did not actually pursue any of its linkage options. The main obstacle
to linkage in the NEP and Iraq cases appears to have been the domestic
political costs involved in sacrificing one issue area in order to improve one's
bargaining position in another. Looking at the process in these cases, and
at the broader pattern over time, it seems that the main factor behind the
change has been the proliferation of domestic coalitions with an interest in
blocking linkages, in accordance with Keohane and Nye's 1977 argument
about the implications of interdependence. This has been reinforced in
important ways, however, by the fragmentation of US foreign-policy decision-
making, and – especially after the signing of the CUSFTA in 1987 – by the
constraining effects of new formal institutions.

Given that the broad argument here is about the importance of the bargaining process, it is appropriate that the case studies look more directly at

the way that the US arrived at specific decisions (or nondecisions) about linkage. Each of the case study chapters therefore also features two kinds of "within-case" tests, designed to get at the institutional and ideational workings of the norm. One is a check on the "activation" of specific domestic political actors within the US foreign-policy making process. During the period in which the network-anchored norm against linkage is expected to have effectively shaped the pattern of outcomes, we should find that the State Department took the lead in identifying and evaluating bargaining strategies, managing the exchange of information among US agencies and officials, and handling contacts with the Canadian government. During the period after the displacement of the norm, the foreign-policy process should be crowded with new players, political leaders and high-level appointees should keep a tighter rein on bureaucratic actors, and there should be coordinated efforts to identify and evaluate linkage options.

This is borne out, for each of the four cases, in the archival records and in interviews with relevant former officials. In the nuclear weapons dispute, State Department officials worked closely with like-minded officials from the Defense Department to effectively co-manage the bargaining process. There was some attention to possible *cooperative* linkages (which ultimately failed), but no coordinated effort to try to identify and evaluate coercive linkages. In the Arctic waters dispute, State Department officials found themselves hard-pressed by the Navy, which pressured the White House to take a more aggressive approach, and proposed a number of linkage scenarios. State Department officials continued to manage the negotiations themselves, however, and maintained a tight grip on key information about legal and diplomatic conditions and – through their Canadian contacts – about the range of incentives and constraints behind the Trudeau government's insistence on a unilateral claim. They were thus able to deflect Navy pressure for linkage, and persuade Nixon and Kissinger that the US had little choice but to carry on with negotiations.

In the NEP dispute, on the other hand, much of the conflict was carried out in the newspapers; informal contacts between diplomats were curtailed and the bargaining process was dominated by cabinet officials; and several different actors (the Commerce Department, the US Trade Representative, some members of Congress) pursued their own, independent investigations of bargaining options. Finally, in the tensions surrounding Canada's decision not to join the Coalition of the Willing in Iraq, there was no coherent American position on how to respond. There was no move toward any particular hard linkage option, but frustration over the way that Canada said no provoked thoughts of revenge in many different quarters, and some high-profile members of Congress evidently put pressure on the White House for an assertive response. But the main way this frustration seems to have manifested itself was in the eruption of soft linkages, which may have had even more severe long-term consequences for Canadian interests than simple retaliation might have had.

The final test is a direct check of the perceptions, rationales, and arguments behind specific decisions about whether or not to pursue certain linkage options, or hard or soft linkages more generally.[31] Where the norm and network are in play, we should expect to find that linkage options are not identified as options at all, or, where they are recognized, that they are rejected on normative grounds. In the period after the breakdown of the diplomatic culture, on the other hand, we should find that decision-makers are more inclined to talk about linkage in much the same way that they talk about any other aggressive bargaining strategy, and that decisions about whether or not to pursue particular linkage scenarios are supported or criticized according to cost/benefit expectations.

Again, these expectations are borne out in the archival records and in interviews with former Canadian and American officials. In the nuclear weapons dispute, US officials did not even recognize coercive linkage options as options per se. With the dispute dragging on for months, they remained convinced that they would have to stick with negotiations, and to appeal directly to Diefenbaker personally. There was some pre-emptive criticism of a possible "heavy-handed" response; more generally, though, it seems clear that hard linkages were simply not on the table. In the Arctic waters dispute, on the other hand, linkages were very much on the table, as the Department of Defense (driven by the Navy) pushed for a more aggressive response to the Canadian claim. State Department officials were able to mount a strong, norm-predicated case against these proposals, however, dismissing them as "bullying" and arguing that they would destroy intergovernmental trust and drive the Canadians to an even more confrontational posture.

In the NEP case, the Reagan administration turned very quickly to consider issue linkages. State Department officials, although strongly opposed to the Canadian position, argued against linkage on grounds in keeping with an enduring commitment to the norm, but their advice was drowned out by other voices. The main line of debate within the US government turned quickly from whether to pursue linkages per se to whether or not to go ahead with specific linkage options. This latter debate, moreover, was carried on mainly in the language of cost/benefit calculations, with specific options endorsed or rejected because they were expected to bring the right mix of strategic effectiveness and domestic political risk.

The pattern is similar in the Iraq case. Because the Chrétien government's abrupt reversal confronted the US with an intractable fait accompli, there was little point in looking at linkage options to force a change. But there was evidently a tendency to think in terms of revenge, and some policy-makers wanted to pursue retaliation as a way to send a signal to Canada and others about the price for defiance. This was not channelled into a coherent bargaining position, however, at least partly because of cleavages within the foreign-policy decision-making structure. To the extent that US officials talked about hard linkage options in this case, they were generally rejected on the ground that they would bring few benefits at a very high cost.

3
Nuclear Weapons, 1959-63

Those familiar with the nuclear weapons dispute are likely to be surprised to find it as the lead case study in a book that sets out to establish the existence and efficacy of a conflict-defusing diplomatic culture in Canada-US relations. The bilateral confrontation leading up to the fall of John Diefenbaker's government in the spring of 1963 is usually seen as one of the postwar relationship's most *un*diplomatic episodes, and it has an established place in efforts to debunk the mythology of the special relationship. In a bilateral relationship generally characterized by goodwill, rule following, and joint pursuit of long-term, common interests, this was unquestionably a dispute driven by mistrust, shortsightedness, and clear-cut violations of some basic diplomatic norms (e.g., quiet diplomacy). That is why it is exactly the right kind of dispute to properly test the diplomatic-culture interpretation advanced in this book.

The Diefenbaker-Kennedy confrontation is best known for the way it ended. On 5 February 1963, Diefenbaker's embattled minority government was defeated in a vote of no-confidence and was forced to call an election. Diefenbaker's Conservatives launched a vigorous, aggressively anti-American campaign, but were narrowly defeated at the polls in April. Many things contributed to this dramatic fall, and many of these were brought on by Diefenbaker himself. But the catalyst for the government's unravelling was a State Department press release that flatly contradicted recent statements by the prime minister on the question of Canada's NORAD and NATO contributions, and its obligation to deploy US-built nuclear weapons. "To put it in the bluntest terms," Canadian newspapers reported, "the State Department publicly called ... Diefenbaker a liar."[1] This triggered an outpouring of indignation in Canada, a fatal split within Cabinet, and ultimately the vote of no-confidence.

Diplomatic historians have, understandably, focused on the question of whether or not the State Department press release actually caused Diefenbaker's fall, and whether or not it had been intended to do so. For the purposes of this chapter, however, the interesting question is not why the US was so aggressive during the early months of 1963, but why it was so *restrained* during the closing months of 1962.

A New Defence Relationship

John Diefenbaker's Conservatives came to power in the summer of 1957, after more than twenty years in the political wilderness, and were re-elected the following spring with a record-breaking majority. Just a few weeks after the 1957 election, the new government formally agreed to the establishment of the North American Air Defence Command (NORAD), a unified, binational air defence system with an integrated command structure. Then in April of 1959, it terminated the development of the Avro Arrow (CF-105) interceptor, thereby tacitly recognizing that Canada could not afford an independent, free-standing defence production capacity. At the same time, the Diefenbaker government initiated talks with the US on the acquisition of alternative, US-made air defence systems, including the Bomarc B anti-aircraft missile and the F-101B ("Voodoo") interceptor.[2] Technically, these were all "dual-use" systems, but military planners on both sides agreed that they had to be nuclear-armed to be "effective."[3] There was an understanding that, pending final negotiations on storage and control, Canada would move quickly to equip these new weapons with nuclear warheads. With these three decisions, Diefenbaker presided over a profound tightening of the bilateral defence relationship, and unwittingly sowed the seeds of the diplomatic confrontation that was to come.

In signing the NORAD agreements, Diefenbaker was deferring to the Canadian military, which had presented it to the new government as a simple extension of existing bilateral cooperation, amounting to little more than "a series of technical decisions."[4] Diefenbaker's quick decision, taken without consulting Cabinet, provoked criticism from the Department of External Affairs and from his parliamentary opposition, thereby stirring the prime minister's resentment and suspicion of the Department of National Defence. In terminating the Arrow and pursuing US-made, nuclear-armed alternatives, Diefenbaker was driven mainly by the perceived need to cut the defence budget without seriously undercutting the country's air defence capability. The intensity of public criticism following the Arrow decision came as a surprise, and made the prime minister anxious and defensive about later defence-policy choices.

Diefenbaker's Delay

There was some friction in the early bilateral negotiations on nuclear weapons, mainly over Canadian concerns about control and storage. But the US Defense Department signalled that it could be flexible on these things, and most observers at the time expected that a mutually satisfactory arrangement would be worked out. Beginning in the fall of 1959, however, Diefenbaker became increasingly reluctant to follow through on these arrangements, and began looking for ways to delay making a final decision. This shift was not caused by any significant change of mind on the part of the prime minister himself. He remained an ardent anticommunist, profoundly mistrustful of the Soviet leadership, skeptical about the prospects for arms control, and generally accepting of nuclear weapons as a crucial component of the Western arsenal.[5] Like many of his major foreign-policy decisions, Diefenbaker's delay on nuclear weapons was driven by domestic political expediency (as he understood it), and later reinforced by his tortured relationship with the new Kennedy administration.[6]

First, the prime minister was deeply concerned that a decision to accept nuclear weapons could be a heavy political liability. The Liberals had overseen an extensive coordination and integration of the two countries' defence efforts, particularly in the last years of the Second World War and the first years of the Cold War. Now in opposition, with Lester Pearson at the helm, the Liberals officially opposed the acceptance of nuclear weapons. The Canadian press had criticized both the Arrow cancellation and the Bomarc acquisition, and was generally seen to be opposed to nuclear weapons.[7] Opinion polls taken throughout this period, on the other hand, showed that the Canadian electorate had mixed feelings about nuclear weapons up until the late autumn of 1962, and then – as I will explain below – were increasingly in favour of accepting them.[8] Diefenbaker was profoundly skeptical of polls, however, and tended to rely on his mail as a measure of the public's views. Since his mailbox was being bombarded by the letter-writing campaigns of a number of peace and disarmament advocacy groups, he was convinced that making a firm commitment to nuclear weapons was politically risky.

Second, Diefenbaker became increasingly concerned – particularly after the autumn of 1960 – that making a decision one way or the other would tear his Cabinet apart. Prior to the Cuban Missile Crisis, Cabinet as a whole was ambivalent about nuclear weapons, and about foreign policy more generally, and usually content to let the prime minister make major decisions on his own. The appointment of Howard Green as Secretary of State for External Affairs in summer of 1959, and of Douglas Harkness as Minister of National Defence in the fall of 1960, created a fault line that would eventually split the Cabinet and cripple the government.

Diefenbaker distrusted both External Affairs and the Department of National Defence, the former for suspected loyalties to his Liberal party rival and the latter for having supposedly "railroaded" him into the NORAD decision. Green and Harkness were seen to be strong ministerial managers who could keep these supposedly willful departments in line and balance each other within Cabinet. Each quickly developed his own agenda, and the two began pulling in opposite directions. Green, with encouragement from

Deputy Minister Norman Robertson, emerged as an active proponent of UN disarmament talks, and took a determined stand against the acceptance of nuclear weapons for Canadian forces, arguing that it would destroy Canada's credibility as a leading advocate of arms control and nonproliferation. Harkness, on the other hand, took up the military's argument that Canada had made a clear commitment to deploy and store nuclear weapons, and pressed Diefenbaker to follow through. The two ministers were soon locked in a struggle for the ear of the prime minister and the support of the rest of the Cabinet, each periodically threatening to resign if his favoured policy was not soon adopted. This tension was heightened by the summer 1962 elections, in which the huge majority of 1958 was reduced to a bare plurality, forcing Diefenbaker to put together a shaky minority government and work under constant threat of a no-confidence vote.

Third, Diefenbaker's inclination to delay was reinforced by his determination not to be bullied by the Kennedy administration. Diefenbaker was not, as many accounts have it – and as he himself denied repeatedly – anti-American. He established a very comfortable personal friendship with President Dwight Eisenhower and a solid working relationship with his administration. Diefenbaker's prejudices and anxieties are better understood, as Basil Robinson has noted, as "anti-establishment."[9] As a small-town public defender and a political outsider, Diefenbaker was profoundly resentful of the privilege and arrogance that he saw in John F. Kennedy's "Camelot."

The intensity of this feeling was clearly evident in his reaction to what might for any other government have been only a minor irritation, quickly forgotten. Departing from a bilateral summit meeting in May 1961, somebody from Kennedy's team carelessly left behind a memo prepared by Walter Rostow, listing for the president "What We Want from the Ottawa Trip." The memo quickly found its way to the prime minister. Diefenbaker was infuriated, not by the positions taken in the memo – which had of course been brought up in the previous day's discussions – but by its recommendation that the president "push" Canada toward the US position on those issues. Diefenbaker's advisers warned him to return the memo with a careful explanation, but he chose instead to hold on to it, as a personal reminder that the Americans wanted to "push Canada around."[10]

Sweetening the Pot, or Poisoning It?

Since the cancellation of the Arrow in 1959, the two governments had been engaged in sporadic talks on a so-called swap deal, by which Canada would receive a replacement force of US-made interceptors in exchange for Canadian-made transport planes. These talks intensified in the weeks leading up to the May 1961 summit, culminating in a US proposal for a new "triangular" deal, in which Canada would receive twenty-six Voodoo interceptors and take over the maintenance of sixteen Pinetree Line radar installations in northern Canada, and the US would sign a $200 million order for Canadian-made transport planes, to be made available to other NATO allies, with the US picking up three-quarters of the costs. This would have filled the gap in Canada's air defences and taken care of part of its NATO contributions, on very favourable terms.

There was one catch, however. US ambassador Livingston Merchant, and later Kennedy himself, insisted that the administration could get the deal past Congress only if it could make the case that it would significantly improve North American air defence, and that would be true only if the Voodoos were equipped with nuclear warheads.[11] The Canadian defence establishment argued that Canada should jump at the chance to get the interceptors on such terms. Diefenbaker was evidently tempted, but ultimately rejected the deal, saying that accepting nuclear weapons at that time would be politically disastrous. Recognizing that the Canadians would not be rushed, and hoping that the transfer would add to the institutional momentum for nuclear deployment, Kennedy authorized US negotiators to push ahead with talks on the triangular deal with no nuclear strings attached.[12]

US officials had seen the original package deal as just that – a simple negotiated settlement, with some conditions for domestic ratification. If there had been any issue linkage, in their eyes, then it was a *positive* one, as the triangular deal itself was so favourable to Canada that it ought to have been seen as an inducement to reassess the domestic political cost of accepting nuclear weapons. Diefenbaker, on the other hand, saw it as a crude negative linkage, in which the Americans had clumsily attempted to tack on new, unwelcome conditions to an established deal.[13]

US officials could be relatively sanguine about the failed negotiation at the time, because Diefenbaker had given his assurance that he would work to prepare the domestic political ground for the eventual acceptance of nuclear weapons.[14] Their confidence was further boosted by Harkness' increasingly vocal behind-the-scenes advocacy of the nuclear option. As a year passed, however, and Diefenbaker became increasingly equivocal, American officials became more and more concerned. A new consensus began to form in Washington that the problem was not in the Canadian electorate but in the heads of a small number of key Canadian officials, particularly Diefenbaker and Green. Green and Robertson had long been written off as proponents of a "naïve" and misguided kind of moralism, bordering on "neutralism," but were recognized as very influential within Cabinet and the civil service, respectively.[15] Diefenbaker, though, continued to profess personal support for the eventual acquisition of nuclear weapons, and US officials still hoped that they could persuade him to try to hurry things along.

The Americans therefore continued to press their main arguments: that Canada had already committed itself to deploy nuclear weapons, that the Bomarc and other post-Arrow acquisitions were virtually useless without them, that Canada's contribution to continental defence was a vital one, and that the domestic political risk associated with making a commitment to nuclear weapons was much less than Diefenbaker believed. Ambassador Merchant took the lead, with substantial follow-up attention from Kennedy and Secretary of State Dean Rusk. With the summer 1962 election approaching, Merchant noted that, despite the difficulties the US had had with Diefenbaker so far, his re-election was still preferable to the most likely alternative, a Liberal-New Democratic Party coalition, which would certainly oppose nuclear weapons and might further undermine NORAD.[16] Frustrations continued to mount after the election, but the US stuck with trying to change Diefenbaker's mind, rather than twist his arm.

Up to this point, most of the major Canadian news outlets had been opposed to the acquisition of nuclear weapons. After the election, however, as Bomarc missiles were being delivered and installed or put in storage, without nuclear warheads, there was a slow but steady increase in the number of editorials criticizing the government's defence policy as clumsy and indecisive. Pressure began to mount within the party ranks for Diefenbaker to make a firm decision to live up to past promises. But the Canadian public was still uninterested, and Cabinet was distracted by more immediate economic problems.

The Cuban Missile Crisis

The Canadian government was informed of the Kennedy administration's decision to blockade Cuba, in a briefing by Ambassador Merchant, just hours before the president's 22 October 1962 television address. Diefenbaker grumbled about the inadequacy of US consultation, but accepted the news gravely and left Merchant with the impression that he would support the administration fully. The prime minister's indignation got the better of him, however, and his speech before the House of Commons that evening suggested the need for independent UN verification and mediation, casting doubt on American intelligence and intentions. Diefenbaker also worried about the public's reaction to close support for Kennedy's risky plan, and shocked Harkness by telling him that the decision to put the Canadian Forces on alert would have to wait for Cabinet approval.

He continued to delay the alert decision even after an angry phone call from Kennedy, and only gave his assent two days later, after US forces had gone to DEFCON 2 and after a Cabinet chamber showdown with Harkness.[17] In fact, Diefenbaker's withholding of formal authorization had little effect on Canada's defence preparedness, because Harkness and the Canadian Chiefs of Staff had secretly initiated a de facto alert right after the announcement of the US blockade. But Diefenbaker's delay had profound political consequences. First, it reinforced the sense of shared grievance, and of common purpose, between Harkness, the Canadian military, and the Kennedy administration. Second, and more important, it got the attention of the Canadian press and public, who were alarmed to hear that their country's primary defences against a Soviet air attack had sat idle during the crisis, many of them in storage, unarmed. The US press and Congress were scathingly critical; the White House smouldered quietly.[18]

This was the crucial turning point in terms of shifting Diefenbaker's position on nuclear weapons from shaky to untenable, but the prime minister did not recognize it as such. Public opinion surveys taken in November and December 1962 showed that a solid majority of the Canadian public believed that their government had undertaken a commitment to deploy nuclear weapons and ought to follow through on that obligation.[19] Diefenbaker remained skeptical of the polls, however, and continued to be influenced mainly by his mail and by close personal advisers such as Howard Green.

The rest of the Canadian Cabinet, however, was alarmed by what had happened and by the public reaction, and they pushed Green and Harkness to start negotiating in earnest. The two governments had initiated informal talks the year before on some kind of compromise settlement, which would allow the Canadian government to set up an effective nuclear capacity without actually becoming a member of the "nuclear club"; the Canadians now pressed for renewal of these talks. Defence planners in both countries were generally skeptical, but, with Harkness' support, they persuaded the Kennedy administration to sign on for the talks in order to generate some kind of forward momentum.[20]

The first idea explored was for a "stand-by" arrangement, in which nuclear weapons would be stored just south of the border, ready to be airlifted to waiting planes and missiles in an emergency. US Department of Defense experts studied a number of scenarios but dismissed each as logistically unworkable. The second idea explored was for a "missing-part" arrangement, in which one critical component of the nuclear warhead would be stored separately in the United States, and rushed to preloaded Canadian weapons in a crisis. The Diefenbaker government could thus give the generals more of what they wanted, without surrendering Canada's "nuclear virginity." US officials were not enthusiastic about this plan either, but were prepared to say that viable schemes might yet be developed, and desultory talks continued on this basis through the winter. At a NATO conference in December 1962, Rusk and Secretary of Defense Robert McNamara met with Green and Harkness, and assured them that the administration was willing to do what it took to help them with their domestic problems, "so long as the solution was not so contrived as to make matters more difficult."[21]

Collision
American frustration came to a head in the new year. On 3 January, retiring NATO commander Lauris Norstad told an Ottawa press conference that

Canada had taken on an obligation to equip its air defence forces with nuclear weapons, and that the Canadian government was thus failing to live up to its NATO commitments. On 11 January, the US Defense Department quietly informed the Canadian embassy that it considered all of the various "missing-part" schemes under consideration to be unworkable, and that, while they were willing to continue the talks, they saw little point in doing so until Canada had developed more promising proposals.[22]

The next day, Pearson reversed his long-standing opposition to nuclear weapons, telling reporters that his party would immediately accept and deploy them in order to live up to Canada's established obligations, and then initiate new negotiations in order to phase them out. Harkness was relieved to hear of Pearson's announcement, thinking that it was now finally politically possible for his government to shift course and accept nuclear weapons. But it only reinforced Diefenbaker's determination to delay. The prime minister, like many of his supporters, saw Norstad's remarks and Pearson's reversal as part of a larger White House plot to topple his government and compel Canada to accept nuclear weapons.

The evidence doesn't support Diefenbaker's conspiracy theory, but it does indicate a marked shift in the US bargaining posture. Norstad's remarks were probably not deliberately orchestrated by the White House, as Diefenbaker believed, but the president's advisers undoubtedly had a sense of what the general was likely to say and did nothing to restrain him. Norstad himself knew that his remarks would cause trouble for Diefenbaker's government, but it seems most likely that he intended only to strengthen the hands of Harkness and other pro-nuclear Cabinet members.[23] Right around the same time that General Norstad was in Ottawa, US officials had begun to hear rumours – through their Canadian press contacts – that Pearson was leaning toward a partial reversal on nuclear weapons, and this would certainly have reinforced their decision to take a tougher stance with Diefenbaker.[24]

Pearson's reversal appears to have been influenced mainly by concern about damage to Canada's long-term relationships with the US and other NATO allies, and reinforced by a November 1962 report by Liberal defence critic Paul Hellyer.[25] The report had described the deterioration of Canada's air defence capacity, its influence in NATO, and the morale of its military services, and it highlighted both what the government had paid for the Bomarcs and what it would have to pay for some kind of non-nuclear replacement. Hellyer's report had also argued that a firm decision against nuclear weapons would almost certainly lead to a deterioration of bilateral defence production cooperation, and hinted at possible economic retaliation.[26] But Pearson need not have taken these latter concerns seriously to have made the decision he did. He recognized that the public tide was now turning against Diefenbaker, and that a commitment to live up to the nuclear agreement could be a powerful weapon against him. The public reaction to

Norstad's remarks confirmed this. Pearson said at the time that his reversal was an act of conscience, not partisanship, but then later reflected that "that was when I really became a politician."[27]

There is no question that Kennedy and most of his closest advisers strongly preferred Pearson, and hoped that he might soon replace Diefenbaker. But the archival record suggests that they were mainly concerned with taking away Diefenbaker's room for manoeuvre, hoping his government would soon be forced to concede or collapse. This was certainly a reasonable expectation. By mid-January, rumours of a split within Cabinet were starting to appear in the press. Harkness' threats to resign had by now become a near-daily event, and other Cabinet members were forming alliances in anticipation of a leadership challenge.

Scrambling to hold things together, Diefenbaker made two major foreign-policy statements designed to deflect Liberal criticism and postpone a decision on nuclear weapons. In a speech on 20 January, he tried to counter the argument that Canada had no choice but to accept nuclear weapons, by arguing that the government had been engaged in talks with the US on a "missing-part" scheme. (He did not mention that these talks had been premised on secrecy, or that the Americans had broken them off just a week earlier.)

On 25 January, he made a complex and confusing speech to the House of Commons, featuring both a promise to work toward the eventual acceptance of nuclear weapons in Canada and a renewed commitment to international disarmament. In the process, he argued that the recent Nassau agreement – in which the US offered Britain the Polaris system as a replacement for the cancelled Skybolt missile – highlighted the receding threat of manned-bomber attack, and the important roles for advanced conventional weapons systems. Because NATO strategic thinking and military burden sharing were in a state of flux, he argued, Canada should suspend any decision on nuclear weapons until after the May 1963 NATO conference. "If ever there was a reason to seriously re-examine every Canadian defence commitment," he later wrote, "this was it."[28] Neither of these statements reflected a new inclination to redirect Canadian defence policy, however; their main purpose was to deflect criticism and set up a credible pretence for delaying a decision until after an anticipated election, in which Diefenbaker hoped to recapture the parliamentary majority he had lost in the summer of 1962.

Angered by Diefenbaker's duplicity and determined to force the issue, Harkness issued a press release on 28 January, "clarifying" Diefenbaker's speech and affirming the Canadian government's commitment to work toward the eventual acceptance of nuclear weapons for Canadian forces in Canada and Europe. The smell of blood was in the water now, and Diefenbaker's government might very well have fallen at this point, without any pushing from Washington.

Meanwhile, however, a small group of US officials who had wanted to take more decisive action against Diefenbaker seized on the 25 January speech and used it to convince higher-level officials in the State Department and White House to take the risk of confronting Diefenbaker directly. Ironically, the initiative came from the US embassy in Ottawa, which had until recently always been a key anchor for the transgovernmental network and a leading proponent of restraint in US policy toward Canada. The recently appointed ambassador, Walton Butterworth, was a notable exception to this rule. His rough manner and confrontational negotiating style alienated Canadian officials and ensured that he – and the embassy more generally – would be kept at arm's length from the rest of the transgovernmental network. Butterworth wrote to Washington condemning Diefenbaker's "masterpiece of deception," arguing that if the US were to "let [Diefenbaker] get away with it," it would make the bilateral relationship harder to manage in the long run, and likely lead to new frictions within NATO.[29]

These arguments resonated with some of Kennedy's key foreign-policy advisers, whose patience with Diefenbaker had all but evaporated. Following Butterworth's advice, Under Secretary of State George Ball had a press release drafted within the State Department, "correcting" a number of aspects of Diefenbaker's 25 January speech, and got White House approval from National Security Adviser McGeorge Bundy and a signature from Secretary of State Rusk.[30] The release, made public on 30 January, flatly contradicted Diefenbaker's recent statements, stating that the "missing-part" talks had been merely "exploratory" and had not been productive, and that the Nassau agreement did not significantly alter US expectations concerning Canada's NATO and NORAD contributions.

Diefenbaker was furious, calling the release an unwarranted interference in Canadian domestic politics. The press reaction was also immediately and overwhelmingly negative, in both countries. The intended beneficiaries of the release, Harkness and Pearson, also publicly condemned it, and both later characterized the statement as not only diplomatically inappropriate but also politically unnecessary and strategically counterproductive. Kennedy, who had not reviewed the release, was also frustrated and embarrassed, and privately castigated Ball and Bundy.[31] Over the next week or so, he worked to distance himself from the press release, without disavowing any of its content.

Aftermath

A few days later, Butterworth was pleased to report that the Canadian press and public reaction had begun to turn.[32] Canadians continued to see the 30 January press release as heavy-handed and intrusive, but many increasingly saw it as an understandable reaction to Diefenbaker's dissembling. A new consensus was emerging in the mainstream Canadian press that the prime minister had been pathetically indecisive, had mismanaged the relationship, and had finally brought out the worst in the Americans.

A few days later, Diefenbaker's Cabinet unravelled. Harkness confronted the prime minister with a final ultimatum, and, failing to secure the firm commitment he insisted on, finally resigned. To his surprise and regret, the rest of the Cabinet rallied around Diefenbaker, believing that he was still the party's best chance in the anticipated election.[33] Nevertheless, the sense of impending disaster within Cabinet was palpable. The axe finally fell two days later, on 5 February, when the government was defeated in a confidence vote in the House of Commons and an election was called for April. A week later, two more Cabinet members unsuccessfully challenged Diefenbaker's leadership and then resigned. Diefenbaker, physically exhausted but driven on by this very personal challenge, focused his campaign on pushing nationalist buttons, raising the spectre of US domination, and attacking Pearson for his close relationship with the Kennedy administration. Pearson's Liberals countered with an attack on Diefenbaker's indecision and duplicity. The campaign stands out as one of the very few in Canadian history in which foreign-policy issues featured prominently. Polls taken at the time, however, suggest that it was not nuclear weapons that divided the voters but rather what Diefenbaker's handling of the issue said about his character and leadership.

Near the end of the campaign, Diefenbaker also got an unexpected boost from the US Defense Department, which chose a bad moment to publish recent Senate testimony by Secretary McNamara, in which he conceded that the Bomarc missile was "an ineffective weapon." The Bomarc did have some strategic value, he said, in that it might draw Soviet missile targeting away from other NATO forces. Diefenbaker was thus able to win points by arguing that Pearson was willing to allow Canada to become a "decoy duck" in a nuclear war. These clever rhetorical flourishes were not enough to bail out Diefenbaker's sinking ship, however; Pearson's Liberals scraped out a bare plurality in the April election, and went on to form a new minority government. Looking back, Pearson later complained that he had probably won the election *in spite of* the Kennedy administration's good intentions.[34]

In retrospective interviews, each of the major US players adamantly denied that the 30 January press release had been intended to topple Diefenbaker's government. "Did we try to knock him over? No, we didn't. We just thought it would solve the problem," Willis Armstrong later reflected, "or at least he would fish or cut bait."[35] This is confirmed in the archival record, including recently opened records of Ball's phone conversations during this period. The officials who prepared and approved the press release knew very well that it would cause an uproar in Canada, but they were surprised and even alarmed by what followed.[36]

It is important, in assessing the decision to go ahead with the press release, to recognize what kinds of risks it involved. It was not hard to see that the release would destroy whatever prospect still remained for convincing the prime minister to take a personal decision in favour of nuclear weapons. There was still the chance that he might be forced to do so under pressure from other Cabinet ministers, but that was a shaky hope at best. Moreover, it was not at all clear at the time that, if an election were soon called, Diefenbaker would not hold on to his plurality, or perhaps even recapture a majority. The election that did follow could have gone either way, and many observers at the time agreed that Diefenbaker's eventual defeat had as much to do with campaign errors as it did with the Cabinet crisis. There was, in other words, the very real possibility that the US might have found itself faced with a Diefenbaker government that was even more intransigent, and with its electoral mandate renewed or even strengthened.

Butterworth later defended the press release decision without reservation. Ball, Bundy, and Armstrong, on the other hand, all publicly conceded that it had been diplomatically inappropriate and probably strategically misguided. This collective reassessment seems to have been driven mainly by criticisms of the move made privately by some of Diefenbaker's domestic opponents, particularly Harkness and Pearson. Nevertheless, while Ball and Bundy later second-guessed the press release decision as a diplomatic move, they both made it clear that they had had no doubts about the accuracy of its contents, and no regrets about its consequences.[37]

When Push Comes to Shove: Explaining US Self-Restraint

At first glance, this case looks like trouble for the diplomatic-culture interpretation. It took place close to what I have identified as the peak of the transgovernmental network's influence over the US bargaining agenda, yet it featured clear violations of some established diplomatic norms (especially quiet diplomacy). Moreover, the ultimate outcome of the dispute itself favoured the American position, as the new Pearson government reluctantly accepted and deployed nuclear weapons. And, as I will explain below, that overall outcome is perfectly consistent with a realist account emphasizing US alliance leadership and the asymmetry of power.

To the extent that these things suggest that it was not surprising that Pearson eventually accepted nuclear weapons, however, they also make it that much *more* surprising that the Kennedy administration allowed Diefenbaker to get away with putting it off for so many months, particularly in the aftermath of the Cuban Missile Crisis. Equally important, it is not at all clear, given what is known about the bargaining in this case, that the final outcome had anything to do with US linkages, either actual or anticipated. Both Pearson's decision to accept nuclear weapons and Diefenbaker's Cabinet split seem to have been driven mainly by domestic political pressures.

The structure of the dispute is exactly the kind in which coercive linkages might have come into play: the US government was aggrieved with the anticipated result of bargaining over the pivotal issue in isolation. The range of possible settlements was limited and discontinuous – basically, Canada would either deploy nuclear weapons or it would not – and the Canadian government would have the last move. Attempts were made to create new settlement points and improve the prospects for a mutually satisfactory compromise, through the "stand-by" and "missing-part" negotiations. But American officials were profoundly skeptical about the technical feasibility of these schemes and were generally reluctant to explore them, both because they believed that the Canadians were already obliged to accept nuclear weapons and because the precedent might complicate nuclear control talks with other NATO allies. At the same time, American officials were reluctant to consider side-payments (i.e., "positive" linkages) as a way to induce Canadian cooperation, because they did not want to reward Canada for living up to established commitments, particularly given the broader NATO audience. If Canada were able to extract new concessions for following through on its alliance obligations, the argument went, surely British Prime Minister Harold Macmillan and French President Charles de Gaulle would be more likely to try to do the same. And, as I will explain below, we can identify a number of apparently viable coercive linkage scenarios. Why then, given the importance the Kennedy administration placed on this issue, were these linkage options (or others) not pursued?

Given the way Diefenbaker reacted to even gentle US pressure, and the desperation with which he held on in the final weeks of the confrontation, we might ask whether *any* kind of coercive linkage could have compelled him to accept nuclear weapons. For the period between General Norstad's press conference and Diefenbaker's electoral defeat, the answer is almost certainly "no." After early January 1963, Diefenbaker was absolutely committed to delay, Cabinet was hopelessly fragmented, and the Canadian public had been acutely sensitized to the question of American "bullying." Any kind of coercive pressure after this time would have made things worse for the US. Prior to the Cuban Missile crisis, on the other hand, American officials were relatively unconcerned about the delay, and fairly confident that Diefenbaker would eventually bring about an acceptance of nuclear weapons. Between these two events, however, there was a two-month period in which one might very well have expected US officials to pursue – or at least seriously consider – coercive linkages.

After Pearson's reversal, Kennedy administration officials began to think about the possibility that the nuclear weapons dispute might be resolved through Diefenbaker's electoral defeat. It had become clear by this point that the prime minister would soon be compelled to call an election, and that he might very well lose. But this was not the case in late 1962. Diefenbaker's Conservatives had lost their impressive majority in the previous summer's election, but they had put together a reasonably reliable parliamentary coalition. The economic turmoil that coincided with the election had begun to settle, and the government's approval numbers, though not strong, were at least fairly stable. Most importantly, Pearson's Liberals still opposed the acceptance of nuclear weapons, so there was no reason to think that a change of government would help the US on this issue.

Nevertheless, it was clear that Diefenbaker was politically vulnerable in another sense. In the immediate aftermath of the Cuban Missile Crisis, the Conservative Party leadership was severely divided, Green was relatively isolated within Cabinet, and Kennedy's popularity in Canada was higher than ever. A clear commitment to withhold or suspend bilateral cooperation in a politically sensitive area might very well have widened the split in Diefenbaker's Cabinet, strengthened Harkness' hand, and forced the prime minister to shuffle Green to a new ministerial post. This would have been risky, as it would certainly have intensified Diefenbaker's mistrust and resentment, and might very well have been leaked to the press, with unpredictable consequences. Nevertheless, if US officials saw serious risks in continued delay on nuclear weapons, as they evidently did, and were skeptical about the "missing-part" talks, as they evidently were, then we ought to have expected them to have at least tested the waters for coercive linkage, by sending some back-channel signals, or at least put some effort into identifying and evaluating some linkage scenarios.

One possible explanation for American negotiators' decision not to pursue linkages in the closing months of 1962 is provided by the realist argument about the logic of strategic restraint, outlined in Chapter 2. The most basic version of that argument is that the US will be more inclined to exercise self-restraint in disputes with Canada during periods when the latter is seen to be relatively valuable as a strategic and diplomatic supporter. The US might therefore have been relatively forbearing in this dispute because it took place during a period when Cold War tensions were high (e.g., Berlin, Laos, Cuba) and the US put a premium on the support of its allies. Canada's value as a strategic and diplomatic supporter had declined somewhat since the early 1950s, however, both relative to that of the Western European NATO members and in absolute terms. The recently signed NORAD agreement highlighted Canada's value as an integrated component in the defence of North America, and the continuing importance of coordinated military decision-making. But it also reflected (and reinforced) an underlying shift from using forward bases to detect and respond to a surprise attack by manned bombers to reliance on a centralized remote-detection and command structure, anchored in the continental US, to coordinate a massive counterattack. The overall effect was a decline in the perceived value of secure access to military bases and infrastructure in northern Canada.

More importantly, the strategic restraint interpretation would expect the US to set aside this more general inclination to be forbearing with allies in disputes where Canadian policies are seen to have a direct, negative effect on core US security interests, particularly where inaction might send a dangerous signal to adversaries or other allies.

The question of control over nuclear weapons was an especially sensitive issue for the United States in the early 1960s, particularly after the Cuban Missile Crisis in October 1962 and the cancellation of the Skybolt missile program in December. That nuclear weapons issues were taken seriously enough to warrant serious consideration of coercive linkages was apparent in the administration's handling of the concurrent confrontation with France. At first glance, the two disputes might seem very different, since the US wanted to push nuclearization in Canada and smother it in France. But the pivotal issue was really the same: US efforts to multilateralize the NATO alliance's nuclear deterrent without giving up control over it.

American officials opposed de Gaulle's effort to develop an independent nuclear deterrent because they thought it would undercut French conventional contributions, encourage Germany to pursue its own nuclear program, and set up dangerous first-strike incentives for the Soviet Union.[38] By the mid-1960s, they had come to accept that there was virtually nothing that could be done to prevent France from building its *force de frappe,* and instead concentrated on trying to make it more stable and more integrated with American and British forces. In the late 1950s and early 1960s, however, they still hoped to discourage de Gaulle from pursuing an independent program, and steer him toward the kind of "dual-key" system being developed for Britain.[39] To this end, the administration encouraged, and the State and Defense Departments pursued, the exploration of scenarios for cooperative and/or coercive linkages.[40] Back-channel signals were sent that French products might be overrepresented in a package of retaliatory tariffs to be imposed on European Community imports during the 1963 "Chicken War" trade dispute. Lengthy delays and embarrassing conditions were imposed on transfers of technology and equipment with any kind of connection to the French nuclear program (e.g., computers). In the end, this was as far as US officials were prepared to go, but this reluctance was a function of their estimation of Charles de Gaulle's determination, and of his apparently unshakable control over French foreign policy, rather than any normative self-restraint.[41]

With respect to Canada, US officials were concerned not only that continuing delay in accepting nuclear weapons would significantly degrade North American air defences but also that it might complicate ongoing NATO negotiations on multilateral nuclear deployment and control. "This is serious enough when we look at it from Washington," one diplomat reported, "it is that much worse when we look at it from [NATO headquarters, then located in] Paris."[42] These latter concerns were heightened by Diefenbaker's statements about the implications of the Skybolt decision, but they were evident even before the Cuban Missile Crisis.

Another possible explanation for US restraint is Keohane and Nye's argument about the implications of interdependence – specifically, their expectation that the US might be held back by resistance from mobilized domestic political coalitions. Because this dispute was strictly about military planning and deployments, however, organized societal groups were simply not an important part of the equation. The only actors with a direct stake in the dispute were the State and Defense Departments, both of which were strongly opposed to Diefenbaker's delay. In terms of the balance of domestic pressures in the United States, then, we might expect to find that there was substantial pressure for assertive action, and virtually nothing holding it back.

Identifying and Evaluating Linkage Scenarios

To properly assess this argument about coalition politics, it is necessary to look outside of the nuclear weapons issue, at the balance of domestic political pressures for each of the most prominent linkage scenarios. There was certainly some anxiety in Canada about the prospect of linkage. Press reports on the leaked existence of the Rostow memo, for example, speculated that it recommended specific threats against American imports of Canadian military equipment, oil, and lumber.[43] In fact, however, the memo had not referred to any of these things, and none of them had received much direct attention in the May 1961 summit. But these issues were not chosen at random. Each was the subject of a concurrent bilateral dispute, each was subject to US executive discretion or control, and each involved very high stakes for a politically sensitive part of the Canadian economy. These were, in other words, the most likely bases for US linkages. In the next few pages, I review each of these parallel issues in turn, with special attention to the domestic political costs and constraints facing each government with respect to that linkage scenario. For each, I will show that the costs of disruption would have been severe for Canada and relatively minimal for the US, that White House officials recognized that they had a measure of bargaining leverage within the given issue, and that they had sufficient administrative discretion or control over the issue to be able to credibly threaten the right kind of disruption. Yet there is no evidence in the archival records of either country that US officials even considered linking them to the dispute over nuclear weapons, let alone signalled any kind of linkage commitment.

The most prominent line of speculation about possible linkages in the nuclear weapons dispute was that the US might respond to a firm decision against the acceptance of nuclear weapons, or to further delay, by clamping down on some of the benefits from the 1957 NORAD agreements and/or the 1959 Defence Production Sharing Agreement (DPSA). These regimes would automatically have been compromised by a Canadian decision against nuclear weapons, since it would mean that certain kinds of technology and intelligence could not be shared. But that was part of the opportunity cost structure associated with the core decision on nuclear weapons, and not a basis for US linkage per se. The original American rationales for these agreements were still in play, and no US administration would have wanted to revoke or otherwise permanently damage either agreement. These original rationales had been undercut by recent technical changes (e.g., declining threat of manned-bomber attack) and by the growing perception of Canadian unreliability, however, and the US might very well have considered an actual or threatened disruption of either or both regimes as the basis for forcing a change to Canada's policy on nuclear weapons. The challenge would have been in working out a temporary restriction that would have imposed severe short-term costs on Canada without risking long-term damage to the regimes themselves.

The purpose of NORAD was to set up a unified command structure, with carefully arranged power-sharing provisions designed to facilitate efficient decision-making and overall US control, while still providing for the information sharing, consultation, and (asymmetric) checks and balances that Canada would need to claim a measure of sovereign control. American officers and officials were generally satisfied with the design and operation of NORAD, and would therefore oppose a threat to revoke the agreements or any other linkage that might permanently damage the institution. But they would have been less concerned about an informal threat to stem the (one-way) flow of military intelligence.[44] That linkage would have had a strong, indirect effect on the Diefenbaker government, as the Canadian military establishment reacted to the anticipated damage to its capacity for independent planning and to the prospect of a more basic attenuation of its influence within the alliance.

The purpose of the DPSA, on the other hand, was to help sustain what remained of Canada's defence production infrastructure after the Arrow cancellation. Diefenbaker's decision to scrap the Arrow had been contingent not only on having worked out a formal deal for immediate replacements (the Bomarc and the F-101B), but also an informal understanding that Canada would have an assured place within an integrated continental defence production system. US officials wanted to make sure that Canada would be able to maintain at least a latent long-term capacity to contribute to defence research and production, and hoped that integrated defence production would help to foster interoperability and reinforce existing inter-service and inter-bureaucratic relationships. Nevertheless, the whole package was considered by many in Washington to have been a favour to Canada that could be revoked at little or no cost to the US. A formal suspension or an informal administrative tightening of DPSA contracting would have been devastating for the defence economy in the politically vital industrial zone of southern Ontario, already reeling from the cancellation of the Arrow. And it would threaten an important source of foreign exchange earnings, exacerbating the country's severe balance of payments problems.

A threat to *terminate* either or both of these agreements would not have been very credible, given the evident and enduring US interest in close, long-term cooperation on these issues, and the obvious political challenges involved in reversing a prominent executive agreement with a close ally. An informal threat to temporarily cut off some of the benefits of these arrangements, on the other hand, would have been very credible. Both the sharing of military intelligence and decisions about the allocations of short-term defence contracts were subject to the administrative discretion of the White House and the Defense Department, and either or both could easily have been temporarily, informally constricted as necessary. American military officials would have been cautious about such a disruption, hoping to avoid a direct confrontation with their Canadian counterparts, but, given the high value that they placed on shifting Diefenbaker's position on nuclear weapons, we might very well have expected them to be prepared to put those inter-bureaucratic relationships at some risk in order to force the issue.

Economic linkages were also a promising option, particularly given Canada's severe balance of payments problems during this period. The Diefenbaker government was still reeling from a forced devaluation just prior to the summer 1962 election, with voters feeling the pinch of an austerity program and the federal government desperate to hold on to foreign exchange earnings. The Kennedy administration had played an important role in helping Canada stabilize its new fixed exchange rate, and had been grudgingly looking the other way on recently imposed import surcharges. This close cooperation meant that US officials were well aware of the vulnerability of the Canadian economy, and – particularly given the shift to a minority government that summer – of Diefenbaker's government.

One of the key sources of potential leverage was the concurrent dispute over US oil import quotas. In setting up the 1959 Mandatory Oil Import Program (MOIP) quotas on foreign oil, the Eisenhower administration had created an "overland exemption" for imports from Canada and Mexico, based mainly on security-of-supply considerations. Partly in response to the incentives created by the exemption, the Diefenbaker government decided in 1961 that, rather than support the building of a pipeline to ship western Canadian oil and gas to eastern Canadian markets, it would encourage the export of western Canadian oil to the lucrative western and midwestern US markets, and allow eastern Canada to import cheaper overseas oil (mainly from Venezuela). This was an excellent arrangement for the Canadian government, as it provided relatively cheap fuel for politically sensitive Quebec and the less-developed Maritime provinces, and raked in desperately needed

US dollars. But it created new problems for the US government, as the White House was swamped with complaints from US domestic producers and from nonexempt suppliers such as Venezuela. Pressure on the White House was spearheaded by the Department of the Interior, which argued that the overland exemption hurt US business by giving eastern Canadian industry an advantage over northeastern US competitors, and put US supply at risk because, in an emergency, Canada was likely to divert oil shipments from the US Midwest to eastern Canada.[45] There had been some bilateral consultation on oil imports, and the Canadians had been somewhat cooperative in agreeing to try to persuade exporters to stick to informal targets, but had not accepted any binding limits.[46] The Canadian government's efforts were doing little to slow the penetration of the American market, and there were more and more calls in the US for a rethinking of the overland exemption.

The White House had administrative discretion over the quota system, and was therefore in a position to make a credible linkage commitment. There was strong pressure from domestic producers and their Congressional supporters for a revocation or reduction of the overland exemption. Those likely to be injured by a restriction, the "northern tier" refiners and midwestern and northeastern consumers, were relatively dispersed and disorganized. The real basis for counterpressure came therefore from the State and Defense Departments, which hoped to support long-term exploration and development in Canada (as a secure source of supply) and to maintain good relations more generally.[47] Domestic producers unsuccessfully attempted to attach an "oil clause" to the Kennedy administration's Trade Expansion Act (TEA) in June 1962, and kept up the pressure in anticipation of a White House decision on oil imports to be made late in the fall. The administration finally made a proclamation in late November, maintaining the overland exemption but changing the quota system in order to make it slightly less advantageous to hold quota-exempt import tickets for Canadian oil.

As with the DPSA, the American rationale for accepting the original, asymmetrical arrangement here was a larger national security agenda – in this case, short- and long-term security of supply. Given the relative stability of the world oil price during this period, and growing concern about Canada's reliability as a crisis supplier, the national security argument had been weakened somewhat between 1960 and 1962, and the US had acquired a measure of unexploited bargaining leverage. An abrupt restriction on imports from Canada would impose high short-term costs on both countries, but these would have been much higher for Canada. A more severe, longer-term disruption – e.g., revocation of the overland exemption – would have been devastating for Canada, as it could compete with foreign oil only on level terms in some small niche markets, and had no promising international alternative markets. The "northern tier" refiners were worried that a sharp restriction would prompt Canada to build the pipeline to Montreal and shut off the supply to the Midwest, but the disruption would have been temporary and the costs of switching to US and Venezuelan oil probably not as severe as they claimed. (The refiners were injured when tight mandatory quotas were finally imposed on Canada in 1970 – as described in the next chapter – but the White House took the edge off through side-payments built into the administration of the quota.)

The third prominent basis for potential linkage, US imports of Canadian softwood lumber, has received far less attention than high politics issues such as nuclear weapons, but it has been enormously important in both economic and political terms for both countries, and has set up some of their most severe bilateral conflicts. During the early 1960s, the sudden devaluation of the Canadian dollar made it possible for Canadian lumber to rapidly capture a much larger share of the US market. The Congressional representatives of hard-hit northwestern states came together to press the administration for some kind of protection, and, like those pushing for restrictions on oil, tried to make a legislative hostage of Kennedy's trade bill.[48]

The administration rejected the imposition of tariffs, and instead offered a package of informal compensations, including a promise to initiate talks with Canada on a voluntary export control regime, increase domestic allowable-cut levels, inject money into road building and other infrastructure development, and amend the Merchant Marine Act to allow for cheaper foreign-flag shipping under vaguely specified "emergency" conditions. Most Congressional supporters of the American lumber industry were generally in favour of free trade, and of the TEA itself, and had been driven to oppose the bill mainly by pressure from the well-organized regional lumber lobby.[49] They were thus easily persuaded to accept Kennedy's "Six-Point Plan," and each of them voted for the TEA, despite the fact that International Trade Commission (ITC) hearings on Canadian lumber were not scheduled to begin until October. The ITC deliberated through the winter and finally ruled in mid-February that the damage to the US industry had not been caused by Canadian tariffs, meaning that domestic lumber would not receive newly established "adjustment assistance" funds. Pressure was renewed, but, without the legislative leverage that came with the TEA negotiations, it went nowhere and effectively ended when President Lyndon Johnson vetoed a country-of-origin bill at the end of 1963.

A restriction on lumber exports to the US would have been devastating for the Diefenbaker government, given its concentrated impact on the party's core constituency region (western Canada) and the likely damage to foreign exchange earnings. One study estimated that lumber exports to the US represented over 10 percent of Canada's total foreign exchange earnings at that time.

The Kennedy administration was well positioned to make a credible linkage commitment, simply by making a lesser effort to block the attachment of protections for lumber in the TEA. A threat to do so would have been made credible by the intensity of Congressional pressure and the high-profile efforts of the US lumber lobby. By following the path of least resistance, Kennedy might have won some political points in the Pacific Northwest, and perhaps secured some additional Congressional support for the TEA. Given that the peak of US frustration with Canada's nuclear delay did not come until after Kennedy had hurdled the lumber lobby and the TEA had been passed, one might argue that lumber restrictions were no longer available as a basis for coercive linkage. A threat to impose restrictions on Canadian lumber was certainly made more awkward, administratively and diplomatically. But Canadian officials offered virtually nothing in bilateral talks on the lumber issue in October and November, the US lumber lobby continued to command the support of some influential senators, and the ITC had yet to deliver its verdict. There was, in other words, still room for the Kennedy administration to use the threat of lumber restrictions as a source of bargaining leverage, if it had been so inclined.

The real key to the question of whether or not lumber restrictions were a viable linkage option is how the administration weighed the importance of forcing a change in Canadian nuclear weapons policy against the cost of a partial compromise of the TEA – or the risk involved in threatening to make such a compromise. There is no question that the administration was opposed to protection for the lumber industry, and – more importantly – to the prospect of a precedent that might encourage other protectionist demands. As I noted above, however, the White House placed a very high priority on shifting Canadian nuclear weapons policy and had the support of top officials in the State and Defense Departments. The extent of their frustration and their willingness to play rough and take risks are reflected in the decision to go ahead with the 30 January press release. So the question of why the administration did not pursue coercive linkages remains unresolved.

The absence of any clear-cut commitments to specific issue linkages in this case does not mean that there were no diplomatic or political consequences, or that the nuclear weapons dispute was entirely self-contained. The tensions surrounding this dispute certainly generated a number of what was referred to in Chapter 1 as soft linkages. In this case, they took the form of a general disinclination to grapple with, or even pay much attention to, Canadian requests on other issues.

Robert Kennedy later remembered that his brother detested Diefenbaker, and had essentially "given up on" him.[50] As the administration's frustration increased, its interest in constructively using and maintaining the established machinery for bilateral policy coordination declined. Leadership and cabinet-level contacts remained extensive until the Cuban Missile Crisis, in spite of sour personal relations between president and prime minister, but were after that reduced to little more than a few bad-tempered telephone calls. Even through this most conflictual period, the day-to-day administration of policy coordination and routine "technical" cooperation among lower-level officials carried on as usual.[51] But the poisonous relationship between president and prime minister suffocated middle-level officials' efforts to resolve new or enduring frictions, and to identify and pursue new joint planning initiatives, in other issue areas.[52] This kind of soft linkage did have important effects on the pattern of bargaining outcomes during this period, but it did not – and was not expected to – change Diefenbaker's position on nuclear weapons.

The fact that the US did not make specific linkage commitments, and thereby made it possible for Diefenbaker to get away with refusing to accept nuclear weapons, is of course consistent with the expectations of the main argument here. In order to show that the right outcome was arrived at for the right reasons, however, I now turn to look more closely at the bargaining *process*. First, I briefly describe the activation of different players within the organizational structure of US foreign-policy making, with particular attention to the individuals and offices that took the lead in identifying and evaluating bargaining options. Second, I report the perceptions and rationales – as revealed in the archival record – behind decisions (and nondecisions) about various bargaining strategies.

During the critical weeks following the Cuban Missile Crisis, US officials debated how best to respond to Canadian delay. The array of available options was very broad, but there were essentially only three kinds of strategic choices: persuasion, inducement, or coercion. Because Diefenbaker himself was seen as the main sticking point, out of step with his country's military establishment and the electorate, US officials naturally gravitated toward persuasion. Most in Washington were extremely reluctant to pursue inducements, because – as they saw it – Canada had already made an informal commitment to deploy nuclear weapons. Offering side-payments to encourage the Canadian government to live up to that commitment was not only morally unacceptable but also likely to set a dangerous precedent for other recalcitrant allies. There were small and halfhearted attempts to pursue a limited kind of positive linkage, through the conditional "swap deal" and the "stand-by" negotiations. Once those failed, and it became clear that persuasion had brought little result over many months, US officials might very well have been expected to turn to coercion. But the US members of the transgovernmental network quietly held the administration to the persuasion option, all the way through the closing months of 1962.

US Decision-making: Actors and Arguments
In all four bilateral disputes reviewed in this book, government officials attempting to "manage" the relationship were undercut by the nature of the

issues in play and by severe tensions between the respective political leaders. This is an important part of what makes these hard cases for the diplomatic-culture interpretation. In the later disputes, however, these case-specific pressures were strongly reinforced by a more enduring domestic political restructuring, which severely challenged the network (Arctic waters) or actually pushed it to the margins (oil and gas, Iraq). In the nuclear weapons dispute, the disruption of the network occurred mainly on the Canadian side and was minor. Moreover, the nature of this disruption – Diefenbaker's personal mistrust of the Canadian foreign service – seems to have reinforced the sense of common purpose within the network, and may have actually invigorated middle-level State Department officials' determination to uphold and sustain the network's defining principles and practices.[53]

As noted above, Diefenbaker was convinced that the Department of External Affairs was still loyal to former bureaucrat Lester Pearson, now leader of the Liberal opposition, and to the Liberal party more generally. He was therefore reserved in accepting the department's advice on both routine and crisis decisions, and was inclined instead to follow his own views and those of close political allies. Diefenbaker was also recognized both by External Affairs officials and by the White House as more likely than most Canadian prime ministers to view even crucial foreign-policy decisions in terms of immediate domestic political expediency, and therefore to be especially unreceptive to veteran External Affairs officials' arguments about the long-term rewards to be reaped by subordinating immediate advantage to "the health of the relationship."[54]

The State Department's influence as a foreign-policy player had declined fairly steadily since the late 1940s. Nevertheless, it continued to be the central agency for foreign policy in the US, with special rights and responsibilities for identifying and evaluating bargaining options and for the conduct of negotiations themselves. The State Department was certainly far more influential in the US foreign-policy process during this period than it would be in later decades, particularly in relations with Canada. In terms of day-to-day contact and bilateral policy coordination, mid-level State officials enjoyed a significant measure of autonomy. Even when it came to more intense, protracted disputes, these well-connected officials were able to exercise substantial influence over the diplomatic choices placed before higher-level officials, and over the way those choices were weighed. This influence came mainly from their expert credentials, a general consensus on means and ends, and the "diplomatic intelligence" they acquired through informal contacts with their Canadian counterparts.

These things were especially true while Livingston Merchant was the US ambassador to Canada (March 1961 to May 1962). Merchant was a core member of the network, with a strong personal commitment to its purposes and principles, strong personal connections with other influential US officials, and strong personal credibility with Kennedy. His replacement, Walton Butterworth, was an outsider who recognized no need for any "special treatment" for Canada. His aggressive style rubbed most Canadian officials the wrong way, and he – and by extension the embassy as a whole – was therefore excluded from many important informal exchanges. Merchant's departure, the long delay in replacing him, and the eventual appointment of Butterworth were not coincidences. The first certainly reflected the overall frustration within the network under Diefenbaker, and the second and third probably reflected the Kennedy administration's frustration with Canada more generally.[55]

Despite these obstacles, US members of the transgovernmental network seem to have played a leading role in framing the way that the administration saw its bargaining options, through their credibility as managers of the relationship and their domination of the bargaining process. Some of the most important formal exchanges were made directly between president and prime minister. Diefenbaker followed his own script in these meetings, but Kennedy was generally cautious and reserved, following the main lines laid down by network-connected Canada experts. The record of the major bilateral meetings indicates that Kennedy's questions and answers consistently reflected the language and logic of State Department briefing materials.[56] Virtually all of the information that found its way to the White House originated in or passed over the desks of leading network members, particularly Livingston Merchant, Willis Armstrong, Rufus Smith, and Ivan White. Their positions were worked out in – and drew much of their credibility from – extensive informal contacts with their Canadian counterparts, particularly Robert Bryce, Basil Robinson, and Ross Campbell. These meetings were "friendly and casual, but deadly serious,"[57] usually one-on-one, over lunch in one capital or the other, or over the telephone. They were not negotiations in the strict sense, since none of the players had the authority to make concrete concessions or commitments. But they were meaningful exchanges, in which information about Cabinet- and official-level perceptions and political priorities was traded, and the basic outlines of a common strategy for conflict management were worked out.

There is no evidence in the archival record – in the files on nuclear weapons or those on the concurrent disputes described above – of any kind of effort by the White House or the State Department to try to identify or evaluate linkage options. Core network members were also responsible for monitoring the concurrent issues and disputes reviewed in the counterfactual scenarios above, and were certainly aware that the US might have some unexploited bargaining leverage in those areas. Armstrong and White, for example, were in the loop for virtually all correspondence and reports on the lumber and oil disputes, and most of the political traffic on NORAD and the DPSA. The State Department's "failure" to identify viable linkage options is thus best understood not as an inability to put the pieces together but rather as a general disinclination to acquire the information in the first place. It suggests, in other words, a shared worldview that made coercive issue linkage unthinkable in the context of the Canada-US relationship.

In this case, the vitality of the norm against coercive linkage is reflected not so much in what US officials said as in what they did not say. There was of course a great deal of talk in Washington about bargaining options during the course of the dispute, but this was limited to a very narrow range of options, and featured very little disagreement on the underlying principles and premises. What comes out of the archival record, up to the end of 1962, is a rapid and enduring convergence among relevant career bureaucrats on what was going on in Canada, and within the Canadian Cabinet in particular, and a fairly straightforward transmission of that picture up the decision-making hierarchy to the political leadership. There is no indication of any sustained disagreement on these questions within the State Department or between the State and Defense Departments. And there is no evidence of any sustained argument for a basic strategic shift from persuasion to either inducement or coercion. The evident lack of attention to a number of readily available linkage options indicates that the norm was so taken for granted within the relevant parts of the US foreign-policy hierarchy at this time that they simply did not recognize linkage options as options at all.

Although there is no evidence that anyone in the US seriously advocated a shift to a coercive strategy prior to January 1963, there were a number of pre-emptive warnings against such a move. Merchant and others dismissed the idea of pursuing (unspecified) coercive moves as "heavy-handed[ness]" or "bullying."[58] At the same time, they warned that threats, no matter how carefully chosen and conveyed, were likely to backfire, because they would trigger Canadian apprehension about US domination. Most of these warnings focused on the importance of not stirring up Diefenbaker's suspicion that the Americans wanted to "push Canada around." But there was also a recognition that Diefenbaker was not working in a political vacuum – that his government was in part a manifestation of growing concern within Canada about the political vulnerability that had come with postwar economic interdependence. An overt coercive linkage would be received in Canada as a sign that the US was now willing to use interdependence as a weapon, and catalyze nationalist pressures that might threaten the entire framework of bilateral policy coordination. Even if the linkage threat were not leaked to the public, it would rupture the reservoir of trust accumulated within the transgovernmental network, and thereby make future dispute management much more difficult.

One might argue that this reflects a simple expected utility calculation, and is therefore readily explained by conventional accounts of bilateral bargaining. It could be explained in those terms. But US officials' assessments of coercive linkage as a general strategy do not seem to have been underpinned by any sustained attention to the likely costs and benefits associated with specific linkage options. Arguments that linkage would not work or would be too risky therefore look like the application of a simplifying rule of thumb, based on a larger, shared perception of the way the bilateral relationship was supposed to work. And this shared understanding seems best understood as a manifestation of the diplomatic culture described here.

Network-connected US officials did not support the "stand-by" and "missing-part" negotiations because of any confidence in the practical utility of the proposed schemes. They supported the talks as a forum for sustaining connections with like-minded Canadian officials and for trying to reach out to new ones. As more and more people were persuaded that Canada had taken on an obligation to deploy nuclear weapons, they hoped, the balance within the Canadian Cabinet might tilt, and Diefenbaker's hand might be forced by pressure from inside. This strategy carried over into the early months of 1963, but in an importantly different way. Beginning in early January, US officials shifted from trying to win Canadian supporters by being as flexible as possible to trying to galvanize established cross-border allies by being conspicuously inflexible. This shift was reflected in Norstad's remarks about Canada's failing to live up to NATO obligations, and subsequent, similar comments by other US officials. This was a riskier strategy, fuelled in part by raw frustration. Ultimately, however, it depended on a sober evaluation of the implications of Pearson's decision to switch to a pro-nuclear weapons position.

It is hard to guess how well this new strategy might have worked in the longer term, because other things had changed and the new situation was inherently unstable. Diefenbaker's provocative comments about the implications of the Nassau meeting created an opening for Butterworth to push for a more open diplomatic confrontation, which eventually took the form of the 30 January press release. This was – as noted above – a risky move, and it was not supported by network-connected, middle-level officials. State Department Canada specialists, who were given only a fleeting opportunity to comment on a draft of the release before it was made public, did not doubt that it was factually correct, but worried that it would be a diplomatic disaster.[59] Like the unspecified linkages that they had warned against in recent months, the press release would not only fail to change Diefenbaker's mind but might in the process inflame Canadian nationalism and set off a mutually damaging cycle of escalating disruptions. Ball and Bundy were only dimly aware of these complaints, and only really came to understand these risks after being confronted with strong, negative reactions from Pearson, Harkness, and other like-minded Canadian officials.

The 30 January press release was a clear violation of established norms against publicly airing grievances over secret negotiations (quiet diplomacy), especially where a public challenge would clearly undermine the other government within the domestic political arena (non-interference). But it does not necessarily undercut the argument that the nature and extent of US restraint in the nuclear weapons dispute is best explained in terms of adherence to a norm against coercive issue linkage. In fact, it reinforces this interpretation, by making the puzzle of "missing" linkages even more puzzling. If the Kennedy administration was so concerned about the implications of Diefenbaker's nuclear delay that it was willing to blatantly violate other long-standing bargaining norms, why did it not pursue – or even explore – coercive linkages? Or, more generally, why pursue *this* risky strategy rather than another one that might be more certain in delivering an immediate policy reversal?

Epilogue: Back to Business as Usual?

The normalization of Canada-US relations happened very quickly after Pearson's Liberals took office. Pearson travelled to Hyannis Port a month after the election, for two days of informal but very carefully arranged meetings with Kennedy, surveying the full range of bilateral issues. Kennedy was well prepared, the frank and friendly personal relationship between the two leaders was deepened, and basic understandings were set down for renewed talks on a number of important issues.[60] The thaw at the top thus reopened the pipeline for everyday problem-solving, and formal and informal contacts between middle-level bureaucrats were rejuvenated. This return to business and the Liberals' receptivity to integrative solutions were reflected in a flurry of new policy coordination agreements over the next three years. Some of these were resolutions of long-standing negotiations that had been paralyzed by the Kennedy-Diefenbaker confrontation, such as the Columbia River Treaty. Others were ambitious new solutions to disputes that had recently erupted, such as those governing civil air routes and auto production. In each of these, the Kennedy and Johnson administrations' main purposes seem to have been to look out for the bottom-line interests of US investors, to avoid public confrontation and avoid harming Pearson's shaky new government, and – as always – to quickly remove distractions from the United States' more pressing foreign and domestic problems.[61]

At the conclusion of their first meeting in January 1964, Pearson and Johnson agreed to set up a working group, chaired by former ambassadors Livingston Merchant and Arnold Heeney, to study what had gone wrong with the relationship in recent years and to identify basic principles for managing bilateral conflicts. The resulting report, published six months later, reaffirmed the core tenets of the postwar transgovernmental network: timely and extensive consultation, quiet diplomacy, pragmatism, and selective integration.[62] In the process, it implicitly assigned blame for the Kennedy-Diefenbaker meltdown on the respective political leaders' failure to adhere to the advice and practices of their officials. Public reaction to the Merchant-Heeney report was mostly negative, particularly in Canada, where it collided head-on with a rising wave of nationalism. It was, however, well received by both the State Department and External Affairs, as a reflection of the way network members continued to see the relationship's essential challenges and their solutions.

Overall, the mid-1960s was a period of bilateral goodwill and constructive problem-solving, but it was not without diplomatic tensions. There was, for example, friction in the post-Diefenbaker negotiation of the nuclear weapons agreement, mainly over the original problem of the sovereignty implications of the proposed storage and control arrangements. US officials never fully understood Canadian sensitivities on these issues, but were willing to make some special arrangements to accommodate them.[63] More intense were the disagreements over maritime boundaries, tax exemptions for magazine advertisements, and the enduring problem of oil imports. Disagreement over US intervention in Vietnam continued to grow, and sometimes came out publicly. Canada did not always get its way in these disputes, but the way that they unfolded tends to reinforce the diplomatic-culture interpretation. In each case, problems were explored quietly and informally at lower levels, American negotiators stuck to the legal and technical merits of the issue at hand, and Canadian officials made decisions about whether or not to press the issue based mainly on anticipated domestic political reactions.[64]

As a civil servant, Pearson had been seen by many as the embodiment of Canada's foreign policy "golden age," and of the distinctive diplomatic culture that had governed Canada's relations with the US in particular. As a politician, this image was a source of both political credibility and political trouble. Most Canadians were inclined to trust him to manage the relationship skillfully, or at least more skillfully than Diefenbaker had done. But others – even those who gave little credit to Diefenbaker's accusations of collusion in the 1963 election – worried that Pearson and the Liberals were too close to the Americans, and would sacrifice Canada's independent international voice and domestic autonomy to the pursuit of an illusory kind of influence.[65] Canada's economic weakness heightened concerns about US ownership of Canadian industry. America's racial conflict, urban poverty and violence, and political gridlock raised serious questions in Canada about the US as neighbour and role model. And the worsening situation in Vietnam seriously undercut Canadian confidence in the US as a strategic and diplomatic partner. These developments would fire Canadian intransigence in a number of disputes in the late 1960s and early 1970s, including those over nuclear testing, Canada's role in the International Commission for Supervision and Control in Vietnam, and joint control of water pollution.

Less visible at the time but more important in the long run were the first stirrings of a larger process of domestic political restructuring that would unfold over the next ten years in both countries. Through the 1950s and 1960s, the transgovernmental network's main challenge in setting the bargaining agenda had been to maintain their connections and influence during periods when particular political leaders were personally skeptical or mistrustful of their contributions, as in the early Truman and Eisenhower years, and under Diefenbaker. Looking back at the mid-1960s, however, we can now see the earliest signs of a more permanent kind of displacement, as the traditional foreign-policy departments were weakened by cross-cutting tendencies toward centralization and fragmentation within the executive structures of both governments. In Canada, Pearson's election bolstered spirits within External Affairs, but it did not lead to the rejuvenation of the department that many had expected. Instead, External Affairs found itself short-circuited by powerful political leaders and confused by administrative reforms.[66] In the US, the relaxation of Cold War tensions in the mid-1960s might have been expected to lead to a general loosening of central executive control over foreign-policy making, but the strains of the war in Vietnam provided an alternative basis for tight White House control.[67] At the same time, the dislocations brought by greater openness to the international economy drove many of the "domestic" bureaucratic departments to develop the means to intervene directly and aggressively in the foreign-policy process, through independent information gathering, interdepartmental diplomatic planning, and direct contacts with foreign counterparts. These early signs of shifts within the executive in both countries were accompanied by the first signs of a deeper restructuring in the US of the relationship between the executive branch and Congress. Congress would continue to be generally passive with respect to strategic and international political issues until the end of the Nixon period. Beginning with the struggle over the Trade Expansion Act in 1962, however, Congressional representatives were increasingly sensitive to pressures from hard-pressed constituents, and became increasingly active in scrutinizing and forcing changes to trade and investment policies.[68]

These cracks in the network's structural foundations were only just beginning to appear in the mid and late 1960s. The challenges they posed for the old informal structure of bilateral dispute management would become brutally apparent in the dispute over Arctic maritime claims, described in the next chapter, but they would not begin to seriously weaken the transgovernmental network, or the diplomatic culture that defined it, for a few more years. It was only in the 1970s that an accumulation of pressures – domestic upheaval, the disaster in Vietnam, and the perception of relative decline – would come together to trigger a more enduring restructuring of the US foreign-policy process, and the proponents of the postwar diplomatic culture would be overwhelmed by a welter of discordant voices.

4
Arctic Waters, 1969-71

Canada-US diplomatic crises sometimes come about as the result of a deliberate push by one government or the other. More often, they occur when the premises underpinning some part of the prevailing tangle of tacit policy coordination understandings are disrupted by something from outside: a diplomatic bump, a market slump, a technological jump, etc. The two governments are thereby forced – usually by a jolt of domestic political pressure – to scramble for a new equilibrium. One shock of this kind was the discovery in 1968 of massive oil deposits under the North Slope of Alaska. The Prudhoe Bay discovery rattled two of the most delicate parts of the prevailing bilateral policy equilibrium: the continental energy market and – once the major oil companies hit on the idea of shipping the oil through the Northwest Passage to East Coast markets – the question of sovereignty and control over Arctic waters. The experimental voyages of Humble Oil's modified supertanker *Manhattan*, in the summers of 1969 and 1970, attracted little attention in the United States but provoked a political firestorm in Canada, and dragged the two governments into what one experienced Canadian negotiator remembered as "certainly one of the bitterest" bilateral confrontations in postwar Canada-US relations.[1]

Under intense domestic political pressure to unilaterally claim sovereignty over all of the waters of the Arctic archipelago, the government of Pierre Trudeau struggled to develop a legal and political formula that would resonate with public concerns about sovereignty and pollution control, and reaffirm and reinforce the country's (heretofore mostly implicit) maritime claims in the Arctic, without triggering an overwhelming reaction from the United States. American officials signalled firm opposition to any kind of unilateral claim by Canada over what the US considered international waters, particularly where such claims might encourage similar claims by other coastal states. After months of complex and often acrimonious bargaining, the Canadian government decided to go ahead with both a unilateral extension of the country's territorial sea and a legally controversial claim to pollution-control jurisdiction over virtually all of the waters of the Arctic archipelago.

As the diplomatic confrontation intensified, so did speculation in the Canadian press and Parliament that the US would try to use coercive issue linkages to deter or roll back the anticipated Canadian claim. The Nixon administration did threaten, and then went ahead with, something that Canadian officials had been anxious to forestall – an explicit challenge to Canada's tacit claim to control over the Northwest Passage – and later followed this up with strenuous international legal and diplomatic pressure. American officials recognized that this would not be enough to deter or roll back the Canadian claim, but that was evidently as far as they were prepared to go. The administration had a number of low-risk linkage options at its disposal, but did not make a clear commitment to any of them, nor even put much effort into investigating them. Canada therefore "got away with" its aggressive unilateral claim. The absence of immediate and direct issue linkage does not mean, however, that there were no consequences. The confrontation catalyzed a deepening sense of frustration and recrimination within the White House, and encouraged American politicians and officials to exact a mild form of revenge by refusing to invest any political capital in other issues that were important to Canada (i.e., soft linkages).

Three aspects of this case make it especially interesting for the purposes of the argument here. First, there is an unresolved historical controversy about whether or not the US government actually pursued hard issue linkages in this dispute. Second, this dispute represents a hard case for the diplomatic-culture interpretation, which expects the US to exercise restraint here, while all the leading alternative interpretations expect the US to bargain aggressively and to pursue coercive linkages as necessary. Third, the diplomatic confrontation represents a pivotal moment in the longer-term transformation of the bilateral relationship, reflecting the beginning of the end of the period when Canada-US relations were effectively governed by the postwar diplomatic culture.

Moving Slowly toward Confrontation

Prior to the *Manhattan* crisis, disagreements between Canada and the United States over maritime claims, resource ownership, and jurisdiction had caused frictions, but had generally been worked out quickly and quietly, through unilateral retractions, tacit compromises, or bilateral consultative mechanisms.[2] As a major maritime and naval power, the US had stuck consistently to the doctrine of freedom of the seas. Canada's position was more ambiguous. Because it relied on the goodwill of major maritime powers on other issues, it had been conservative and generally supportive of the US and Britain in international legal fora. But because it was a coastal state, acutely concerned with fisheries and continental shelf development, it also looked for opportunities to incrementally strengthen and extend its control over its own bays and straits.

The US had been opposed in principle to Canada's tacit claim to sovereignty in the Northwest Passage, but in practice had chosen not to challenge it, mainly because there had been no pressing practical or legal reason to do so. Only a few surface ships had ever gone through the ice-jammed passage, and those transits had taken months or years. The discovery of oil on Alaska's North Slope changed all that, and the oil companies and (some parts of) the US government quickly took an interest in the possibility of shipping Alaskan oil by reinforced tanker through the passage to the eastern US. Just a few months after the Prudhoe Bay discovery, Humble Oil (made part of Exxon in 1972), with financial support from other oil companies, proposed to send a refitted tanker, the *Manhattan,* through the passage the following summer.

The prospect of tanker traffic in the Northwest Passage evoked mixed feelings within the Canadian government. On the one hand, a successful transit might stimulate oil and gas exploration and open the way for infrastructure development in the Canadian north. On the other hand, it could help to displace Alberta oil in US midwestern and northeastern markets, and could set up the risk of catastrophic environmental damage to the fragile Arctic ecosystem. Canadian officials recognized – as did their American counterparts – that a small number of uncontrolled tanker transits would tend to undermine Canada's tacit claim to effective control over the passage, but that one or more sanctioned and controlled transits would tend to reinforce it.

There was tension in Washington during this period as well, but far less uncertainty about where US interests lay. Each of the major players in Washington focused on a different problem, but all agreed that the US should oppose any unilateral Canadian claim to the waters of the Arctic archipelago. The Transportation and Interior Departments worried that a Canadian claim might interfere with the possibility of moving newly discovered Alaskan oil by tanker, through the passage, to eastern US markets. The Navy was uneasy about possible complications to its submarine operations in Arctic waters. And the State and Defense Departments were concerned that a Canadian claim to the Northwest Passage – particularly if it were made unilaterally and without significant legal or political sanction – would encourage other coastal states to make similar claims over more important strategic straits in the Middle East and Southeast Asia.[3]

The first sign of potential bilateral trouble came almost immediately, when the US Coast Guard announced that it would send an icebreaker, the *Northwind,* to assist the *Manhattan,* but did not formally request Canadian permission. Canadian officials quietly went to Washington to ask that the US formally request permission for the transit and for Canadian icebreaker assistance, and were politely but firmly turned down. In Ottawa, it seemed that Canadian resolve was being tested, and the government found itself unprepared, with little legal or logistical planning in hand.[4] The Canadian public had not yet been roused, and would not be for another six months, but the government hurried to explore its domestic and international legal options, and to mobilize bureaucratic and military resources that might be necessary to make a display of effective control.

Trudeau broke the public silence in a speech to the House of Commons on 15 May, assuring the home audience that Canada's position in the Arctic was not being challenged. The powerful Canadian icebreaker *John A. Macdonald* had been sent to assist the *Manhattan,* he announced, and the two governments were cooperating to make the experimental voyage a success. Ottawa had decided, in other words, that although the US had declined to formally ask permission for the transit and for icebreaker assistance, Canada would give both, and treat the entire project as a joint venture.[5] The speech was immediately followed up with a diplomatic note along the same lines, evidently based on the hope that the US might be satisfied with assurances of access to the passage and not press on to challenge Canada's tacit legal claim. That hope was undone a few days later, when the US sent a formal reply, insisting that the Northwest Passage was an international strait, that any unilateral claim to the contrary would be prejudicial to vital US security interests, and that the US government would be compelled to oppose any unilateral extension of Canadian jurisdiction. In late June, Under Secretary of State for Political Affairs U. Alexis Johnson went to Ottawa for talks with Canadian Secretary of State for External Affairs Mitchell Sharp. Sharp explained that the Canadian government was primarily interested in mitigating the risk posed by unregulated tanker transits to Canada's legal position and the Arctic environment, but that there would undoubtedly be intense public pressure for a more expansive claim to sovereignty. Finding little room for compromise, each side affirmed its determination to avoid conflict and its willingness to pursue further consultation, and promised to meet again in the autumn.[6]

Between a Rock and a Hard Place
Canadian nationalism and anti-Americanism had been on the rise through the 1960s, and both were certain to be inflamed by the impending diplomatic confrontation over Arctic waters. The *Manhattan* pushed all of the Canadian public's buttons. It appeared to directly threaten what Canadians imagined as "their" northern frontier – as a pristine wilderness area, integral to Canada's sense of its own national distinctiveness, and as an untapped storehouse of natural resources promising future prosperity.[7] And, given the

US government's open opposition to the Canadian claim, it was also seen by many as a test case for Canadian autonomy. Editorial and parliamentary pressure on the Trudeau government had been building during the late summer of 1969, but in September, as the *Manhattan's* first voyage was launched, it erupted. The three major Toronto newspapers printed a series of incendiary editorials attacking the prime minister's 15 May speech and urging the government to go ahead with a unilateral claim to the waters of the entire archipelago.[8] The editorials started to feed off each other, stimulated by vague reports of tough talk from Washington. Opinion polls showed that a majority of Canadians believed their country had an established claim to the waters of the Arctic, and expected the government to take decisive action to protect it.[9]

In parliamentary debate, Trudeau rejected calls for an expansive, unilateral claim as a shameful and dangerous form of national "chauvinism." Meanwhile, there was an implicit consensus within Cabinet and in the Department of External Affairs that Canada's legal footing was not sure enough at that time for a unilateral claim to the waters of the entire archipelago.[10] The prime minister promised that the government would soon draft legislation to protect Arctic waters, and policy-makers began debating what kind of limited legal or jurisdictional claim would satisfy the Canadian public and safeguard the country's long-term legal position, without provoking an overwhelming American reaction.

Most cautious was the recently created Department of Energy, Mines and Resources (EMR), which – with support from the province of Alberta and the oil companies – opposed any kind of unilateral extension, fearing that the US might retaliate by restricting imports of Albertan oil.[11] The Department of External Affairs, with support from the Department of Transport, argued for an extension of the territorial sea from three to twelve miles. This would be difficult for the US to challenge legally or politically, since it had already tacitly accepted similar extensions by dozens of other coastal states. And it might contribute to the incremental strengthening of Canada's long-term claim to sovereignty, by creating a new territorial sea "gate" at the eastern end of the Northwest Passage (to complement the existing "gate" at the narrower western end).

But Trudeau's closest advisers argued that the extension of the territorial sea would not necessarily give Canada any new control over American ships, since the US would undoubtedly maintain that the Northwest Passage was still an international strait, and therefore by definition open to "innocent passage." They wanted to make an expansive claim to pollution-control jurisdiction over most of the region, arguing that this would directly address the danger of an environmental disaster while satisfying the public's appetite for a big claim. Trudeau, looking for an opportunity to rally a divided public, concerned about the latent threats to Canadian sovereignty and the Arctic environment, and willing to take diplomatic risks, was convinced by these arguments.

Mitchell Sharp, who had been among those opposed to a more provocative claim, now made a series of public statements explicitly denying that the Northwest Passage was an international strait and referring to "Canada's sovereignty over Arctic waters." In the October 1969 Speech from the Throne, Trudeau announced the government's intention to go ahead with (unspecified) pollution-control legislation, speaking grandly of Canada's historical responsibility to protect the Arctic and flatly stating that Canada "would not bow on the Arctic to the pressure of any state."[12]

The State Department responded to the Throne Speech with a diplomatic note urging Canada to forgo a unilateral claim, and calling for bilateral consultations to prepare for an international conference on Arctic pollution control. The Canadian response was polite but noncommittal, kicking off what would later became a far-ranging diplomatic contest, as each side attempted to manoeuvre the dispute into a favourable international forum and win the support of other interested states.[13] At the November conference of the International Maritime Consultative Organization (IMCO), the Canadian delegation actively pushed for an international pollution-control agreement that would allow coastal states to make and enforce decisions against polluters. After a blistering attack on the representatives of the major shipping states, they succeeded in securing the kind of agreement they wanted, but were ultimately unsatisfied with the liability provisions and so tried to rally other coastal states to defeat the entire agreement. The Canadians were later able to use this diplomatic "failure" as evidence of the inadequacy of prevailing international law, and to claim that it was this that had driven them to take action unilaterally.[14]

Last Chance

The new year opened with mixed signals from Washington. US embassy and State Department officials assured the White House that the Trudeau government was exercising "considerable restraint" in resisting "substantial public and parliamentary pressure" for a much broader claim, and that constructive bilateral talks were continuing.[15] The US must therefore try to avoid forcing Trudeau's hand by publicly saying anything that would further stir up Canadian nationalism. State Department officials informally let their Canadian contacts know that they were trying to keep a lid on things, but also made it clear that the US remained firm in its opposition to any unilateral extension. The embassy's advice notwithstanding, a number of US government and military officials went to the press with their complaints, hinting at a determination to challenge Canada's control over the passage or to pursue some unspecified retaliation. In January, former Under Secretary of State

George Ball told reporters that the US would insist on a right of access to the Northwest Passage as part of a proposed continental energy agreement, implicitly holding Canada's privileged access to the American oil market as a hostage to concessions in the Arctic.[16] Then in mid-February, President Richard Nixon's State of the Union address highlighted the need to take a strong legal and political stand to "head off the threat of escalating national claims over the oceans." These rumblings from Washington were taken very seriously by the Canadian press and parliamentary opposition, which condemned US strong-arm tactics and renewed their calls for the government to go ahead with a unilateral claim to the entire archipelago.

Canadian officials responded by ratcheting up their own rhetoric. In early February, Sharp welcomed the impending return voyage of the *Manhattan*, saying that it would help the government to learn more about the use of "Canadian waters." Transport Minister Don Jamieson insisted that the *Manhattan* could make the transit only with Canadian icebreaker assistance, and that this would be forthcoming only if it complied with the yet-to-be-tabled pollution-control legislation. Humble Oil agreed to accept Canadian safety guidelines and to accept the authority of the Canadian icebreaker captain in making the final decision about whether to terminate the voyage under adverse conditions.

The day after Jamieson's remarks, the Canadian commitment to the pollution-control zone concept was powerfully reinforced when a Liberian-registered tanker, the *Arrow*, ran aground just off the coast of Nova Scotia, spilling thousands of barrels of oil. Canadians had been appalled by the disastrous spill created by the foundering of the *Torrey Canyon* in the English Channel in 1967, and now reacted angrily to the dramatic television news footage of the *Arrow* wreck.

Legal experts in External Affairs argued that the planned claim to jurisdiction for the purposes of pollution control would be vulnerable to legal challenge, and that if the government planned to go ahead with it, it would have to submit a partial reservation to the jurisdiction of the International Court of Justice (ICJ). Those in Cabinet who opposed the pollution-control claim also objected to the ICJ reservation, arguing that it would undermine Canada's legacy and reputation as an international institution builder; unhappy with these new developments, they now tried to reopen the debate. After a brief but intense battle, the prime minister made the decision, on 19 February, to go ahead with both the extension of the territorial sea to twelve miles and the pollution-control zone, and to take an ICJ reservation covering the latter.[17]

The Canadian government had now chosen the form that the claim would take, and had initiated the process that would culminate in a public commitment through the tabling of legislation. Time was running out for the

US to persuade, induce, or compel Canada to back down. In mid-February, the State Department issued a press release amplifying its call for an international conference to create a multilateral regime for Arctic pollution control, and signalled the possibility of a compromise based on a Canadian extension of the territorial sea to twelve miles, as long as it was embedded within a larger international settlement guaranteeing freedom of navigation through international straits. Transportation Secretary John Volpe and Navy Secretary John Chafee wrote to Secretary of State William Rogers to press for more information about the Canadian position, an urgent renewal of bilateral talks, and a tougher bargaining stance.[18]

The last, best chances for US officials to make a deal or force a retraction came at two secret intergovernmental meetings, on 11 March in Washington and on 20 March in Ottawa. The 11 March meeting was small and relatively informal. The new Canadian ambassador, Marcel Cadieux, was accompanied by the prime minister's adviser, Ivan Head, and the lead Canadian maritime law expert, J. Alan Beesley. The US team was led by Under Secretary Johnson, with support from State Department's maritime law expert, John R. Stevenson, and a small number of other State officials. The meeting, Head and Trudeau report, was "friendly and very candid," with each side reviewing its legal and political options and exploring possible compromises.[19] Deadlocked after eight hours, they reaffirmed their commitment to work out a satisfactory settlement and agreed to meet again soon.

Less than a week later, Nixon telephoned Trudeau to say that the imminent prospect of a unilateral Canadian claim was raising the temperature in the White House, and informing him that the US would immediately send a negotiating team to Ottawa for renewed talks.[20] The resulting 20 March meeting was larger, more diverse, and more confrontational, with less attention to complex legal issues and more to simple political problems.[21] Johnson and Stevenson again took the lead for the US, but were accompanied this time by senior officials from Defense, Interior, the Navy, and the Coast Guard. The Canadians obviously took this meeting very seriously, sending Sharp (as acting prime minister), plus another Cabinet minister, three of the prime minister's closest advisers, the current and former ambassadors to the US, two legal experts from External Affairs, and high officials from the Departments of Transport and Fisheries.

Johnson began by pointing out that the primary US concern was the potential international legal precedent, and flatly stating that the US simply could not accept the expected 100-mile pollution-control zone. He then moved on quickly to talk about possible compromises, mentioning that the US might be prepared to accept a much more limited pollution-control zone. Johnson and Stevenson said that they understood that the Canadian government's two main concerns were domestic political pressure and pollution control, and argued that the best way to deal with both would be to set up a bilateral joint commission to oversee the upcoming return voyage of the *Manhattan* and work toward a conference on Arctic development and pollution control. The Canadians turned this aside, saying that the Canadian public would not tolerate any kind of shared control or jurisdiction. If he were seen to have settled for anything less than exclusive Canadian control of the passage, Sharp remarked, he would be compelled to resign.

The Canadian position was essentially that the government was now locked in to going ahead with its legislative package, including the pollution-control zone, and that backing down at this point would amount to political suicide; once the package had passed, they argued, they would be able to restart negotiations and try to address some of the US concerns. The US team made it clear that they were not satisfied and would continue to oppose any unilateral claim, without actually specifying what form this opposition might take. In his report to Nixon, Johnson advised that the US team had succeeded in getting the Canadians to rethink some aspects of the legislative package, but that, given the weight of domestic political pressure, they should not expect much in the way of changes or delay.[22]

Fait Accompli

On 7 April, the day before the tabling of the Canadian legislative package, Canadian officials, worried that their American counterparts would be angered by their apparent failure to fulfill vague promises of further consultation, hurried to advise them of the imminent legislative push and try to smooth things over. Canadian ambassador Ed Ritchie met with Under Secretary Johnson in Washington and outlined the details of the legislation. Johnson told him that the US was "disappointed" by the Canadian decision and would "find it necessary to manifest [its] opposition in some way."[23] Trudeau tried to arrange a call to Nixon later that day, but, Head and Trudeau say, Nixon was not available, and Trudeau talked to Rogers instead.[24] The phone call degenerated quickly, as Rogers said that the US would be compelled to try to defy the Canadian claim to effective control, "with a submarine if necessary," infuriating Trudeau. Both calmed down quickly, though, with Trudeau apologizing for the original diplomatic miscommunication and assuring Rogers that, now that the legislation was in and public pressure was settling down, it would finally be possible for the Canadian government to engage itself in talks toward an international conference.

The next day, the government introduced the Arctic Waters Pollution Prevention Act (AWPPA), and simultaneously deposited a reservation to the jurisdiction of the ICJ on all matters relating to maritime pollution control. The opposition parties criticized the legislation as a "half-measure" that would ultimately undermine Canada's long-term position.[25] But the package was overall a major domestic political success, earning rave reviews in editorials and opinion polls. After extensive behind-the-scenes wrangling over legal details, the legislation was passed unanimously by the House, with the reporting of the results carefully staged to highlight the political impossibility of reversing the decision.

The final legislative package represented a partial compromise between US and Canadian positions, but ultimately there was not enough overlap between the two countries' interests for a mutually satisfactory negotiated arrangement. The Canadian government had chosen not to pursue what the US most strenuously opposed – a unilateral drawing of straight baselines around the entire Arctic archipelago – partly because of concern about the US reaction, but mostly because of a basic lack of confidence in the legal foundation for such a claim.[26] The legislation included provisions for the government to exempt categories of ships from AWPPA control, as long as they were "substantially in compliance" with its standards, thereby creating a loophole for unrestricted passage of US Navy vessels. And both the legislation and the subsequent push for diplomatic support emphasized that Arctic waterways had to be treated differently from other kinds of maritime areas, because the permanent cover of ice effectively blurred the distinction between land and water. This reinforced the rationale for Canada's unilateral action while undercutting legal and political precedents that the US wanted to avoid.

These gestures did help to take the edge off for US officials, but they did not address their bottom-line concerns. The main problem with the Canadian legislation in American eyes was that it was unilateral, and – Canadian arguments about the special properties of ice-covered waters notwithstanding – it established a precedent that was likely to encourage other coastal states to make similar claims over more important strategic straits. The US responded to the announcement of the Canadian legislation with a stern diplomatic note, which passed quickly over the extension of the territorial sea and focused its fire on the proposed pollution-control zone: "This action by Canada, if not opposed by us, would be taken as a precedent in other parts of the world for other unilateral infringements of the freedom of the seas ... Merchant shipping would be severely restricted, and naval mobility would be seriously jeopardized."[27] A *Wall Street Journal* report that the note had been very aggressive in tone, with a veiled threat of unspecified economic sanctions, set off ripples in the Canadian Parliament and press. Close examination of the archival record, however, reveals that this report was unfounded. The most threatening passage in draft versions of the note – a reference to the United States' intention to "take legal and appropriate steps to safeguard the integrity of its position" – was removed in the late stages of drafting, soon after it passed over Henry Kissinger's desk.[28]

A few days later, in public testimony before the House External Affairs and National Defence Committee, former prime minister Lester Pearson urged the government to follow through on its Arctic agenda, with the expectation that the US would complain bitterly, and not be intimidated by unsubstantiated reports of impending retaliation. In keeping with established norms, he assured the committee, the US had not made, nor would it make, coercive linkages between the Arctic dispute and other issues.

When Push Comes to Shove: Explaining US Self-Restraint

Canada had a number of important issue-specific bargaining advantages in this dispute, which forced the US to choose between pursuing linkage and giving way. The obvious weight of domestic political pressure on the Canadian government greatly strengthened the credibility of its commitment and convinced US officials that Trudeau would be willing to take significant risks in order to stake out an ambitious claim. Because they were aiming for something less than the public demanded, Canadian officials were able to present their position as a compromise between two extremes, and to convince their State Department counterparts to try to join in working out a settlement along their lines.[29] Nevertheless, many US negotiators believed that the Canadians were reaching for more than they were being compelled to, and expected them to accept some domestic political risk in order to work toward a mutually satisfactory settlement.[30] There were important divisions within the Canadian Cabinet and among various bureaucratic actors, but these were for the most part well concealed, and US officials could not find a crack to wedge open the Canadian position.

Canada also drew advantage from some aspects of the progress and results of the *Manhattan* voyages themselves, which tended to reinforce its tacit claim to effective control over the Northwest Passage. The US Coast Guard icebreaker was generally ineffectual in support of the *Manhattan,* and the transit might have failed without assistance from the much more powerful Canadian icebreaker and aerial reconnaissance. (While the crisis was unfolding, both countries initiated crash programs to build more powerful icebreakers.) Extensive damage to the *Manhattan's* empty outer hull compartments tended to reinforce arguments about the risk of an environmental disaster. And Humble Oil's readiness to accept Canadian oversight and safety conditions reinforced the Canadian claim to effective control, while undercutting the potential US argument that Canada was imposing undue restrictions on commercial shipping and development in the Arctic. The major weakness in Canada's claim to effective control over the passage was that its military presence was spread very thin across vast Arctic spaces, and it did not have the means to detect or intercept US Navy vessels operating in Arctic waters, particularly submarines. The US therefore had the option to try to challenge the Canadian claim by surfacing a submarine in the Northwest Passage. State Department officials did raise the idea on a number of occasions, both before and after the passage of the Canadian legislation, and Secretary of State Rogers apparently hinted at it in his telephone confrontation with Trudeau, but there is no evidence that the idea ever went beyond the hypothetical in US strategy debates.[31]

The nature of Canada's claim made it a difficult target for US diplomatic pressure, in spite of its debatable international legal foundations. The focus on pollution control was a public relations success in every relevant arena, satisfying Canadian voters, winning over American observers, and giving other sympathetic governments a basis for supporting the Canadian position. Awareness of the dangers of marine pollution – and particularly oil tanker accidents – was rising all over the western world, and the foundering of the *Arrow* in February 1970 cemented broad public approval for aggressive pollution-control measures, even where those measures might stray outside established legal boundaries. Canadian officials argued that they were not breaking international law but rather "developing" it, on grounds of self-defence and environmental stewardship.[32] When US officials attacked Canadian unilateralism, Ottawa launched a counterattack on American diplomatic hypocrisy, starting with a long list of past incidents in which the US had flouted international agreements or rejected the authority of the ICJ. In multilateral fora, Canadian negotiators effectively played up the fact that the US had already tacitly accepted more than fifty other states' unilateral extensions of their territorial sea to twelve miles or more, and got considerable mileage out of the parallel between their argument about legal "innovation" and similar themes in President Truman's 1945 proclamation on the continental shelf.

Given this difficult bargaining position, and a clear reluctance to try to induce Canadian cooperation through side-payments, why did the Nixon administration "fail" to pursue coercive linkages as a means of deterring or rolling back the Canadian claim? This is more puzzling because of the personal philosophies and personal relationships among the key players. Trudeau was not by any means a jingoist prime minister, and his approach to foreign-policy making was generally cautious during his early years. But his interest in showing off the dynamism of the federal government and his environmental convictions encouraged him to take risks and to be inflexible in the Arctic waters dispute. Nixon, on the other hand, felt no sense of special obligation to Canada, and personally disliked and mistrusted Trudeau and his key advisers.[33] Moreover, he and Kissinger were well known as proponents and practitioners of realpolitik, and both had talked publicly about tactical issue linkage as an important part of their strategy for arresting America's relative decline and shifting adjustment costs to major allies and trade partners.

Thinking about this case in terms of the realist interpretation and the logic of strategic restraint only deepens the puzzle. The entrenchment of détente, superpower summitry, and the stabilization of the nuclear confrontation under the doctrine of mutually assured destruction had combined to under-cut the importance for the US of soliciting and maintaining the support of smaller allies, and Canada's value in particular had clearly declined. As US military planners' concern shifted in the 1960s from manned-bomber attack to intercontinental ballistic missiles (ICBMs), the strategic importance of Canadian bases and interceptors had steadily deteriorated. Meanwhile, Canada's military contributions to the alliance continued to decrease, in both relative and absolute terms, and were further scaled back by Trudeau's 1968 decision to reduce the Canadian military contingent in Western Europe. While there was some appreciation in the State Department and White House for Canada's role in the International Commission for Supervision and Control (ICSC) in Vietnam, US officials had grown increasingly frustrated by the Canadian contingent's reluctance to take a more partisan role as the de facto "western" member of the commission.[34] Canada had won points in Washington in the mid-1960s in its role as peacekeeper and diplomatic go-between, but Trudeau had recently signalled his intention to turn away from the "helpful fixer" role in favour of a foreign-policy agenda driven by a narrower conception of the national interest.

More importantly, the anticipated Canadian claim threatened established US interests in secure access to strategic materials, particularly oil, and un-restricted naval and commercial access to strategic maritime areas. Renewed instability in the Middle East had greatly increased US concern over the security of foreign oil supplies, and many US officials – particularly in the Transportation and Defense Departments – were concerned that a Canadian claim would compromise the prospect of establishing a short-term link from the newly discovered Alaskan reserves to eastern US markets. This was also a time of concern about naval mobility, as the superpowers had renewed their naval arms race and shifted their nuclear arsenals toward submarine-based missiles, and some Navy officers worried about possible complications for submarine operations in the North Atlantic and the Arctic Ocean. An extension of the territorial sea would technically require US submarines to surface at the "gates" of the Northwest Passage, but that problem could be solved – as a practical political matter – by having Canada look the other way. More importantly, the Canadian claim would reinforce the Soviet Union's standing claims to Arctic waters, which the US explicitly rejected.

These concerns about the direct implications of the anticipated Canadian claim to jurisdiction over the Northwest Passage were overshadowed by concerns about its *indirect* implications. State and Defense Department of-ficials were gravely concerned that a Canadian claim would encourage other coastal states to make similar claims over more important strategic straits in the Middle East and Southeast Asia. This apprehension, it turned out, was not unwarranted.[35] Less than a year after Canada made its claim, Iran annexed the Tamb Islands, capturing effective control over the entrance to the Persian Gulf, and soon afterward claimed a fifty-mile pollution-control zone, which would theoretically allow it to intercept all ships passing through the Strait of Hormuz. The following year, the government of Indonesia passed legislation prohibiting the transit of large oil tankers through the Strait of Malacca. And at the third round of UN Law of the Sea talks, beginning in 1973, a number of coastal states presented arguments for legal and jurisdictional extensions that reflected some of the language and logic behind the Canadian claim. US negotiators found themselves obliged to offer additional concessions to some coastal states in order to secure support for a revision and extension of the right of innocent passage through international straits. Overall then, a focus on strategic calculations should lead us to expect the US to have been *more,* rather than less, likely to have bargained aggressively with Canada, and to have pursued linkages as necessary.

Keohane and Nye's argument about interdependence and the proliferation of blocking coalitions cannot help us solve the puzzle either. The depth and breadth of bilateral interdependence between the US and Canada, already extensive by the early 1960s, grew markedly through the decade, catalyzed by multilateral tariff reductions and a series of integrative policy coordination agreements governing the sale and production of autos and parts, civil air routes, and new defence cooperation arrangements. As Keohane and Nye expected, this further interpenetration of the two societies generated or strengthened a number of coalitions with a stake in the bilateral relationship. Because of the nature of the pivotal issue, however, nongovernment actors were not an important part of the equation here. The multinational oil companies with a big stake in Arctic oil development – particularly Standard Oil of New Jersey and Atlantic Richfield – wanted to keep open the option of tanker transit through the Northwest Passage, but were not especially concerned about the larger legal precedent. Humble Oil and its partners were prepared to accept the safety and oversight conditions set by the Canadian government, knowing full well that these would tend to reinforce the Canadian claim to effective control of the passage.

As in the nuclear weapons dispute, the principal players in the US struggle over how to respond to the Canadian challenge were bureaucratic ones, and the balance of pressures tilted solidly against the Canadian position. The principal proponents of a more aggressive bargaining stance were the Navy, acting through the Department of Defense, and the Coast Guard, acting through the Department of Transportation. The State Department, on the other hand, advocated a more cautious approach, with a clear commitment to reaching a negotiated settlement. The bureaucratic clout of the State Department, however, had been severely undermined during the 1960s by the ongoing shift to the National Security Council, which had accelerated under Nixon and Kissinger.

There was a great deal of speculation in the press and in the Canadian Parliament that the Nixon administration would try to force Canada to back down by threatening to disrupt one or more of the areas of bilateral co-operation in which it was particularly vulnerable. In the next few pages, I will evaluate three of the most prominent of these linkage options: restriction of imports of Canadian oil, revision or abrogation of the bilateral auto production agreement, and disruption of the established reciprocal defence production agreement. I conclude that although at least two of these options might have been viable ones, there is no evidence in the archival records of either country that the US actually made coercive linkages to other issues, either as a deterrent prior to the tabling of the Canadian legislation or in reprisal afterward. Moreover, as I will show below, the evidence suggests that some of these options were explicitly rejected in terms that fit neatly with the expectations of the diplomatic-culture interpretation.

Identifying and Evaluating Linkage Scenarios

The most commonly cited of the specific issue linkages anticipated by Canadian officials, reporters, and opposition members of Parliament was a threat to unilaterally restrict Canadian access to the American oil market, and Edgar Dosman has argued that Nixon himself actually made an explicit linkage between Arctic waters and oil imports.[36] In fact, although it is entirely possible that Nixon made an undiplomatic reference to oil restrictions in his efforts to deflect the Canadian Arctic legislation, there is no evidence that this was part of a larger, coordinated bargaining strategy. If there was any kind of linkage, then it was a "soft" one – that is, a grudge that translated into a more inflexible approach to ongoing talks toward a continental energy agreement.

In Chapter 3, I described the way that, in the early 1960s, Canada took advantage of its exemption from the Mandatory Oil Import Program (MOIP) to capture a larger share of the US market and to profit from its "two-price" policy. Canadian penetration of the US market expanded rapidly in the mid-1960s, partially displacing domestic producers and important foreign suppliers like Venezuela. The two governments soon settled into a pattern of periodic meetings to informally set short- and medium-term targets for Canadian oil. In 1967, they signed a secret agreement, in which the Canadian government agreed to try to keep exports to a fixed schedule in exchange for US approval of a pipeline extension to the Chicago market. US demand rose sharply over the next three years, and the voluntary control system broke down. The Department of the Interior, under intense pressure from US domestic producers, pressed the State Department to force the Canadian government to bring exports back to the level set in the 1967 agreement. American negotiators complained about the widening gap between the price paid for Venezuelan crude in New England and that paid by industrial competitors in eastern Canada, and sent increasingly blunt signals that the US might eventually be compelled to impose mandatory controls, effectively removing the so-called overland exemption. The Canadian government made an effort to restrain exports, but argued that the terms of the 1967 agreement were no longer an appropriate measuring stick, as the demand from refiners in the US Midwest continued to increase rapidly, and categorically rejected the idea of mandatory controls.[37]

The long-delayed report of the US Cabinet Task Force on Oil Import Control, chaired by Secretary of Labor George Shultz, was finally released in late February 1970. It criticized the existing quota arrangements as anticompetitive and inefficient, unfair to New England industry, and shortsighted in failing to address the possibility that Canadian supplies might be diverted in an emergency. And it recommended that the US government immediately initiate talks with Canada on amendments to the "two-price" policy and toward a continental energy policy, adding that "pending the outcome of discussions on these subjects, the United States must decide what arrangements it is prepared to make unilaterally."[38] Specifically, it recommended that the US gradually tighten quotas for the next six months, and then relax them over the following eighteen months, "providing that a mutually satisfactory energy pact had been concluded by then." The White House accepted the basic logic of tightening and release, but rejected the report's relatively "gentle" strategy and timetable. On 10 March, Nixon announced that, pending the resolution of talks on a continental energy deal, the US would immediately impose mandatory controls on Canadian crude, at a level far below the current import numbers and well below the modest cut proposed in the Shultz task force's report.

Nixon's abrupt shift to mandatory controls was widely seen as a cynical pressure tactic, designed to soften up Canada for further rounds in the ongoing talks on an integrated continental energy market. Most Canadian observers assumed that the US was holding out for better terms on long-term oil and gas contracts, but a few worried that the US might intend to demand a much larger package, including bulk water sales or "guaranteed rights of access for overland (e.g., Trans-Canadian) or Northwest Passage transportation routes."[39] Dosman reports that an explicit linkage was actually made between Arctic waters and oil. In a telephone call a week after the imposition of mandatory controls, he says, Nixon warned Trudeau to back away from the most provocative parts of the proposed Arctic legislation or expect "further retaliation."[40] The form of the threat fits with common ideas about what was distinctive about the Nixon/Kissinger bargaining style, as reflected in, for example, the August 1971 import surcharge announcement. The idea of making the relaxation of oil import controls contingent on the establishment of a satisfactory continental transport system, including free access to the Northwest Passage, was clearly making the rounds in Washington at that time, appearing in both the Shultz task force report and the State Department "talking paper" prepared for Under Secretary Johnson for the 20 March meeting on Arctic questions. And of course there were rumours swirling in the newspapers and in Parliament.[41]

There are reasons to question, however, whether such a threat would have constituted a "real" bargaining linkage. First, any connection made by Nixon between oil restrictions and the Northwest Passage would have been – and would have been received as – little more than "cheap talk." It carried no specific commitment and did not set up any domestic political or institutional costs for failing to follow through. There is no evidence in the archival record that it came out of any larger plan for coercive linkage, or that any kind of discussion or preparation had been done to translate the threat into action. Like Secretary of State Rogers' veiled reference to a submarine challenge, this would seem to have been a case where a high-level negotiator – in this case, the president – raised the possibility of linkage, not so much as a "real" bargaining move but rather as a way to vent personal frustration and highlight the seriousness with which the White House took the issue.

Second, while the 10 March announcement may have had some value to the United States as a lever in the ongoing energy talks, it was not well suited in form or effect as a way to deter the Canadian Arctic claim. There is no question that Canada was vulnerable to short- and long-term disruptions of its access to the American oil market. A temporary cutback would exacerbate the trade imbalance and intensify tensions between Ottawa and the western provinces. And a longer-term restriction or outright removal of the overland exemption would lead to the permanent displacement of expensive Canadian crude by cheaper overseas suppliers.[42] But Nixon's tightening of the oil quota was not severe enough to force radical changes in Canadian policy. The new quota was set at a level well below what Canada had said it could achieve through voluntary controls, but it was still much higher than that specified in the 1967 agreement, and not far from that proposed by US negotiators in the most recent round of bilateral talks.[43] When the Canadian Cabinet met the day after Nixon's announcement, there was a basic consensus that while the cuts were painful and likely to rock the domestic political boat for a while, they were not unexpected and not unbearable. Western Canadian producers could be brought to accept the new quota, it was agreed, as long as Canadian negotiators could secure assurances that it would probably be relaxed in the near future.[44]

Whatever leverage the US derived from the new quota came not from the expectation of further tightening but from Canadian uncertainty about long-term relaxation. US officials were pointedly noncommittal about the timetable and the conditions for the eventual loosening of the restrictions, and many Canadian officials saw this as a bargaining ploy. But they were generally confident that growing demand in the Midwest and New England, and the high price of domestically produced oil, would eventually generate enough political pressure to force the US to loosen the restrictions. The restrictions announced on 10 March, in other words, were a problem for the Trudeau government, but not a disaster.

It seems clear, however, that the Nixon administration *could have* used oil restrictions as an effective basis for coercive linkage if it had been so inclined. It would have been administratively difficult and would have involved some domestic political risk, but it could very well have been a viable option. We know that Nixon could impose tight mandatory controls on imports of Canadian oil, because he did. The real question is whether he could have imposed even tighter ones, as a way to get more extensive bargaining leverage. The tightening of controls on Canadian oil was strongly supported by the well-funded and well-connected US domestic oil lobby and by other countries competing for a share of the American oil market, primarily Venezuela. It was opposed, on the other hand, by a small number of Midwest refineries and by unorganized consumers in mostly Democratic northeastern states.[45] Congressmen from these states moved quickly to pressure the White House for a relaxation of the quota, on the grounds that the expected restrictions would raise fuel costs in these markets and that expert projections anticipated a growing supply shortfall that would increase the importance of secure foreign sources. Canadian officials were probably right to think that these pressures would eventually compel the administration to give some relief to these groups, but Nixon was able to shrug them off for several months and could probably have done so for a longer period.

If the Nixon administration had been determined to put pressure on Canada, it might very well have done so by threatening to pursue a long-term structural displacement of Canadian oil from the US market, in a way that would minimize domestic political pressure. This could have been effected by arranging for formally or informally subsidized use of domestic oil in the Midwest and Northeast, and/or shifting a large part of Canada's share of the overall import allowance to Venezuela (and perhaps also Mexico). It could have been rationalized in terms of some combination of the 1967 agreement, concern about possible Canadian diversion in an emergency, and the trade-distorting effects of the price gap between the US Northeast and eastern Canada. The best time to do this would have been in January or February 1970, *before* the release of the Shultz task force report. If US negotiators had privately made an explicit linkage between Arctic waters and severe oil restrictions, backed it up with a concrete plan for structural displacement, and tied their own hands by making the commitment through the Schultz task force report, then the Trudeau government might very well have been compelled to retreat to a less ambitious claim (i.e., less stringent pollution-control zone). The fact that this was not tried, or even explored, seems to indicate that US officials were not looking seriously for linkage options.

A second prominent linkage scenario involved the Canada-US Automotive Products Trade Agreement, or Auto Pact, which had created a single, rationalized continental market for autos and auto parts, but with special incentives for the major auto companies to settle a substantial share of production in Canada. It ensured a large pool of jobs and a solid manufacturing base in central Canada, and a growing source of export earnings that helped Ottawa cope with its chronic trade imbalance. The deal was seen as very big and very beneficial for both sides when it was signed in 1965, but its economic benefits tended to gravitate back and forth across the border, pulled by shifting production, investment, and demand patterns. In the late 1960s and early 1970s, the flow turned sharply in Canada's favour, stirring complaints in the US; some argued that the deal had been a bad one for the US and should be scrapped altogether. In fact, speculation that the US would threaten to kill the Auto Pact surrounded virtually all of the major bilateral disputes during this period, including the reduction of Canada's NATO contribution, and the disagreements over Canadian participation in the ICSC in Vietnam. A major disruption of the agreement would have been devastating for the Canadian government, causing massive layoffs in southern Ontario and exacerbating ongoing balance of payments problems. Midwestern auto workers and their Congressional supporters pushed strongly for revision of the agreement during this period, and a linkage could therefore be rationalized in terms of serving their interests. This would have been an extremely risky option, however, because the Big Three auto companies had a great deal invested in the established continental production structure, and would have resisted any major disruption. There is no evidence that the White House ever seriously considered using a threat to revise the Auto Pact as a tool of linkage in the Arctic waters dispute.[46]

There was also scattered speculation that the US might try to deflect the Arctic legislation, or retaliate for it, by disrupting certain aspects of long-standing continental defence cooperation, most likely intelligence-sharing or defence production agreements. CBC News, quoting an unnamed American source, reported that the US might punish Canada for its Arctic legislation by killing the Defence Production Sharing Agreement (DPSA). A revocation of the agreement, or even a severe tightening of the way that contracts were awarded to Canadian firms, would have been painful for the Canadian government, as these contracts were not only vital to the continuation of the industry but also an important source of employment and export revenue in politically sensitive regions. Because the rules for awarding contracts to Canadian firms were somewhat vague, readily susceptible to executive interference, and implemented in secret, it would have been relatively easy for the administration to disrupt the agreement informally – and perhaps even formally – as long as it had the support of the US defence establish-ment. Since the latter was strongly opposed to the Canadian challenge in the Arctic, it is not hard to believe that they would have been prepared to allow for short- or perhaps even long-term disruption of the Canadian de-fence industry as a way to deter an expansive Arctic claim. The secrecy sur-rounding defence contracting makes it virtually impossible to directly assess the possibility that the Nixon administration pursued linkages through the DPSA. White House and State Department records indicate no evidence of any formal planning or directions for a concrete linkage to the agreement, however. Historical analyses of the bilateral defence relationship show that US support for the DPSA generally declined through the late 1960s and into the 1970s, but there is nothing to indicate any major disruption in the early 1970s.[47]

US Decision-making: Actors and Arguments

The Arctic waters dispute occurred at the beginning of the end of the period when the transgovernmental network was consistently able to shape the bilateral bargaining agenda, and played an important role in catalyzing the dramatic acceleration of the network's displacement in the 1970s. In Chapter 3, I described the way that the Department of External Affairs had been held at arm's length by Prime Minister John Diefenbaker but then recaptured some of its past stature and influence under Lester Pearson. Under Trudeau, the department was again pushed from the centre of the foreign-policy process, but for different reasons and in a more decisive and apparently permanent way.

First, Trudeau cut back the department's overseas missions and initiated a series of management reforms that in theory were designed to stimulate creativity at lower levels and streamline decision-making, but which, in short-term practice, tended to create new bottlenecks and increased confu-sion and resentment.[48] Second, and more important, Trudeau presided over an acceleration of the ongoing transfer of foreign-policy agenda setting and policy coordination from External Affairs to the prime minister's staff.[49] One manifestation of this shift was Trudeau's appointment of a political outsider, Ivan Head, as foreign-policy adviser within the Prime Minister's Office (PMO). An expert on Arctic sovereignty issues, Head took a very high profile role in Canada's Arctic policy during this period, in both the development of policy and the conduct of negotiations. Canadian policy meetings and diplomatic teams were thus almost always made up of both PMO representatives and External Affairs experts. This created some friction, but – in contrast to some later disputes – it did not seem to significantly compromise the Canadian position nor interfere with senior External Affairs officials' efforts to keep up and make use of their network contacts. By the late autumn of 1969, External Affairs had set aside its reservations about the legal and political defensibility of the pollution-control zone, and worked closely with the prime minister's advisers.[50]

Like the Department of External Affairs, the State Department had been increasingly undercut as the lead agency for foreign policy in the United States, and was especially weak at the time of the Arctic waters dispute, as Secretary of State Rogers carried little weight in the cabinet and Nixon tended to rely on the counsel of Henry Kissinger and a few other close advisers.[51] Nevertheless, most of the development of bargaining options, inter-bureaucratic coordination, and intergovernmental negotiations in the Arctic dispute were handled by a small number of key State Department officials, led by Under Secretary Johnson and the State Department's resident Law of the Sea expert, John Stevenson. Johnson reported regularly and directly to the White House, with major decisions cleared by Kissinger. Johnson, Stevenson, and many of the leading State Department officials in this dispute had little personal knowledge of or direct experience with Canada. However, some of the other State Department officials consulted – notably Philip Trezise, Julius Katz, and Willis Armstrong – had been leading players in some of the major bilateral negotiations of the mid-1960s (e.g., civil aviation agreement, Auto Pact). These men had a solid appreciation not only of the particular political and developmental problems confronting the Canadian government but also of the established rules of the game for Canada-US bargaining. Overall, the US embassy in Ottawa was relatively weak during this time, because the ambassador was a political appointee with few important contacts in Washington.[52] His deputy, Rufus Z. Smith, however, had been the director of the State Department's Canada section, was very well connected in Ottawa, and was aggressive in pushing the embassy's network-anchored view on Washington.

Although the political importance of the issues in play meant that decision-making moved up fairly quickly to higher levels of the US government, lower-level officials connected to the transgovernmental network continued to play an important part in shaping the agenda on both sides of the border. External Affairs officials acted as a brake on the proponents of an expansive jurisdictional claim, solidified the legal underpinnings of the AWPPA legislation, developed the marginal concessions offered at the 20 March bilateral meeting, and pressed Cabinet to follow through on its promise to participate – however halfheartedly – in the diplomatic preparation for an abortive US-sponsored international conference on Arctic pollution.[53] Canadian network members had to walk a fine line between assuring their American counterparts that they were doing what they could to dampen domestic political pressure for a more expansive claim, and trying to use that pressure as a lever to reinforce the Canadian bargaining position. In the major bilateral meetings, and in less formal preparatory contacts, Canadian negotiators self-consciously cultivated a sense of mutual identification with their American counterparts, as professional problem-solvers caught in the middle between pressure groups that didn't really understand the legal and political ramifications of their own demands, and could not place the dispute within the context of "the relationship." They were generally successful in this, as State Department negotiators were receptive to the image of bureaucratic professionals working together to prevent politicization and pursue a negotiated settlement.[54] This started to wear thin through the early months of 1970, as US officials came to believe that much of the domestic pressure on the Trudeau government was of its own making, but they continued to see External Affairs as sharing with them a middle ground between two extremes.

Given their weakened position within the US foreign-policy making process, network-connected officials in the State Department could not expect to win a head-to-head policy struggle with their bureaucratic rivals in the Departments of Defense and Transportation. Instead, they had to try to intervene "earlier" in the policy-making process, by steering the identification of available bargaining options and shifting the way those options would be evaluated. As in the nuclear weapons case, US members of the transgovernmental network had two main assets. First, despite its partial displacement by the National Security Council structure, the State Department still had special bureaucratic responsibility and resources for collecting and sharing information about bargaining options, and for the conduct of the bargaining itself. Second, their informal relationships with their Canadian counterparts gave State Department officials an advantage in collecting diplomatic intelligence about Canadian perceptions and priorities. Network members used these resources to good effect in the Arctic waters case, deflecting pressures for linkage and keeping the US on the negotiating track through the crucial early months of 1970.

As in the nuclear weapons dispute, there is no evidence here of any formal, organized effort within the US government to investigate and evaluate specific linkage options. The White House, however, was under pressure from various individuals and offices for a more assertive approach, up to and including coercive issue linkages. The Defense Department, and the Navy in particular, pressed the administration for a more aggressive challenge to the Canadian claim, both before and after the passage of the AWPPA legislation. A small group of senior officials, primarily policy and legal experts attached to the Defense Department, attempted to make interdepartmental alliances with like-minded officials from the State Department (with some success), and to press their superiors for a tougher line. This group had informally discussed specific linkage scenarios and made a number of off-the-record proposals for loosely specified linkages to oil and/or defence cooperation.[55] The State Department leads accepted the argument that the US could not allow the Canadian claim to go unchallenged, but strongly opposed arguments for coercive linkages. Instead, they argued that the US should maintain a very firm, public opposition to any kind of unilateral Canadian claim, and work doggedly toward a negotiated settlement based on persuasion and political compromise.

Network-connected American officials made two kinds of arguments against linkage. First, they recognized coercive linkage as a trigger for Canadian autonomy concerns, which might actually make it harder for the US to get what it wanted from Canada, in this dispute and in the future. On one hand, they worried that a linkage threat would provoke a severe domestic political reaction in Canada, making it harder for the Canadian government to back down. Under Rufus Smith's direction, the Ottawa embassy pushed hard to raise awareness in Washington of the weight of public pressure on Trudeau and his Cabinet, and the ratcheting up of public expectations that followed from each new public commitment.[56] Lower-level Canada experts within the State Department made it clear to their superiors that, given the way that the Arctic waters issue had become bound up with Canadian anxiety about national sovereignty, American pressure tactics were likely to backfire, by increasing pressure on the Trudeau government and making it virtually impossible for it to accept any kind of negotiated settlement.[57] Their success in getting this message across is reflected in Johnson's advice to the president against "open threats" and on the importance of sticking with quiet negotiation.[58] On the other hand, State Department officials were concerned that recourse to coercive linkage would damage network relationships and cut off the flow of inside information about Canadian perceptions and priorities. This is reflected, for example, in the many references, in relevant State Department correspondence, to the importance of maintaining "trust" and "confidence."[59] A breakdown of established personal relationships was considered an especially bad prospect during this period, as many American officials were concerned about perceived undercurrents of neutralism and autarkism within the Trudeau government, and hoped that close relations with upper- and middle-level External Affairs officials might help them monitor and defuse those tendencies.

Second, US network members' arguments against a more aggressive posture also indicated a rejection of coercive linkage on normative grounds.[60] An embassy report prior to the crucial March 1970 meetings, for example, referred to talk of economic retaliation as "heavy-handed" and its (unidentified) proponents as "toughs." Johnson's reports to the White House said much the same thing (albeit in more temperate language), dismissing calls for a more aggressive bargaining posture as "extreme" and "inappropriate." Stevenson and his legal team also worried that taking a tough line with Canada would be perceived by other states as bullying, and contribute to a polarization of multilateral Law of the Sea talks.

Epilogue: Crisis and Adjustment

As in the nuclear weapons dispute, the absence of specific coercive linkages in the Arctic waters dispute did not mean that there were no consequences for Canada. US frustration again manifested itself in various soft linkages. Former Canadian officials recall that the Nixon administration "put [Canada] in the deep freeze" in the spring of 1970, by discouraging US officials from following through on new or ongoing talks on various forms of cooperative policy coordination and from "going to bat for Canada" in Congress.[61] Bilateral management was virtually paralyzed for weeks, until tensions abated and mounting pressure to fix day-to-day problems brought a gradual return to established patterns. Moreover, the Nixon administration's frustration with Canadian unilateralism almost certainly contributed to an evident lack of receptiveness to Canadian requests for special consideration within subsequent US policy initiatives, including the balance of payments measures announced in August 1971.

US members of the transgovernmental network were profoundly frustrated by the outcome of the Arctic waters dispute, and there were some acrimonious exchanges in the weeks that followed. It did not lead them to seriously question the value of the network, however, or of the normative framework that sustained it. Instead, they interpreted what had happened as a result of the kind of politicization that the network had originally been formed to prevent, much as they – and, in some cases, their bureaucratic predecessors – had done after the Kennedy-Diefenbaker confrontation over nuclear weapons. There was, however, a broader perception among political elites in both countries that some of the premises underpinning the postwar system of bilateral dispute management were unravelling, particularly the general presumption in Washington that bilateral disagreements with Canada were always essentially technical ones, which could be resolved through quiet diplomacy.

This sense of crisis and change was reflected in the relationship's two defining moments of the early 1970s, the Nixon shocks of August 1971 and Nixon's speech to Parliament in 1972. Canadian officials thought at first that their inclusion in the list of countries subject to the new US import surcharge and investment controls was an oversight, and were shocked to find that Treasury Secretary John Connally had had them very much in mind.[62] Inter-bureaucratic talks and technical arguments did little to sway Connally, and it was only after a successful summit meeting and direct intervention by Kissinger that Canada was able to secure a conditional exemption. Canadian officials were shaken by the experience, many of them lost whatever faith they still had in the old quiet diplomacy, and some turned seriously toward the idea of reducing Canada's vulnerability to the twists and turns of US policy by containing foreign investment and seeking political and economic counterweights in Europe and Japan.

When the Trudeau government's preoccupation with recognition of national sovereignty and reduction of vulnerability met the Nixon administration's interest in reducing its share of the burdens of alliance and international economic leadership, the result was Nixon's extraordinary address to Parliament. In a carefully prepared speech, with Trudeau's tacit endorsement, Nixon argued that the time had come for a more "mature" relationship, in which the two countries recognized their separate interests, accepted the prospect of conflict, and committed themselves to working out cooperative solutions. Many interpreted the speech as a eulogy for the old special relationship, and in some ways it was.

But this reassessment of established practices of network-driven management and quiet diplomacy mattered less in the long run than the fact that domestic political restructuring was making those practices unworkable. Congress had become increasingly assertive in trade and investment matters during the 1960s, and was encouraged by the Vietnam debacle and the Watergate scandal to try to wrest a bigger share of control over high politics issues as well. The new exposure of the US to the international economy stimulated the expansion of the external concerns and capabilities of various "domestic" agencies (e.g., Commerce, Interior), which captured a sizable share of the State Department's traditional bureaucratic turf.

There was, in other words, a profusion of new players within the US foreign-policy making process, many of whom had little or no knowledge of – and no incentive to prioritize – the bilateral relationship as a whole. Moreover, there was a marked increase in the amount of public oversight over foreign policy, driven by new media activism and the involvement of constituency-driven actors. And finally, there was an increase in the number of policy areas subject to the oversight, enforcement, and procedural timetables of quasi-judicial entities such as the International Trade Commission. These developments accelerated the weakening of the postwar transgovernmental network and the informal system of dispute management that went with it, and replaced it with a new, more fragmented system, driven by political cross-currents, with ambiguous effects on the process and patterns of bilateral bargaining. On one hand, these changes increased the number of actors that might be able to successfully pressure the White House into making coercive linkages, or even to make their own linkages. On the other hand, they also empowered a wider variety of blocking coalitions and a profusion of new institutional chokepoints. Overall, the process and outcome of bilateral bargaining promised to be driven less and less by the old rules of the game, and more and more by constantly shifting constellations of domestic political pressure in the United States.

The weakening of the transgovernmental network in the 1970s was not immediately followed by an eruption of coercive linkages. The nationalist wave in Canada rolled on, fuelling efforts to pursue a more "independent" diplomatic posture and "Canadianize" the economy. The US continued to struggle with prolonged economic malaise and new domestic dislocations. These trends generated a substantial number of bilateral disputes, virtually all of them over trade and investment practices, and most of them exacerbated by intra-state jurisdictional conflicts. None of these disputes pressed hard on core US interests, and most were readily contained and quickly resolved, usually through a tacit agreement to disagree.[63] Bilateral disputes were dampened by the general passivity of the Ford administration, strong personal relationships and policy convergences between Jimmy Carter and Trudeau, and the renewal of the Canadian federal crisis, which distracted Canadian attention and encouraged US restraint. This surface calm concealed the quiet consolidation of the new configuration of US foreign-policy making described above, obscuring both the undermining of the informal institutional bases for US bargaining restraint and the resulting constriction of the space for the exercise of Canadian policy autonomy.

The first clear sign of this new diplomacy came in the confrontation over Canada's Bill C-58, between 1979 and 1981.[64] This was another iteration in the long-running dispute over Canadian efforts to protect its "cultural" industries, particularly magazines and television broadcasting. The bill targeted US cable television broadcasters by permitting Canadian cable suppliers to strip US programs and replace them with "simulcast" Canadian retransmissions; US border broadcasters were thus robbed of their signals and of Canadian advertising revenues. Congress put pressure on the White House for action and then turned to explore its own retaliatory options, but could not figure out a way to effectively punish Canadian broadcasters. Eventually, the well-organized and well-financed US border broadcasters' lobby hit on the idea of punishing Canada by suspending the tax exemption for US conventions held in Canada. Canadian officials fumed about this blatant linkage, and pressed their contacts in the White House and State Department to derail it. Canada stuck to its guns and, at the last minute, the bill was unexpectedly withdrawn.[65]

This dispute is important here not because of the scale or intensity of the diplomatic confrontation but rather because of what it reflects of the underlying dynamics of bilateral bargaining after the 1970s. Canadian policymakers came to recognize that policies that injure organized interest groups in the US could trigger dangerous Congressional reactions, out of proportion to the original provocation and developed without consideration of prior policy trade-offs or of the risk of an escalating cycle of disruptive linkages.[66] Moreover, it became clear that close relations with the White House and State Department would not always be enough to deflect these pressures. Finally, a dangerous precedent seemed to have been set, raising apprehension in Ottawa that this kind of coercive linkage might become an ordinary feature of Canada-US bargaining. These changes became even clearer, and had a more decisive impact on bargaining outcomes, in the early 1980s, particularly in the dispute over the National Energy Program. As I will explain in the next chapter, recognition of these new conditions seems to have had a profound effect on the way that Canadian officials have since thought about the risks involved in pursuing policies at variance with those of the United States, and played an important role in Canada's surprising turn toward formal, integrative forms of bilateral dispute management.

5
Oil and Gas, 1980-83

Officials at the Canadian embassy in Washington and those in Ottawa charged with monitoring and managing the bilateral relationship have a lot to keep track of. Because American foreign-policy makers have so many different issues and relationships to deal with, because Canada is usually far down the list of countries for them to worry about, and because the American political system is so complex, policy decisions are frequently made in Washington with little or no attention to their (often enormous) implications for Canada.

Canadian policy-makers, on the other hand, are acutely conscious of a policy's impact on the bilateral relationship, and they are usually very careful to try to anticipate and respond to possible US objections. Sometimes they go ahead with something they consider vital to Canada's interests, knowing it will provoke a strong American reaction. From time to time, however, they pursue a potentially provocative initiative without giving adequate thought to the US reaction, and the result is usually diplomatic and domestic political disaster. One of the most dramatic examples of this is the hastily designed and highly controversial National Energy Program (NEP) of 1980, and the intense bilateral diplomatic confrontation that followed from it.

At the end of the 1970s, the Canadian government found itself confronted with rapidly increasing oil prices and a bitter struggle with the major producing provinces over pricing and revenues. Ottawa responded with a package of measures designed to insulate eastern Canada from rising world prices, strengthen the hand of the federal government in the domestic energy market, and reduce foreign (primarily American) ownership of the oil and gas industry. The US government was prepared to accept these goals in principle, but objected strenuously to the means by which they were to be pursued, including direct subsidies, discriminatory contracting and investment incentives, and retroactive appropriation. The newly elected Reagan administration, under pressure from the oil companies and Congress, attacked the NEP with diplomatic protests, a challenge under the General

Agreement on Tariffs and Trade (GATT), and, ultimately, threats of diplomatic and economic retaliation.

This case is of a different kind from those described in Chapters 3 and 4, and plays a different kind of role within this study as a whole. In the nuclear weapons and Arctic waters cases, the pivotal question was why the US was so restrained in confrontations over Canadian policies that cut deeply into core American interests. Why, given the high stakes, the difficulties in reaching a negotiated settlement, and the availability of viable coercive linkage options, did US officials *not* pursue linkages in order to try to deter or roll back these Canadian challenges? In the NEP case, on the other hand, the key questions are: (1) Why was the US so quick to resort to overt coercive linkages, particularly given that the Canadian initiative was arguably less damaging to US national interests than those in the nuclear weapons and Arctic waters cases? (2) Why, once US policy-makers had turned to retaliatory threats, did they apparently have so much difficulty in effectively making an effective linkage?

In the nuclear weapons and Arctic waters disputes, American officials were prepared to make "soft" linkages, by withholding executive attention and support on issues important to Canada, but chose not to pursue "hard" coercive linkages. For most American policy-makers, in fact, the idea of twisting Canada's arms through overt, direct linkages was all but unthinkable. By the early 1980s, however, hard linkages had become very "thinkable." The Reagan administration turned almost immediately to threats of retaliation, both in terms of the way they identified and evaluated their diplomatic options and in terms of the way they talked with their Canadian counterparts. In fact, they seemed to go out of their way to make it clear that there would be no holds barred, and that Canada would not be treated differently from any other country that tried to "hijack" American investments.

It seems, moreover, that Canada's partial retraction of its foreign investment agenda was driven in large part by the anticipation of escalating linkages. It is difficult to say for certain how important this was to the shift in Canadian policy, because that shift was also driven in part by domestic political pressures and changing market conditions. And it is difficult to say how far the US would have pursued its linkage options, because the Canadian government withdrew several of the program's most provocative elements *before* the US was able to settle decisively on any effective linkage commitment. The crucial point is that the US was clearly inclined to pursue linkages vis-à-vis Canada in a way that it would not have been during the 1950s and 1960s, and that this new tendency appears to have had important implications for the process and outcome of bilateral bargaining in the decades that followed.

The Reagan administration's aggressive opposition to the NEP was partly a reflection of the new government's ideological hostility to the program's interventionist agenda, but it was also a reflection of a longer-term transformation of the management of the Canada-US relationship. The postwar generation of American officials that had so successfully guided and sheltered the bilateral relationship with Canada was leaving the stage, and being replaced by a new cohort that knew less and cared less about Canada, and had little patience for the idea that there was a special way of doing business within the Canada-US relationship. Those who remained, and those younger officials who had been socialized to think along the same lines, found it increasingly difficult to maintain network connections with their Canadian counterparts, and to manage the relationship according to the old rules of the game.

Vietnam and Watergate had broken the imperial presidency and catalyzed a resurgence of Congressional involvement in all aspects of foreign policy. The long-term deterioration of the State Department's always shaky position as the "central" agency for foreign policy had been accelerated by Henry Kissinger's personal dominance of the agenda under both Richard Nixon and Gerald Ford, and by new encroachments by ostensibly "domestic" agencies such as Commerce, Energy, and Agriculture. More players were crowding their way into the cozy world of the Canada-US relationship, and more and more of these new players had reasons to challenge established bargaining norms.

The NEP: Problem and Solution

As noted in previous chapters, Canada decided at the end of the 1950s against building a pipeline to move Alberta oil to eastern Canada, and chose instead to supply the eastern provinces with oil from Venezuela in order to maximize exports to the lucrative US market. This was an enormously beneficial arrangement for Ottawa, but it started to break down in the late 1960s, as Washington began to press Canada to restrain exports to the US. Then in 1973 the Organization of Arab Petroleum Exporting Countries (OAPEC) mounted an oil embargo against the west, and the North American energy market was turned upside down. The US, recognizing that it had nearly exhausted its domestic reserves, and increasingly worried about political vulnerability due to its reliance on overseas suppliers, pressed Canada for more of its oil. Canada, on the other hand, realized that it had overestimated its reserves, and signalled that it would restrict exports and try to move toward a self-contained national market.[1] "Clearly," the authors of the National Energy Program would later write, "any country which can disassociate itself from the world oil market ... should do so, and quickly."[2]

The Canadian government's announcement that it intended to restrict oil and gas exports to the US provoked indignation in Washington, and several American politicians remarked that this was just one more indication that the days of the "special relationship" were over. But moves toward export restrictions were effectively blunted by opposition from Alberta and recognition in Ottawa that oil export revenues were badly needed to shore up the country's balance of payments and offset the cost of subsidizing oil imports for eastern Canada.[3]

When the world oil price doubled again in 1979-80, so did the level of economic apprehension in Canada's eastern provinces and the political tension between Ottawa and Alberta. Canadian officials began exploring more ambitious policies, designed to engineer a gradual movement toward the world price (while insulating eastern consumers through subsidies), capture a larger share of expected windfall profits, and generally increase federal government control over the oil industry.[4] As a reaction to the oil crisis, Charles Doran has noted, these moves were very much in line with those of comparable countries.[5] As in other major oil-consuming countries, the Canadian government tried to shelter industry and voters from rising world oil prices. As in other major oil-producing countries, it moved to exercise greater control over production and pricing, and a bigger share of the economic rent. In fact, Canada was the last of the major producer governments to try to force new terms on the oil companies.

Compounding these concerns about development and consumption was a mounting concern about American ownership of Canadian industry generally, and in strategic sectors like oil and gas in particular. Anxiety about the concentration of US ownership had been growing in Canada since the late 1950s, but had not yet gone much beyond a very broad academic debate over whether or not high levels of foreign ownership would retard the country's economic development and/or compromise its political sovereignty. By the late 1970s, however, the question of foreign ownership of oil and gas had become urgent. Recent studies had shown that the repatriation of profits from American energy holdings in Canada was outstripping new investments, causing a net drain on the Canadian economy.[6] As prices rose, so did Ottawa's concern that the anticipated windfall profits would be captured by US firms. If those profits were withdrawn, they might escape virtually untaxed; if they were pulled out suddenly, it might cause severe economic dislocation. If, on the other hand, those profits were reinvested in exploration and development, they might further crowd out potential Canadian investment and reinforce Canada's overall dependency.

To respond to this dilemma, Prime Minister Pierre Trudeau's Liberal government initiated a number of moves to exercise greater control over strategic sectors of the Canadian economy. In 1974, it established the Foreign Investment Review Agency (FIRA) to certify that proposed foreign investments would bring a "net benefit" to the Canadian economy. In 1975, it launched a national public oil company – Petro-Canada – to be the federal government's "window" on the energy sector, and its vehicle for strategic investment. The NEP was one more step in that same direction, and was proposed as part of a larger aspiration to Canadianize strategic sectors of the economy and to extend the reach and strength of FIRA.

The third and final layer of the problem was the energy sector's pivotal role in the larger struggle over political power within the Canadian federation. The hallmark of the Trudeau governments was a near-obsessive preoccupation with reversing – or at least slowing – the shift of political and economic power from Ottawa to the provinces, which had become so apparent during the 1960s. When it came to oil, Ottawa found itself facing a clear choice between east and west. Alberta wanted to protect the very profitable arrangements it had secured in the tax and revenue agreements of 1975, and to reaffirm the constitutional provision for provincial control over natural resources. Its new prosperity fuelled resentment of the federal transfer payments system, and of federal government efforts to try to capture oil revenues in particular. Ontario and Quebec, on the other hand, were horrified by skyrocketing oil prices and clamoured for federal government protection.

This was an easy choice for the Trudeau government.[7] The Liberal party's electoral base was concentrated in Ontario and Quebec, which were hardest hit by high fuel prices and most concerned with the question of US ownership. Quebec's concerns were particularly important, because separatist forces were rebounding from the failed sovereignty referendum of 1980, and the Trudeau government hoped to win the province's support for its controversial plan to patriate the constitution. On the other hand, Liberal support in the western provinces was already virtually nonexistent, and not likely to improve any time soon, so Trudeau had no political incentive to defer to Alberta.[8] (He did, however – as I will explain below – have strong reasons to be concerned about Alberta's capacity to cause trouble in other areas.)

In the 1980 federal election, Trudeau and his supporters had campaigned on stability, centralism, and state-led development. Many voters had responded positively to their proposals for jumpstarting the economy through major investments in energy development and infrastructure-building megaprojects. After the election, world oil prices continued to increase, and renewed price and revenue-sharing talks with Alberta quickly broke down. Frustrated by Alberta's intransigence, federal officials decided to accelerate their timetable for the centralization/nationalization ("Canadianization") of the oil and gas sector. Ottawa would simply take what it needed, by rushing to draft major new provisions into the fall 1980 federal budget.

Time Bomb

The National Energy Program, introduced as part of the 1980 federal budget, was a complex policy initiative, but there were a few core provisions that grabbed US attention: (1) a commitment to "self-sufficiency," which called for a substantial reduction of exports over the next ten years, and (2) a series of specific regulatory and tax policies designed to bring foreign (i.e., American) ownership in the oil and gas sector down from about 70 percent in 1980 to below 50 percent by the end of the decade. Specifically, the NEP called for restrictions on production licences for companies with less than 50 percent Canadian ownership, a new system for allocating exploration grants according to the level of Canadian ownership (the Petroleum Incentive Program, or PIP grants), incentives to encourage reliance on Canadian suppliers, and – most provocative of all – a requirement (to be applied retroactively) that all oil and gas firms turn over 25 percent of their holdings to the Canadian government ("crown interest" provisions).

Despite the signals the Trudeau government had been sending about its intention to take a more assertive role in the energy sector, the NEP provoked surprise and indignation in Washington and in Alberta. Because it had been put together in response to the sudden increase in world oil prices and the breakdown in talks with Alberta, and because it was done through the budget process, the NEP was developed hastily, in secrecy, by a small group of federal officials. In order to maintain budget secrecy and avoid "complications," Minister of Energy, Mines and Resources Marc Lalonde deliberately avoided interdepartmental consultation, excluding officials from External Affairs, Finance, and Industry, Trade and Commerce.[9] It was not only that there was no consultation with the US prior to the unveiling of the NEP; not much thought had been given even to the likely US reaction, or to relevant international commitments undertaken through the Organisation for Economic Co-operation and Development (OECD) and GATT. The dispute was thus intensified, partly because specific diplomatic provocations were not anticipated and tempered, and partly because of the psychological effect of the surprise itself.[10]

Because the NEP's announcement coincided with the US presidential election, the initial American reaction was deceptively mild. The lame-duck Carter administration was not in a position to bargain effectively with Canada, but State Department officials travelled to Ottawa to express their shock and anger at the proposed initiatives. By subsidizing consumer demand and dampening pressures for exploration and development of crucial non-Organization of Petroleum Exporting Countries (OPEC) supplies, they argued, Canada was breaking ranks with the anti-embargo coalition operating through the International Energy Agency (IEA). And by imposing discriminatory requirements on foreign investors, Canada was egregiously violating the OECD commitment to the principle of "national treatment."[11]

Canadian officials countered by saying that the US ought to have seen the NEP coming, since the Trudeau government had been increasing its controls on foreign investment for years and had affirmed its intention to extend them into the oil and gas sector in the Throne Speech the previous year. The NEP was contrary to the spirit of the IEA counter-cartel, they conceded, but Canada was not like other IEA countries. More importantly, its oil industry had been dominated by foreign firms, and those firms had recently been draining the Canadian economy by repatriating oil revenues faster than they were investing. As for OECD investment standards, they argued, Canada had signed on to a joint declaration, not a formal treaty. In signing the 1976 declaration, Canada had explicitly reserved its position on oil and gas, citing its extraordinary dependence on foreign investment and the continuing need for developmental interventions.[12]

US officials were not happy with these arguments. They continued to complain about Canada's violation of the national-treatment principle, arguing that Canada's proposed policies would set a dangerous precedent and encourage other countries to impose arbitrary restrictions on investment. US objections focused mainly on the discriminatory effect of the PIP grants and the expropriatory effect of the "crown interest" rules. The objection to the latter was not so much to the requirement that new investments hand over a 25 percent interest to the Canadian government as to the fact that it would also be applied to established claims that had not yet been developed. US officials referred to this as the "back-in" provision, and bitterly condemned it as "confiscation," or – more colourfully – as a "hijacking" of US investments. US officials also complained about the trade implications of the NEP. The suppression of domestic oil prices, they maintained, amounted to an indirect subsidy to Canadian exports. And the revised procurement requirements, they argued, were an unfair restriction on US goods and services, in direct violation of GATT standards.[13]

The NEP provoked a good deal of indignation in Washington but not much action in the final months of 1980. Two things changed in the new year, galvanizing the US government into a much more aggressive posture. First, the relatively sympathetic Carter administration was replaced by the Reagan administration. The new president was largely ignorant of Canada and its priorities but generally supportive of closer relations. Most of his advisers also knew little or nothing about Canada, but they were familiar with the NEP and they recognized its developmentalist approach as anathema to their own pro-market principles. Ronald Reagan and his advisers believed that previous administrations had allowed other countries to get away with predatory trade and investment practices, and they were determined to stand up for US investors.

Second, Canadian moves to wrest control over the oil and gas concerns of the US-based multinationals provoked a severe – and largely unanticipated – Congressional backlash, which heightened the administration's determination to force Canada to back down. Emboldened by NEP incentives and protections, Canadian oil companies quickly moved against their American competitors, either pursuing hostile takeovers of the US firms' Canadian subsidiaries or trying to force the sale of subsidiary firms by buying up stock in the parent companies.[14] The most dramatic of these campaigns was Seagram's torrid (but ultimately unsuccessful) pursuit of Conoco, which was closely covered by the business press on both sides of the border through the spring and summer of 1981. The target companies rushed to Congress – and in some cases, directly to the White House – to press for protection against Canadian "piracy." The NEP requirements, they argued, were driving down the value of US subsidiaries, making them vulnerable to NEP-fattened Canadian rivals, while FIRA investment controls were preventing the American targets from protecting themselves by interfering with their attempts to make defensive buyouts.

The wave of hostile takeover attempts thus set up a new connection, in the minds of US decision-makers, between the NEP and FIRA. The investment review regime, which US officials had grudgingly come to accept over the half-dozen years since its formation, was now very much back on the table, and by the summer of 1981 US officials were in the same breath calling for the scrapping of both NEP and FIRA. This was not issue linkage, strictly speaking, because it was in US policy-makers' minds all part of the same issue and the same basic complaint: violations of the principle of national treatment for foreign investment. US officials looked again at what Trudeau and his associates had been saying about their state-led development agenda, and didn't like what they saw. Pressure began to mount for assurances that the NEP model would not be carried over to other sectors, and that existing FIRA investment-screening procedures would not be tightened.[15]

As the targets of Canadian takeover attempts began to converge on Washington and the US business press became increasingly indignant, Congressional wheels started turning. A number of "protective" legislative initiatives were launched, including a requirement that foreign firms comply with US margin requirements, a suspension of all foreign takeovers in the energy sector, a delegation of authority to give the Secretary of the Interior discretion to block foreign energy takeovers, and a revocation of Canada's reciprocal status under the Mineral Lands Leasing Act.[16] None of the Congressional initiatives was considered a strong legislative prospect, and some were explicitly opposed by the White House on the grounds that they were just as incompatible with OECD investment guidelines as the NEP itself. It seemed that Congressional pressure would continue to increase, however, and this certainly played an important part in spurring the administration to adopt a more confrontational stance.[17]

Opening Moves

In its initial diplomatic moves, the Reagan administration weaved back and forth between toughness and conciliation. Aggressive demands were sent and then quickly withdrawn. Bargaining positions were left vague or shifted erratically. This was due in large part to the foreign-policy inexperience of new administration appointees, but it probably also reflected the general fragmentation of executive decision-making since the late 1960s.

In early March, the State Department sent a letter, signed by Secretary of State Alexander Haig, to Canadian ambassador Peter Towe, conveying US opposition to the "unnecessarily discriminatory" provisions of the NEP and delivering a veiled threat: "Should the balance of concessions be disturbed, the United States would be obliged to consider how a new balance might be achieved."[18] Canadian diplomats expressed surprise at the aggressive tone of the letter, and suggested that it be withdrawn.[19] The White House also disapproved, as it hoped to establish a positive tone for bilateral summit meetings to be held the following week.[20] The letter was quietly returned, but bilateral tensions remained high and were intensified by new recriminations and disagreements within the US executive. When Reagan visited Ottawa a few days later, the NEP was left off the agenda for his talks with Trudeau. It was taken up instead in a parallel meeting between Commerce Secretary Malcolm Baldrige, US Trade Representative William Brock, Canadian Minister for Industry, Trade and Commerce Herb Gray, and Canadian Minister of State for Trade Ed Lumley. Baldrige and Brock laid out US objections to the NEP in some detail, but did not make clear what kinds of changes might be satisfactory and offered few ideas about how the diplomatic impasse might be resolved. The next day, Brock sent a follow-up letter to Gray, reiterating US concerns and putting Canada on notice that the administration intended to pursue formal consultations through GATT Article 22.

The State Department sent another strong note to Ambassador Towe at the beginning of April, requesting assurances that the Canadian government would not discriminate against US firms in awarding contracts for energy megaprojects. Three days later, this letter was also withdrawn.[21] The same day, senior Canadian negotiators met with their American counterparts in Washington. The US team was clearly divided on what to press for and how, and failed to present the Canadians with the position paper they had promised. Towe offered assurances that Canada had not violated its international legal commitments, and that it was being careful to adhere to GATT conventions in drafting the NEP legislation.[22] In a follow-up letter to Gray, Brock and Baldrige again outlined US concerns about the NEP and FIRA, concluding with another warning: "We are concerned that failure to deal with these types of problems could lead to FIRA becoming a significant irritant in our bilateral relationship."[23] Gray met again with Baldrige and Brock the next day, but no real progress was made.

At the end of April, Towe signalled Canada's intention to make minor changes to the proposed legislation in order to accommodate US concerns without compromising the core purposes of the NEP. Two weeks later, Lalonde formally announced two major revisions. First, the wording of the procurement provisions was changed to make it clear – in accordance with

GATT requirements – that there would be no discrimination in the awarding of megaproject contracts. In the new formulation, project developers were required to consider Canadian firms, but would do so on a competitive basis. US pressure probably accelerated this change, but Canadian officials had already recognized the GATT conflict and had resolved to make the change.[24] Second, although the Canadian government would maintain the "crown interest" provisions, and refused to recognize any obligation to provide formal compensation, it would now offer *ex gratia* payments to leaseholders with established discoveries.

On 1 June, Brock wrote to Towe, welcoming the announced revisions but making clear that the US still had major grievances with the NEP. The oil companies were not satisfied with the procurement system because it still required project managers to explain why they were choosing American suppliers over Canadian ones, which was sure to bias contracting against the former. Neither the companies nor the US government was satisfied with the *ex gratia* payments. Canada refused to acknowledge expropriation or to offer compensation per se. The payments themselves were not even adequate to cover the asset value of the discoveries themselves, the oil companies argued, let alone underlying exploration costs. US officials were angry that Canada offered so little in compensation and was so inflexible on the terms; Canadian officials were angry that the Americans didn't seem to recognize the concessions as such.[25]

Pressure on the administration continued to build. Brock was compelled to testify before the Senate Finance and Banking committees, and to offer assurances that the administration would take a harder line against countries attacking US investments and aggressively enforce US trade laws. A *Wall Street Journal* editorial condemned the NEP, and pressed the president to force its retraction: "The prime lesson ought to be that you can't promulgate the kind of xenophobic national energy program that Canada is currently pressing without driving away foreign capital and reaping a backlash from the nations you are turning against."[26]

Two sets of top-level meetings were held in July, first during a short visit by Trudeau to Washington, and then again at the Group of Seven (G7) summit in Ottawa. Again, the NEP and FIRA were not on the agenda for the president and prime minister, but they were raised by US negotiators in parallel meetings between key advisers. The Canadians complained that US officials had not taken account of the policy distortions and domestic political risks entailed in the changes that Canada had already made to the NEP, and argued that the US had not made a convincing case for its contention that the program was incompatible with Canada's commitments to the OECD and GATT. Baldrige and Brock warned that the recent changes to the NEP had not addressed core US concerns, and warned that they would have to have further concessions in order to pacify the oil companies and their

Congressional supporters.[27] Soon after the summit closed, the Trudeau government went ahead with the passage of one part of the NEP legislative package, locking in the PIP grants and procurement requirements. The final component, including the so-called back-in provisions, was expected to come before Parliament at the end of the summer. Time was clearly running out for American officials to persuade or compel the Canadians to make changes to the most provocative parts of the NEP.

By the end of July, the massive outpouring of Canadian dollars caused by the takeover attempts was starting to take its toll on the economy. The finance minister intervened to ask Canadian banks to cut back the funds available to finance the takeovers, which quickly came to an end. Corporate pressure on Congress slackened almost immediately, and so in turn did Congressional pressure on the administration.[28] The weight of domestic political pressure was thus lifted from the White House, but US diplomatic pressure did not slacken, as the Reagan administration continued to fight for the principle of national treatment.

The Pot Boils Over

In the late summer of 1981, US officials passed the word to reporters that the administration was actively considering coercive linkages.[29] "The US administration is not going to sit by and do nothing," one warned. "Canada has been firing off salvo after salvo. At some point, Americans are going to react." Another unnamed US official told the *Wall Street Journal* that the administration considered Canada to be an important test of its determination to oppose harassment of US foreign investment. "If the US allows Canada to get away with its new policies, what about Mexico? It's not something we can just sit by and not fight." "It's not a question of *if*," warned one US official, "but *what* action will be taken." Some of this was just hype – the sideshow of leaks and unauthorized statements that always swirls around the diplomatic process.[30] But within this barrage there was an embedded signal – of frustration, certainly, but also of resolve, and of an underlying willingness to complicate the agenda and take risks.

These were not just idle threats. In July, the administration set up an interdepartmental committee to investigate linkage options. The Commerce Department and the Office of the United States Trade Representative (USTR) also pursued their own independent studies and made their own proposals to the White House.[31] US officials privately signalled their Canadian counterparts that they were considering various linkage options, and even highlighted some specific scenarios. Access to lucrative American defence contracts might be smothered. The US might be compelled to pursue a formal GATT challenge, or even massive trade retaliation through Section 301 of the Trade Act of 1974.[32]

By the end of August 1981, the Trudeau government had decided on a strategy to defuse conflict over the NEP. First, they would make whatever concessions were necessary to reach a short-term settlement with the oil-producing provinces. Ottawa made a renewed push for agreement with Alberta in September and, after a week of intense negotiations, was able to negotiate a new deal on production and taxation that would gradually lift the domestic oil price up to the world price, and shift revenue shares away from the companies and from Ottawa toward the producing provinces.[33] Alberta still harboured a number of grievances, but the agreement effectively closed this front in the conflict over the NEP. It also took some steam out of US objections, by gradually removing whatever subsidy effect might have come from lower oil prices in eastern Canada.

Second, the Trudeau government would move to alleviate American concerns about further investment restrictions by privately assuring US officials that they would not follow through on their publicly stated intention to extend the NEP model to other sectors of the economy and to strengthen the monitoring and enforcement provisions of FIRA. Back-channel signals were sent in late August, and Finance Minister Allan MacEachen followed up with an explicit commitment in mid-September.[34]

The two governments held another summit meeting in early September, and Reagan and Trudeau exchanged promises to "tone down the rhetoric" and renew efforts toward a mutually satisfactory understanding.[35] This was followed by further exchanges of diplomatic notes and another flurry of formal and informal bilateral meetings. Just as they had done in early June, US officials welcomed these Canadian assurances but made it clear that they only scratched the surface of US concerns about the NEP. Under Secretary of State for Economic Affairs Myer Rashish warned Canadian officials that pressure was mounting in Washington for "action," and presented a list of "retaliations" the administration would be compelled to consider. Deputy US Trade Representative David MacDonald cautioned them that the US was moving toward a formal GATT challenge, and that the administration "may have an obligation to publicize the risks of investment in Canada."[36]

Frustration was building in Ottawa over US officials' apparently growing demands: "Given the current intransigent stance being taken at least at the senior officials level of the US administration, it is difficult to see how further concessions on the NEP, unless they were in key policy areas, which we would not want to change, would improve dramatically bilateral relations."[37] Secretary of State for External Affairs Mark MacGuigan told Canadian reporters that it was "very important [that] we not lose our nerve ... Certainly the Government won't alter its policies because of what you call 'sabre-rattling.'"[38] Rashish countered by telling American reporters that the bilateral relationship was "sliding dangerously toward crisis," and that "sentiment is strong in favor of countermeasures against Canadian energy and investment policies. The dangers are real."[39]

Treasury Secretary Donald Regan wrote to MacGuigan, warning that the situation had become "urgent and extremely serious." "The President's primary objective," he wrote,

> is to avoid a circumstance in which the United States and Canada find themselves in a situation where actions lead to counteractions with serious damage to the overall relationship. I am personally convinced that this outcome can be prevented, but it will require the dedicated and concentrated effort on both sides, and frankly, I fear that time is running out ... if we cannot make progress in these discussions, the situation will almost certainly become more serious, and management of it far more difficult.[40]

A few days later, on 13 October, Regan and US ambassador Paul H. Robinson met again with Canadian officials and pressed for two additional concessions. First, they requested a public statement of the private commitment MacEachen had recently given that the Canadian government would not apply the NEP model to other sectors of the economy. Second, they asked for provisions for greater transparency in the awarding of procurement contracts on energy megaprojects.[41] MacGuigan said little about the former request, but reacted angrily to the latter, arguing that the underlying problem was discrimination by US oil company subsidiaries in Canada, which routinely awarded construction and supply contracts to the same US companies used by the parent companies, without considering local alternatives.

One of the recurring themes in US complaints about the NEP was that Canada's "Third World" investment policies did not sit well with its membership in the club of advanced economies. Some US officials even suggested that Canada be kicked out of the club, and implied as much in bilateral talks. These remarks were taken seriously by some in Ottawa, provoking a rush of anger and alarm. In September, US officials told reporters that Canada's informal request for an invitation to a major trilateral summit, to be held in New York the following month, was being turned down. No explicit connection was made to the dispute over the NEP, but the rejection was generally interpreted as "a gesture by somebody in Washington we don't like very much."[42] In December, Brock told reporters that Canada would not be invited to another trilateral meeting, to be held in Key Biscayne, Florida, in January 1982.[43] At the last minute, the administration changed its mind and renewed Canada's invitation.

Drawing the Line
Canadian officials were shaken by American pressure tactics but resolved to push ahead with the final component of the NEP legislative package. To

smooth the way, they made one final conciliatory gesture, acceding to one of the two requests made by US officials in the 13 October bilateral meeting. As part of the government's November 1981 budget speech, MacEachen made an explicit, formal commitment not to extend the NEP model to other sectors of the Canadian economy or to expand the reach and capabilities of FIRA. The NEP itself was not altered, but the Trudeau government had publicly renounced the developmentalist agenda it had proclaimed on coming to power in the 1980 elections. This would be the final concession, Canadian officials resolved; Canada had been driven down to its bottom line and would not be pushed any further.[44]

On 4 December, a week before the crown interest/"back-in" portion of the NEP legislation was to come before Parliament, Brock sent a toughly worded letter to the Canadian embassy, pressing for additional revisions to the NEP and FIRA.[45] This was the culmination of a protracted struggle among various US officials and agencies to resolve disagreements over goals and strategies, and to respond to Canadian complaints about shifting US demands, by presenting a final, structured set of concerns and priorities. It welcomed the formal disavowal of any extension of the NEP and FIRA, but went on to list a number of specific features that the US still wanted "eliminated." Again, the main targets were the "back-in" provisions and the PIP grants.

The Brock letter set off another wave of anger in Ottawa, with Canadian officials fuming about American negotiators' presuming to dictate specific policies, and making veiled threats of retaliation. On 10 December, as planned, the Trudeau government held the vote on – and passed – the core legislative component of the NEP, with the crown interest ("back-in") provisions intact. In the media scrum that followed, Lalonde again denied unfair expropriation, arguing that the oil companies had reaped windfall profits through their Canadian subsidiaries and could afford to give something back to Canada.[46] The final component of the NEP legislative package – including the PIP grants and procurement requirements – was due to come before Parliament in just a few weeks.

A little less than a week later, the State Department received an equally provocative letter from Canadian ambassador Allan Gotlieb. Canadian officials, he wrote, were deeply frustrated by the Americans' apparent refusal to recognize the May and November concessions as such. The crown interest provisions and PIP grants were absolutely essential – as Canadian officials had already explained – to the purposes of the NEP, and would not be compromised. FIRA had been on the books since 1974, he added, with virtually no US complaint. The message was clear enough: Canada was not prepared to bend any more, and, if the US thought that it had a sound legal case to make against what was left of the NEP, then it should go ahead and make it.[47]

Later that same day, the two sides held a meeting in Ottawa. Tempers were high and the talks were not very productive. The American negotiators raised the same points that they had in previous meetings, and were frustrated to find the Canadians growing impatient and threatening to suspend negotiations. Acting Under-Secretary of State for External Affairs de Montigny Marchand complained that the US had not given any indication that further concessions could actually bring an end to US pressure, and grumbled about the Americans' "nasty habit ... of making linkages."[48] "Canada does not accept the charge that it is not living up to high standards," he fumed, "and finds statements that it is no longer worthy to be a member of the club [of advanced economies] to be highly offensive." The talks ended where they began, with both sides frustrated and no prospect of settlement in sight.

In January 1982, Canada went ahead with the remaining major component of the NEP legislative package, containing the PIP grants and procurement requirements. The US initiated a formal consultation through GATT, but did not press for an immediate panel judgment and did not initiate any new diplomatic challenges. The bilateral diplomatic struggle gradually slackened, with both sides aggrieved and resentful.

A number of developments in the closing months of 1981 took the pressure off US negotiators, and in turn they began to ease up on their Canadian counterparts. Canada had made a series of significant concessions, including the *ex gratia* payments and the promises not to extend the NEP and FIRA. The number of Canadian takeover attempts had dwindled, and so had the intensity of Congressional outrage. The oil companies had begun to adapt themselves to the new Canadian requirements, and signalled that they would be able to live with the NEP.[49] And, perhaps most important, now that the Trudeau government had gone ahead with the legislation, US policy-makers understood that it would be virtually impossible for the Canadians to back down without risking domestic political disaster.[50]

In early 1982, the world oil price fell sharply, and the overextended companies rushed to Ottawa and Washington for relief. In May, Lalonde announced new tax breaks and incentives for Canadian oil and gas exploration, to try to get the companies through the depressed market and recession and to stave off public criticism that the NEP had damaged the industry. In the June 1982 budget, MacEachen announced that the FIRA review process would be streamlined in order to attract new investment. These changes were driven primarily by changing market conditions rather than US diplomatic pressure.[51] The NEP agenda had been predicated on continually increasing oil prices. When the recession deepened and oil prices dropped, the prospects for further Canadian takeovers disappeared. The government's efforts to deflect these pressures meant that most of the burden fell on federal and provincial revenues, but substantial blame still landed on the NEP itself.[52] In the 1984 election, Brian Mulroney's Progressive Conservatives campaigned aggressively against the NEP and FIRA. Buoyed by strengthened support in western Canada and new inroads in Quebec, Mulroney trampled Trudeau's designated Liberal successor, John Turner, and swept to power. The NEP was immediately scrapped and replaced with a substantially deregulated national oil policy, and FIRA was reinvented as an investment promotion agency (Investment Canada).

The Canadian Decision to Scale Back the NEP

It is difficult to assess the role played by the anticipation of US linkages in the Canadian decision to scale back the NEP, because pressure from Washington converged with equally intense pressure from Calgary. Past studies of the NEP have tended to focus almost entirely on either the intergovernmental conflict or the federal-provincial conflict. It is better, however, to see the Trudeau government's position as a "two-level game," where Ottawa needed to find a deal that would be acceptable to both domestic constituents and American diplomats.[53] In the first half of 1981, strong public support in Ontario and Quebec made this a relatively easy game for Ottawa to play;[54] as the year went on, however, pressure increased from both sides, and the Canadian government's bargaining position deteriorated.

The NEP agenda was originally conceived mainly as a way to strengthen Ottawa's hand in the domestic energy game, and in federal politics more generally. Alberta saw it as a blatant attempt to grab western resources and funnel them to Liberal Party constituents in Ontario and Quebec, and it was not far wrong. The pre-NEP tax and revenue system for oil and gas, negotiated after the first OPEC crisis in 1973, strongly favoured the interests of the oil companies and the producing provinces. As prices turned sharply upward in 1979, Ottawa had felt itself increasingly pressured to shield the oil-importing provinces, but it also saw an opportunity to capture a larger share of the enormous profits and to use those revenues to further ambitious regional development projects.

The announcement of the NEP in October 1980 was received in Alberta as a declaration of war, and the province was prepared to fight back.[55] Oil production in the province was immediately cut by 15 percent, driving up prices across the country, particularly in Ontario. A provincial moratorium was imposed on the promising oil sands megaproject, which Ottawa had hoped would be a vehicle for long-term federal revenues and northern development. Alberta, and the western provinces more generally, had virtually no electoral leverage over the Trudeau government, but they did have other kinds of political leverage. Ottawa was in the midst of delicate constitutional negotiations on the patriation of the constitution, and needed to maintain the support of as many provinces as possible. It was also battling a severe recession and needed provincial support to implement unpopular wage and price controls. Alberta Premier Peter Lougheed stubbornly withheld support for these federal initiatives throughout the spring and summer of 1981, giving way only after the September pricing agreement was signed. In the end, the federal and provincial governments were compelled by exasperated business interests to reach an agreement; they cut off a slightly bigger slice of the oil revenue pie and split it between them.[56]

Pressure from Alberta helps to explain the desperation in Ottawa in the summer of 1981, but it cannot explain the nature and timing of some of the major changes to the NEP. If the government had wanted only to pacify Alberta, it would have limited itself to shifting the tax and revenue arrangements, and perhaps compensating investors through restructuring of the *ex gratia* payments. The changes to the procurement requirements for megaproject contracts, the terms of the *ex gratia* payments, and the public revocation of the NEP model and strengthened FIRA were all initiated in response to the demands of the United States.

Stephen Clarkson's influential account describes the partial retraction of the NEP as a "collapse on the Rideau."[57] The Trudeau government, he argues, was shortsighted and overcautious in the summer and fall of 1981, and gave away much of its developmentalist agenda – and its bargaining leverage – without actually being confronted with any credible and substantial hard linkages. There is no question that Canadian officials were taken aback by the severity of US pressure, and by the Reagan administration's often undiplomatic handling of the dispute. They did offer significant concessions, in the form of the *ex gratia* payments and the revocation of their public commitment to extend the NEP model to other sectors and to strengthen FIRA. But while one could make the argument that Canadian "appeasement" might not have been a sound strategy, it was not driven by the kind of spinelessness that Clarkson implies. Past experience suggested that the US would generally accept a quiet settlement in this kind of bilateral dispute if the deal responded – formally or informally – to its major substantive concerns, particularly if it were set up in a way that helped the administration deflect its own domestic critics. This strategy's partial failure in this case reflects how much had changed over the preceding decade, in the political context for Canada-US bargaining. The White House and State Department did not like any part of the NEP, but they would have been prepared to live with it if it had been brought into line with relevant legal standards for national treatment of investment. However, inflammatory coverage in the US business press and intense Congressional pressure made it much harder for the administration to be seen to settle for anything less than the total destruction of the NEP, and this was reflected in the way US negotiators responded to Canadian concessions with greater and greater demands. The ride was made much rockier for Ottawa, moreover, by the general incoherence of the US bargaining position, which can in turn be traced to the splintering of decision-making among the State and Treasury departments and the USTR, and to the direct, mostly uncoordinated interventions by various cabinet secretaries in formal bilateral negotiations.

The question of whether or not Canada backed down because of US linkage is important to a proper understanding of this dispute. For the purposes of this book, however, the more important question is whether and why the US was prepared to go ahead with coercive issue linkages. The record indicates that the administration was inclined to pursue linkages, and, while it had some difficulty in identifying viable linkage scenarios, its apparent determination to do so was credible enough to drive the Trudeau government toward a partial retraction.

When Push Comes to Shove: US Aggression and Self-Restraint

Given that linkage is generally assumed to be an ordinary feature of international bargaining, we might say that there is no puzzle to solve here. The more pressing question, for the purposes of this book, is not why the US was inclined to pursue linkages but rather why it was inclined to pursue linkages *in this case, given that it was not prepared to do so in earlier, weightier disputes.* The process and outcome of the NEP dispute confound the realist argument about the logic of strategic restraint, albeit in a different way than the disputes over nuclear weapons and Arctic waters. The process and outcome in this case are essentially consistent with the expectations of the diplomatic-culture interpretation, if only negatively. And they highlight the way that, where the diplomatic culture is less salient, specific outcomes may be best accounted for by the pushing and pulling effects of domestic political coalitions.

The realist interpretation outlined in Chapter 2, emphasizing alliance politics and strategic restraint, expects the US to be more forbearing with Canada on low politics issues (trade, investment) during periods when international strategic competition is most intense, and the support of small allies is therefore most valued. Thus, we might expect the US to have been inclined to take a relatively cautious approach to resolving bilateral disputes with Canada during this period, because the Soviet invasion of Afghanistan had reinvigorated the Cold War confrontation, the US was struggling to maintain the support of NATO allies in the face of controversial new strategic doctrines and deployments, Canada had recently increased its defence spending, and US military planners hoped to use Canadian territory for cruise missile testing.[58]

But a realist should also expect the US to be tough with Canada on issues directly related to US national security concerns, and a case could be made that US concern over security of supply for oil and gas was so intense at this time that it ought to be treated as a high politics issue. The NEP was designed to reduce the US-based multinationals' stake in the Canadian oil and gas industry, and would thus undercut the American government's capacity to indirectly influence exploration, pricing, and export decisions in this important supplier country. But the Canadian share of overall US oil imports had been declining during this period, and no one in Washington seriously expected the NEP to lead to dramatic pricing shifts or jeopardize the overall security of imports from Canada. Archival records and interviews indicate, moreover, that American officials did not frame their arguments for or against linkage in terms of national security calculations, in inter- or in intra-governmental contexts.

The NEP case is perfectly compatible with the diplomatic-culture interpretation advanced here, not only in the sense that the US was clearly inclined to pursue linkages in this post-fragmentation case but also in the sense that the decision-making process in Washington reflected the fragmentation itself.

The limited archival record and interviews with former Canadian and American officials confirm that US reservations about issue linkage in the NEP dispute were anchored in practical political calculations and not normative compunctions. When specific linkage options were ruled out, they were opposed on the ground that they did not impose costs severe enough to change Canadian priorities, and/or that they might impose unacceptably high political costs on the administration. The most common versions of the latter objection were that a particular option would trigger a dangerous reaction from powerful domestic interest groups (e.g., Auto Pact) or would be a violation of an important domestic or international legal commitment (e.g., retaliatory investment restrictions).[59]

Moreover, the administration deliberately played up its investigation of linkage options *as linkages,* in order to draw Canadian attention to the seriousness of its opposition.[60] This probably reflects what we might call the "sunset effect" of the norm against issue linkage: by drawing attention to the way that the US was willing to pursue linkages, and framing them as such, the administration sent the signal that it recognized the norm's past importance but that it would not be bound by the old rules of the game. A number of US officials recognized that their Canadian counterparts would still attach special meaning to linkages, and deliberately made use of that meaning as a signal of their resolve. Some of them recognized that crossing this threshold entailed a real risk of inflaming nationalist elements in Canada and triggering a dangerous escalation of the dispute. Others did not, and simply barrelled ahead with coercive diplomacy in much the same way they would with any other country.[61]

The diplomatic confrontation over the NEP is probably the clearest example we have of the post-Nixon deterioration of the Canada-US transgovernmental network and the bargaining norms that defined it. The Department of External Affairs had, over the previous few years, come to a new modus vivendi with Trudeau and his advisers, but it had far less in-dependent influence over the direction of foreign policy than in the 1960s. The department, as noted above, had been completely excluded from the original formulation of the NEP itself. That had much to do with the secrecy requirements of the budget process, but the department's career officials were also relegated to a supporting role in the dispute over the NEP, as a small number of prominent Cabinet ministers – especially Marc Lalonde and Herb Gray – took the lead in strategic planning and negotiation.

The State Department took a prominent role in shaping US goals and strategies, but it was not in a position to "manage" the issue as in the past, primarily because of cross-cutting pressures from the USTR, the Treasury and Commerce departments, and other bureaucratic agencies. Each of the various departments made its own assessment of US priorities, initiated its own investigation of bargaining options (including hard and soft linkages), and set up its own channel of contact to the White House. The USTR, for example, naturally pressed for a focus on the trade distortions caused by differential fuel prices and on procurement discrimination. Commerce, on the other hand, took a very strong stand on the principle of national treatment of investment. The result was a near-complete failure on the US side to arrive at a unified, structured negotiating position.

There was no real disagreement about which parts of the NEP were objec-tionable, but much disagreement about what changes to insist on and what kind of pressure to bring to bear.[62] Despite the complexity of the NEP and its effects, and despite the diversity of the various departments' concerns, the US never effectively compartmentalized its bargaining position. Instead, all of the various grievances were heaped in one pile, and then dumped on Ottawa that way. The US failure to segment and prioritize its demands was intensely frustrating for the Canadians and almost certainly got in the way of a number of possible compromise settlements. In the early stages of the dispute, it probably strengthened the US position by heightening anxiety in Ottawa and encouraging the Canadians to offer some concessions. By late November, however, it only reinforced the perception that the US had no bottom line, and reinforced Canadian officials' determination not to make any further concessions.[63]

The White House did not do much to steady and strengthen the hand of US negotiators. The new administration was slow to make appointments, and provided little direction to the various departments. The dispute carried on for over a year, but the administration never actually made a decision on which department to designate as lead agency.[64] In the early months, the White House put a high priority on cultivating leadership relationships and making bilateral summits "successful" (i.e., nonconfrontational), and so deliberately deflected efforts to raise the NEP's diplomatic profile. The State Department felt that it was being undercut (sometimes publicly), Congress became convinced that the administration was being passive, and Canadian officials were left confused about the severity of US objections to the NEP.[65]

In both capitals, middle-level officials with established transgovernmental connections were kept on a very short leash, as leadership advisers and cabinet officials took a very hands-on approach to both strategic planning and negotiations. Bilateral summit meetings of top officials took on greater importance, as informal meetings were curtailed and rendered unimportant by tight administrative controls. The result was that the high-level meetings were filled with unpleasant surprises and frustrations, and eventually devolved into venues for reading official statements rather than seriously exploring settlement options.

Further complicating the US position was the sustained Congressional pressure during the spring and summer of 1981. Congress was generally dissatisfied with the Reagan administration's support for American firms threatened by foreign trade and investment restrictions. The furor over the NEP reinforced this feeling, and generated a number of bills designed to show that Congress was doing something about the wave of takeover attempts and to "light a fire" under the White House. This undoubtedly strengthened the administration's hand vis-à-vis Canadian negotiators, by setting up significant domestic audience costs and reinforcing the perception of American resolve. In bilateral meetings, US officials often took the position of the "good cop" who needed to have some concession to take back to Washington in order to deflect harsher demands at home and derail possible retaliation.[66] The identity of the "bad cop" was usually left unspecified, but it was no secret that they meant Congress and the politically powerful oil multinationals. The high drama of the takeover attempts and the target companies' calls for help, combined with Congressional vitriol, greatly increased media coverage of the dispute and raised the domestic political stakes for the administration. Thus Congressional pressure almost certainly reinforced the administration's inclination to consider coercive linkages.

The diplomatic-culture interpretation developed here can explain only US willingness to consider hard linkages vis-à-vis Canada in this dispute, not whether any specific linkage scenario was actually pursued or the success or failure of linkages in forcing changes to Canadian policies. With the postwar diplomatic culture stripped away, US decisions about linkage were bound to be driven by ad hoc calculations of diplomatic efficacy and political risk, shaped largely by the configuration of domestic coalition pressures in each of the various linkage scenarios. Domestic blocking coalitions (like those identified by Keohane and Nye) appear to have been decisive in steering the administration away from making linkages to the Auto Pact and the Defence Production Sharing Agreement (DPSA), for example, and probably ruled out a wide variety of other options that did not receive much attention from the interdepartmental strategy committees. The threat to exclude

Canada from the club of advanced economies was more credible – and therefore more effective – because the administration had some direct discretion over it, and because it would not directly harm any powerful domestic interests. The threat of unspecified trade retaliation was also relatively credible – or would have been if the US had had a stronger legal case – but might have broken down when it came to identifying specific retaliatory restrictions and thereby stirring up a hornet's nest of domestic interests.

Identifying and Evaluating Linkage Scenarios

At several points in the dispute, US negotiators threatened to formally challenge the trade effects of the NEP, raising the possibility of retaliation within the context of the multilateral trade regime. USTR officials raised the possibility of a GATT challenge soon after the announcement of the NEP, and reiterated it several times through the spring and summer of 1981. This was not a particularly effective threat. Canadian officials doubted the United States would go ahead with a formal challenge to Canadian investment policy while they themselves were ignoring a number of high-profile GATT decisions.[67] Even if such a challenge were made, Canadian officials believed, no fault would be found with the NEP's trade-relevant provisions.[68] (The one exception was the wording of the procurement requirement provisions, which Canadian officials had revised almost immediately after the program was launched.) In the end, the US did initiate GATT consultations, but did not push for a panel judgment.

US officials also raised the possibility of a unilateral challenge through Section 301 of the Trade Act of 1974. If the NEP had been found to have discriminatory effects that injured US producers, the president would have been directed to impose retaliatory restrictions on imports from Canada. Pursuit of a Section 301 challenge would have required a concurrent GATT challenge, however, and a GATT judgment against the NEP would have required a clear chain of evidence linking it to material injury of US firms, which would have been extremely difficult in this case. Both sides therefore recognized that formal trade retaliation through Section 301 was "not a serious proposition."[69]

The very first weeks of the NEP dispute coincided with the final weeks of the long-standing dispute over the failed East Coast fisheries agreement, and one might argue that the new administration's decision to withdraw the agreement from Senate consideration in March 1981 was driven by frustration brought on by the NEP. But the fisheries agreement was headed for trouble anyway, and the Reagan administration had good reasons to pull the plug on it without looking beyond the agreement itself.[70] Congressional opposition was driven by just two senators from New England, but those two were very determined and had gathered a substantial number of allies, and the White House's preliminary head-counts found a substantial majority opposed to ratification. The Reagan administration was not particularly inclined to try to rescue the deal either, because the ambitious, binational conservation management agency that it would create did not sit well with their anti-regulatory, small-government instincts.

The sectoral managed trade agreement for autos and auto parts negotiated in the mid-1960s (the Auto Pact) was generally beneficial to both countries, but – as noted in Chapter 4 – the balance of benefits shifted back and forth across the border, depending on demand for different types of cars and other market conditions. In the late 1960s and early 1970s, the balance had tilted strongly in Canada's favour, and US officials pressed for a renegotiation of the agreement. By the end of the 1970s, however, the balance had turned in favour of the United States, and Canadian officials were the ones pressing for renegotiation. When the Reagan administration took office at the beginning of 1981, it assured the Trudeau government that it was willing to at least talk about the possibility of changing the terms of the agreement.[71] Canadian officials continued to press for negotiations through the rest of that year, but without any appreciable results.

The Auto Pact was one of the issues raised in US officials' early speculation about possible retaliation: the logic, presumably, was that if Canada refused to make compromises on the NEP, it would jeopardize whatever support it had from the administration on possible renegotiation of the Auto Pact. This idea was kicked around in the State Department but never got beyond the hypothetical, and no overt connections were made in negotiations with Canadian officials. US officials must have recognized that the threat to withhold White House support for renegotiation of the Auto Pact would not have held much water with the Canadians, since there had been little evidence of any real support to begin with. More importantly, the politically powerful auto companies would have strenuously opposed any state intervention to change the terms of the agreement, particularly in the face of a looming economic recession.

As in the nuclear weapons and Arctic waters cases, the asymmetrical benefits of the DPSA were raised in the NEP dispute as another possible basis for US leverage.[72] Again, disruption of the agreement – including informal disruption through administrative restrictions – would have had severe consequences for Canada, particularly in terms of lost foreign exchange earnings and loss of jobs in politically important southern Ontario. Such a disruption would have brought significant short-term adjustment costs for the United States, because the US military had built a number of systems on components and maintenance by Canadian defence contractors. But these costs might have been borne if the stakes were thought high enough. In the event, there is no evidence that any serious thought was put into any kind of hard linkage involving defence production.

The linkage scenario taken most seriously in Ottawa was the veiled threat to informally suspend Canada's membership in the club of advanced economies, by blocking its participation in upcoming international economic summits. This was the threat, Ambassador Gotlieb remembered, that "had some people [in Ottawa] running scared."[73]

Losing Canada's seat at the summit table would have been a foreign-policy disaster because it would have undercut the government's capacity to influence the development of the world economic order, and removed it from an important forum for informal diplomatic engagement and coalition building. It would also have been a domestic political disaster, slicing deeply into the Canadian public's insecurity about their international status and raising questions about the government's management of foreign economic policy.[74] The threat was relatively credible, moreover, because it would have been fairly easy for the administration to follow through with it. There were no formal institutional obstacles to withdrawing invitations to events hosted by the US, and the administration might very well have been able to convince (or compel) other countries to withdraw invitations as well. No domestic interests, and few bureaucratic agencies, would have seriously opposed a temporary exclusion of Canada from the summit system. The primary drawback would have been alarm and possible opposition from other summit participants worried about a dangerous precedent, but the administration might very well have taken this risk if it thought that the threat would have changed Canadian policy.

Ultimately, the Reagan administration decided that it probably would not, and the summit invitations were restored.[75] This was, in other words, just another step in the series of difficulties US officials experienced in searching for linkage options that would be weighty enough to force changes to the Canadian position without violating standing international commitments or stirring up domestic opposition. Canadian officials knew all about these dead ends; they had read about them in the press and heard about them from their contacts in Washington.[76] In the end, warnings about revoking invitations to summit meetings were ineffective in changing the Canadian position, but they did have important diplomatic implications. First, they exacerbated ongoing debate within Canada about the Trudeau government's developmentalist agenda, fuelling opposition arguments that the government was pursuing "Third World" policies that were likely to damage the Canadian economy and provoke American reprisals. And second, they convinced many in Ottawa that the US was determined to keep pressing, and stirred anxiety that it would eventually find its way to something that offered the right mix of effectiveness and risk.

Linkages between the NEP dispute and summit participation did not begin until after – and thus played no part in catalyzing – the May 1981 decision to offer the *ex gratia* payments and revise the procurement requirements. But they did precede, and probably played an important part in, the November decision to publicly disavow the extension of the NEP and FIRA. According to one well-placed former Canadian official, it was the threat of "excommunication" – and its direct diplomatic and domestic political implications – that spurred Canada's decision to offer these additional concessions.[77] It is more likely, however, that the threat to withdraw future summit invitations was important mainly as a signal of the administration's willingness to pursue more extreme options. This, a couple of former Canadian officials admitted off the record, definitely played an important part in the government's decision to disown the NEP/FIRA model right before passing the NEP legislation.

Epilogue: Adjusting to the New Washington

The fallout from the NEP had a chastening effect on the Trudeau government. If the world oil price had continued to rise and the government had been able to reach its goal of 50 percent Canadian ownership, the entire project might have been a political success despite the resentment in Calgary and in Washington.[78] When the recession deepened and the price of oil collapsed, however, the NEP agenda unravelled completely. The May 1982 decision to bail out the oil industry, and the June 1982 decision to "streamline" the NEP, amounted to a recognition that the developmentalist agenda laid out in the 1980 budget had run out of steam.[79]

In the immediate aftermath of the NEP dispute, difficult questions were asked about the Trudeau government's management of the economy, federal-provincial politics, and Canada-US relations. In September 1982, Trudeau shuffled his Cabinet, replacing each of the key ministers from the NEP drama – MacGuigan, Lalonde, and Gray – with a group of more "pragmatic" party heavyweights: Allan MacEachen, Jean Chrétien, and Ed Lumley, respectively.[80]

The tumult over the NEP and the subsequent explosion of protectionist attacks on Canadian exports heightened Canadian concern over the new assertiveness and unpredictability of the US Congress, and reinforced long-standing doubts about whether the White House was still willing and able to go to bat for Canada. With encouragement from its new ambassador in Washington, Allan Gotlieb, the Canadian government made a substantial new investment in the Washington embassy and directed its officials to place a higher priority on cultivating influence in Congress.[81] One of the main themes of this new push was to do more to keep track of the balance of domestic coalition pressures within the US on various issues of interest to Canada, and to cultivate ad hoc transnational alliances with groups whose interests converged with those of Canada. This was a direct contradiction of the way Ottawa had managed its relations with Washington during the

1950s and 1960s, and it reflected a deeper recognition that the old informal system of transgovernmental network connections had broken down.

The suspension of the NEP and the "streamlining" of FIRA were just the first steps in a series of moves by the Canadian government toward a more integrative, less confrontational approach to relations with the US, which began even before Pierre Trudeau passed the reins to the more pragmatic, more thoroughly pro-business leadership of John Turner. In 1983, for example, the Department of Finance began to develop the negotiating points for sectoral trade liberalization that eventually became the diplomatic foundations for the 1987 Canada-US Free Trade Agreement.[82]

Brian Mulroney campaigned on his rejection of Trudeau's supposedly reckless and unnecessary provocations of the US, and promised voters that "good relations – super relations – with the United States would be the cornerstone of [his] foreign policy." Mulroney's personal relationship with Reagan was warm and constructive, and the overall tone of the bilateral relationship was very positive during the 1980s. The Mulroney government did press ahead with a number of provocative policies – including a polite no to participation in the Strategic Defense Initiative and open disagreement on sanctions against South Africa – but overall the number of bilateral conflicts in the decade after the NEP dispute was relatively low. Many Mulroney supporters believed that making a deliberate strategic decision to avoid pursuing policies at odds with the US would increase Canada's capacity to influence policy outcomes in Washington. The Mulroney government's experience with acid rain, however, and the rough ride it had in the negotiation of the free trade agreement, raised serious questions about whether the US was willing or able to make these kinds of cooperative linkages.

When the Soviet Union collapsed in 1991, some worried that the end of the Cold War would undercut the US rationale for diplomatic self-restraint and weaken the Canadian bargaining position in Washington. But bilateral relations remained quiet and generally harmonious through the 1990s, even after Mulroney was replaced by the much more confrontational and ostensibly nationalistic Jean Chrétien. The new prime minister talked tough about his intention to "scrap" the free trade agreement and made a point of not being seen to be too close to President Bill Clinton, but he actually initiated very few policies that were provocative to the US, and the relationship hummed along peacefully through the 1990s.[83] It was not until after the terrorist attacks of 11 September 2001, and – more specifically – with the severe diplomatic confrontation over America's push to war in Iraq in 2003, that Canada-US relations again experienced the kind of frustration and resentment seen in 1963, 1970, and 1981, and the question of linkage came to the forefront once again.

6
War in Iraq, 2002-4

A few days after the first bombs began falling on Baghdad, signalling the start of the second US-Iraq war, the American ambassador to Canada went to Toronto and dropped one more. Many in Washington were "disappointed" and "upset" by the Chrétien government's decision not to support the war, Paul Cellucci told a crowd of corporate executives, and Canadians needed to understand that in the post-9/11 world, "security trumps trade."[1] Alarm bells started to ring. "The Americans," historian J.L. Granatstein warned, "are furious at Canada now, as angry as they have ever been and, as soon as the dust in Iraq settles, they will exact their revenge."[2] Speculation about the form that revenge might take ranged from tightened border security protocols to tougher restrictions on imports of Canadian lumber. Bilateral meetings were hastily arranged, and things were quickly smoothed over. Ambassador Cellucci went back to tell reporters that the US hadn't really intended any kind of coercive linkage between issues, and Canadian officials swore they had neither perceived nor expected any.[3] Yet, in virtually the same breath, the Chrétien government announced that Canada would make a major contribution to postwar reconstruction in Iraq, and would soon expand the sharing of border-crossing information that the US deemed essential to the post-9/11 "War on Terror."

Was this a textbook case of America resorting to direct, coercive ("hard") linkages to compel Canada to change its tune on a crucial national security issue? There is no solid evidence that overt threats were ever made, and Canada was not actually compelled to change its stance on Iraq. But perhaps, as some have supposed,[4] the Chrétien government was alarmed by the prospect of future linkages and therefore backed down, not by reversing itself and sending a contingent of ground troops to Iraq – which, given the level of public opposition in Canada, would have been politically impossible at that point – but rather by making other policy changes designed to show Canada's usefulness and reliability as an ally in the broader US-led campaign against terrorism. There is no doubt that the government embarked on a number of new policy initiatives after March 2003 that it might not otherwise have pursued, and that these were intended to improve Canada's image in Washington and repair some of the damage done to the bilateral relationship. These moves are better understood, however, as part of a unilateral Canadian effort to find a new bilateral equilibrium, rather than as concessions extracted under duress.

The Bush administration evidently had no problem with making threats and twisting arms in order to put together its somewhat ironically named "Coalition of the Willing."[5] And there is no question that the Canadian decision to say no to war in Iraq was intensely frustrating to many in Washington. Yet, based on what we know so far – which is actually quite a bit, thanks to a number of timely leaks and subsequent interviews – there is no evidence that the US tried to twist Canada's arms. If in international politics, as Thucydides said, "the strong do what they can and the weak accept what they must," this raises the question of why the Bush administration "failed" to do whatever it needed to do – including resorting to coercive linkages, if necessary – to force Canada into line.

One part of the explanation was that it was not entirely clear in Washington that there *was* any problem with Canada that might need to be fixed through aggressive bargaining. The Chrétien government – like the governments of France, Germany, and Russia, among others – had made it clear that they were uncomfortable with the Bush administration's talk of preventive war and regime change, and that they expected the US to secure United Nations approval for war in Iraq, just as President Bush's father's administration had done in 1991. Unlike France and Russia, however, the Canadian government sent mixed signals about how firmly it would insist on explicit, direct UN approval. Chrétien himself maintained that "Canada [would] insist on UN approval," but sometimes implied that the crucial factor was really the strength of the evidence against Iraq, and his foreign minister, Bill Graham, hinted that Canada might be prepared to support an invasion with UN Security Council consensus, as it had done in Kosovo in 1999. Canadian military officers privately reassured their American counterparts that they expected their government to sign on to the Coalition of the Willing, and that they expected to fight side by side with them as they had in the past. The result was that there was still some uncertainty in Washington about what Canada would do, right up to 17 March 2003 – just three days before the start of the US-led invasion – when the prime minister announced in the House of Commons that his government definitely would not support war in Iraq without a specific UN Security Council authorization.

A second part of the explanation for US self-restraint was that Canada's decision not to offer direct support for the war in Iraq had to be weighed against its value as a supporter for other aspects of the American agenda in the Middle East and the broader US-led War on Terror. While the Chrétien government refused to offer direct support for the war in Iraq, it did offer *indirect* support for American involvement in the region, including the leadership of a naval task force in the Persian Gulf and – most importantly – a commitment to take command of NATO forces in Afghanistan. American defence planners were frustrated by the lack of Canadian support in Iraq, but they were prepared to live with it, based on the expectation that Canada's ambitious contributions in Afghanistan would free up American forces for redeployment to Iraq. This is an important part of the story, but – as I will explain in greater detail below – it is not enough to thoroughly explain US self-restraint in this case. The Bush administration certainly welcomed Canada's assistance in the Persian Gulf and in Afghanistan, but it just as certainly could have carried on without it. What the White House wanted most from Canada in the spring of 2003 – as with all of its traditional allies – was diplomatic endorsement of the push to war in Iraq, to shore up the perceived legitimacy of the administration's strategy, in the eyes of the international community and the American public. And that was the one thing that the Chrétien government was conspicuously determined to withhold.

The third and final part of the explanation for US self-restraint is the administration's assessment, in strict expected-utility terms, of the political pros and cons of pursuing coercive linkages vis-à-vis Canada in this case. There is no doubt that the White House had bigger fish to fry in March 2003, and that Canada's position – whatever it might eventually turn out to be – was less important than that of France, Germany, or even Mexico (as one of the elected members of the Security Council at the time). But if Canada's importance was small relative to others, it was still large in absolute terms. "You should have no doubt about this," one US official reflected. "We told every Canadian that we talked to the same thing: 'we care about what you do and say about Iraq. It matters to us.' This was not just striking poses. It was serious stuff."[6]

There were a number of ongoing negotiations and disputes in the spring of 2003 that represented potential vehicles for hard linkages, including the awarding of potentially lucrative contracts for postwar reconstruction in Iraq, the expected tightening of border-crossing rules and procedures, and ongoing restrictions on imports of Canadian lumber and beef. As I will explain below, however, none of these most prominent scenarios were viable ones for the US in strict cost/benefit terms. The potential benefits, in terms of changing Canada's position, were too low or too uncertain, and the potential costs and domestic political risks were too high. With respect to border security, for example, there were powerful interests on both sides of the issue in the US, and it is this domestic political struggle – rather than anything that Canada has done or not done – that has tended to drive US decision-making on this issue. The importance of latent "blocking coalitions" in cost/benefit calculations about potential issue linkage tends to support Keohane and Nye's argument about the implications of extensive inter-dependence (see Chapter 2). But there were mitigating factors in this case that would have made it much harder for the US to force a change to Canada's policy, and made it easier for the US to live with Canada's decision, so the outcome here does not necessarily support the more sweeping argument that interdependence rules out linkages altogether.

American officials shied away from pursuing linkages for *practical* – mostly domestic political – reasons, not normative ones. As I have shown in previous chapters, US policy-makers adhered during the early Cold War decades to a special set of bargaining norms in their dealings with Canada, which featured a strict norm against hard linkages between unrelated issues. This normative self-restraint created a great deal of space for Canada to pursue policies at odds with those of the United States, and in some cases even to openly challenge American leadership in wider multilateral contexts. Based on what we know so far about the diplomatic showdown over Iraq, however, it is clear that very few American officials saw any particular reason to treat Canada differently from any other potential supporter, or to observe any special rules of the game for bilateral bargaining. In fact, the speed and ease with which American officials turned to consider coercive linkage scenarios in the Iraq dispute, and the wide variety of different political actors in the US that actually pursued some kind of indirect retaliation, powerfully highlights how much has changed in Canada-US relations since the early 1970s.

9/11, the War on Terror, and the New "Fortress America"
The terrorist attacks of 11 September 2001 revitalized a sense of mutual identification and support between Canada and the United States – at least for a little while. In the immediate aftermath of the attacks, Americans expressed gratitude for Canadians' having spontaneously welcomed into their homes hundreds of US-bound airline passengers who had been stranded by emergency flight diversions, and Prime Minister Jean Chrétien declared that Canada was "standing shoulder to shoulder with the United States." Canada was quick to support the invocation of NATO's collective defence mechanism, and made a substantial contribution to the initial joint military intervention in Afghanistan. These feelings of solidarity and common purpose with the US quickly evaporated, however, just as they did in many other western states, in the heat of subsequent diplomatic frictions over war in Iraq.

While most Americans continued to see Canada as a close friend and partner after 9/11, the terrorist attacks stirred up long-standing anxieties in some corners of Washington about Canada's reliability as a strategic and diplomatic ally. US policy-makers had been frustrated with the perceived inadequacy of Canadian defence spending since the 1960s, and increasingly critical of Canada's relatively permissive immigration and refugee policies since the early 1990s. Rumours that the 9/11 hijackers had entered the United States through Canada – which were groundless and repeatedly refuted by the Canadian government – were strikingly persistent, and were often repeated by American elites who were in a position to know better, even months afterward.[7]

America's instinctive response to 9/11 was to close the border and start building walls. The temporary closure of the border in the immediate aftermath of the terrorist attacks hit the profoundly export-dependent Canadian economy hard. Over the previous decade, the Canada-US and North American free trade agreements (CUSFTA and NAFTA) had encouraged Canadian and American companies – particularly those in highly integrated sectors such as energy and auto parts – to build intricate cross-border production and distribution systems, and the post-9/11 border closures were said to have cost some firms as much as a million dollars per hour.[8]

The Chrétien government moved quickly to try to work out a new understanding with the White House that would reopen the fortress gates and protect Canadian companies' access to the American market. Intensive negotiations between Deputy Prime Minister John Manley and Homeland Security Director Tom Ridge transformed ongoing border security talks into the Smart Border Accord of December 2001, a plan for joint action that was supposed to enhance border security and streamline crossings at the same time. But Congress – in the grip of a broader anti-immigrant movement and popular desire to achieve "perfect security"[9] – continued to press for tougher standards and tighter rules, holding out the prospect of additional restrictions on trade and travel that could have had crippling effects on the Canadian economy.

While Americans were annoyed by Canada's supposed free-riding, Canadians were increasingly frustrated and alarmed by signs that the US was turning its back on leadership of the multilateral institutions it had built during the Cold War. Before 9/11 – and even before George W. Bush moved into the Oval Office – many Canadians had been critical of America's opposition to the landmine ban treaty, the Kyoto Protocol, the International Criminal Court, and other multilateral institutions. The Bush administration then offended many in Canada almost immediately after 9/11, when the president gave a speech thanking the many nations that had offered their support after the attacks, but left Canada off the list. Just a few months later, the administration did it again, by not making much of an effort to express contrition, or to demonstrate a clear commitment to holding responsible parties accountable, after a "friendly-fire" incident killed four Canadian soldiers on a nighttime training exercise near Kandahar.[10]

These perceived slights against Canada, along with some thinly veiled criticisms of Bush's foreign policy by Canadian officials, drew out and reinforced a sense of grievance and mistrust on both sides of the border. The root cause of the bilateral tensions during this period, however, and of the parting of ways over Iraq, was an underlying divergence of perceptions and priorities between the two countries after 9/11. Americans were profoundly affected by the idea that they could be hit hard and without warning, even at home. They granted the White House sweeping new powers through the USA PATRIOT Act, diverted enormous financial and administrative resources into the building of a new Department of Homeland Security, and were generally inclined to put national security considerations ahead of all other political priorities. Canadians also felt the impact of 9/11, but saw the nature and scope of the challenge differently. The most urgent concern for the federal government, the business community, and the general public in Canada was to try to restore and protect the country's vital economic links with the US. Canadians also demanded that their government take action against the terrorist threat, but the rationale behind most of the specific policy initiatives during this period was the need to reassure Washington that Canada was doing all it could to prevent itself from becoming a staging area for terrorist attacks against the US.

After 9/11, Americans began to see new potential threats all over the world, their anxieties about known threats were intensified, and many saw menacing connections between all of these otherwise scattered and diverse sources of danger. Both inside and outside the Washington beltway, there was a powerful impulse to find ways to "do something" about terrorism, to strike back, and to make it plain that the US had both the will and the muscle to defend itself. Under these conditions, it was possible for those in the Bush White House who had long been arguing for a more aggressive response to Iraq to take the reins, and steer the US toward a "preventive" approach to containing weapons of mass destruction, coupled with a demand for "regime change" in Iraq.[11]

They sought a mandate for this more confrontational approach from the UN Security Council, but when it became clear that some of America's traditional allies – most notably France and Germany – would not support them, the Bush administration decided to turn the tables: rather than allowing the UN to be the test of the policy, they would treat support for the policy as a test of the UN itself.[12] The US had already secured a measure of UN approval through Resolution 1441, which declared that Iraq was "in material breach" of past resolutions. This latest resolution had given Iraq "a final opportunity to comply" with UN investigation of Iraqi weapons programs, and a warning that failure to cooperate fully would lead to "serious consequences." When subsequent UN reports judged that Iraq was continuing to obstruct the weapons inspection program, the Bush administration argued that the Security Council was obliged to take direct action. France, Germany, and Russia maintained that the US would need to obtain an additional resolution to explicitly authorize the use of force, but the White House rejected this argument.

The Bush administration had drawn a line in the sand, and – although Canada was not on the Security Council at this time – the Chrétien government would have a tough choice to make about where it would stand. On one hand, they understood that good relations with the United States are always in Canada's best interests. On the other hand, Canada had always prided itself on its support for the United Nations, and multilateralism more generally, and many in the Liberal caucus were committed to the idea that Canada must do whatever it took to rescue the UN from being torn apart by feuding great powers.

"With Us or against Us"

America's pursuit of UN approval for war in Iraq had nothing to do with any need for help on the battlefield. Operation Desert Storm had easily demolished the Iraqi army in 1991, and the already enormous gap in the two countries' respective military capabilities had grown much wider since then. And military contributions from smaller allies – with the partial exception of the British – were probably more of a liability than an asset for the United States, since they were not nearly as capable as US forces and could not coordinate with them effectively, and were thus less likely to further the American advance than to be run over by it.[13] As every government at the UN understood implicitly, the main thing the Bush administration wanted from other states was their diplomatic approval, partly because this might draw out the support of other countries (including strategically important Middle Eastern states), but mostly because it would reinforce the perceived legitimacy of the intervention in the eyes of the American public.

This was equally – perhaps especially – true when it came to Canada. American defence planners knew that Canadian forces were well trained and would work well with their US counterparts, but they were also well aware that the Canadian military had atrophied over the past twenty years and would be hard-pressed to send anything beyond a token force. The Canadian navy had been playing a meaningful support role in the Persian Gulf, and the US hoped it would continue to do so. Overall American expectations about a potential Canadian military contribution in Iraq were very low, however. In fact, the White House sent signals that it hoped Canada would put the military resources that it did have into Afghanistan instead, since the US was trying to reduce its troop commitment there in preparation for the coming conflict in Iraq. In early January 2003, Janice Gross Stein and Eugene Lang report, Secretary of Defense Donald Rumsfeld told Foreign

Affairs Minister Bill Graham that the White House could accept a Canadian decision not to go to Iraq, based on the expectation that Canada would take over a leadership role in Afghanistan.[14]

The Bush administration's expectations were fairly high, however, when it came to the question of diplomatic support. American foreign-policy makers have traditionally expected that Canada – along with fellow "Anglosphere" cousins Britain and Australia – would be among the United States' most loyal supporters, based on shared history, values, and commitments to international institutions. US officials therefore tended to assume that Canada would be on side for Iraq, or, at the very least, would not openly oppose them. This was particularly important in the context of US domestic politics, because, as a country with similar values and a long history of defence collaboration with the US, Canada's endorsement of the war would carry more weight with American voters than that of Poland or Nicaragua.

Washington's expectation that Canada would come through in Iraq was reinforced through the final months of 2002 by informal connections between American and Canadian military officers, since many of the latter also tended to assume, notwithstanding some posturing by policy-makers in Ottawa, that Canada would ultimately support the US in Iraq. This was made plain enough after the fact, as a number of Canadian military officers publicly expressed shock and frustration when Chrétien announced that Canada would not go to war without a second UN resolution, and at least one high-ranking officer resigned in protest.[15]

Chrétien and his Cabinet associates, moreover, did little to dispel these expectations, in Washington or in Canada's National Defence Headquarters. They were consistently clear that they thought the Bush administration was practically and morally obliged to work through the UN and to hold out for explicit authorization for the use of force in Iraq. At the same time, however, they were also very clearly trying to keep their options open, and they dropped a number of hints that the Canadian government might ultimately be prepared to support war even if there were no such direct authorization. On a few occasions, Chrétien suggested that the crucial criterion for Canadian support was not really whether or not the UN Security Council approved, but whether or not the US were able to provide clear proof of Saddam Hussein's violations of past UN resolutions.[16]

No one within the prime minister's inner circle agreed with the Bush administration's regime change agenda for Iraq, but there were sharp divisions between those who thought the government should follow its multilateralist convictions and those who thought that Canada should "go along to get along" with the US. A substantial part of the Liberal party rank and file was adamantly opposed to war without UN sanction, particularly junior members of Parliament representing urban areas and in Quebec.[17] These tensions within the party were dangerous for the prime minister, because his finance minister, Paul Martin, was openly challenging his leadership of the party and pressing him to step down after ten years in office. Nationally, polls showed that over half of Canadian voters were skeptical of President Bush's case for war, and most wanted Canada to stay out of Iraq.[18] Popular opposition was concentrated, moreover, in some of the areas that were seen to be pivotal to the Liberals in an upcoming election, including the Toronto suburbs, southern British Columbia, and most of Quebec.

It is not particularly surprising that Chrétien ultimately chose to put domestic politicking ahead of the bilateral relationship, given his reputation as a hard-boiled political pragmatist. In fact, tensions within the Liberal party were so intense and public opposition to the upcoming war was so extensive that virtually any prime minister would probably have chosen to say no to Iraq. But the way that Canada said no was just as important, in American eyes, and the way it was done in this case had a lot to do with the prime minister's personal priorities and leadership style. Since taking the reins of government in 1993, Chrétien had mastered the traditional practice of building up Canada through unflattering comparisons to the US, and by posturing against American policies. "I make it my policy ... to stand up [to the Americans]," he bragged at a NATO summit in 1997 (not realizing that his every word was being picked up by a nearby microphone); "it's popular." As tensions with Washington grew and the challenge from Paul Martin and his supporters intensified, Chrétien was increasingly inclined to try to rally supporters by picking a fight with the US. At the same time, he was more and more inclined to cater to anti-American impulses within the Liberal caucus, as seen in his toleration of some high-profile cheap shots taken by staffers and party members: Carolyn Parrish's seething about American "bastards," Françoise Ducros' dismissal of Bush as a "moron," and Herb Dhaliwal's pronouncement that the president was a "failed statesman" who had "let the world down."

Although Chrétien's response to the US push to war was certainly crusted with political opportunism, it is important to see that there was something more substantial beneath. Like many of their European counterparts, the prime minister and his closest advisers simply did not believe that the US had made a compelling case for war, and they were deeply troubled by America's drift toward unilateralism and the long-term implications of a direct circumvention of the UN Security Council. Even the most cynical members of Chretien's inner circle recognized that this was a turning point for the postwar multilateral order, and they understood implicitly that Canada could not stand by and watch that order crumble.[19]

Going Separate Ways

On 14 November 2002, Secretary of State Colin Powell met with Foreign Minister Bill Graham in Ottawa, and Powell expressed his hope that Canada would be part of an emerging "like-minded coalition" for a more aggressive strategy against Iraq.[20] Graham made it plain that Canada wanted to be supportive of the United States, but that his government wanted to give the UN weapons inspectors more time, strongly disagreed with the administration's insistence on regime change in Iraq, and was convinced that pressure on Iraq could be successful only if it enjoyed broad international support, which – if it came to war – would ultimately require some kind of explicit UN authorization.[21] This was consistent with the way the Canadian government had been publicly framing its position during the closing months of 2002: insistence that there was no alternative to the UN, but without actually saying explicitly that Canada would not support war without explicit UN approval.[22]

Chrétien sat down with his Cabinet in January 2003 to clarify the government's position on Iraq, both in terms of what would be done and in terms of what would be said to the Canadian press and public. Canada should do all that it could to hold out for formal UN authorization, they agreed, but the government must also recognize that the US might go ahead in the face of a "capricious veto" by France or Russia, just as it had done in the face of Russia's threat to veto intervention in Kosovo. If that happened, it was agreed, Canada might sign on, as long as there was a strong case for war and a substantial international coalition.

Just a few days later, the new minister of national defence, John McCallum, faced a press scrum in Washington and plainly spelled out the position that the prime minister had outlined.[23] Several Liberal MPs expressed outrage at the party leadership's apparent abandonment of Canada's traditional support for the UN, and Chrétien was forced to do some damage control, telling reporters that the inexperienced defence minister had answered a "hypothetical question" and had since "clarified" his position.[24] Even as he was correcting McCallum, however, the prime minister subtly made the connection to the Kosovo precedent again, thereby leaving the door open for Canadian involvement even without formal UN authorization.[25]

As the politicians were scrambling to keep their options open, the military were trying to get things settled. Most of the military leadership in Canada expected that the coming war in Iraq would be brief and overwhelmingly successful, while the intervention in Afghanistan was certain to be long and draining, and therefore hoped that Canada would involve itself primarily in the former and not in the latter. The expectation was that, in addition to naval frigates, the Canadian Forces might provide a special forces contingent (JTF2) and a small mechanized infantry force for Iraq. Based in part on these expectations, the Chief of Defence Staff approached Defence Minister McCallum in January 2003 to ask about sending Canadian officers to sit in on a US planning session at US Central Command (CENTCOM) headquarters in Florida. US field commanders wanted the Canadians to be there, but the

White House was not so sure, given Canada's nonresponse to Powell's previous requests. None of that mattered, though, because Chrétien and Graham would not authorize the trip, worried that the Canadian military's views were getting too tangled up with those of their American counterparts, and that the Canadian public might get wind of the meetings and misinterpret Canadian participation as a sign of Ottawa's support for the war.[26]

Meanwhile, Canadian diplomats were facing their own challenges in Washington and New York. Powell laid out the administration's case against Iraq in a speech at the UN on 5 February. The Chrétien Cabinet was not impressed by the evidence that Powell offered,[27] and the reaction was similar in France, Germany, and a number of other traditional US allies. With his main diplomatic ally, British prime minister Tony Blair, under severe domestic political pressure, Bush reluctantly agreed to try to secure an additional Security Council resolution. A split was developing within the Security Council, and many observers worried that the UN itself might be fatally damaged, regardless of which side ultimately carried the day. Ottawa therefore felt compelled to try to broker some kind of compromise.

On 19 February, Canada's ambassador to the UN, Paul Heinbecker, presented a proposal for a new Security Council resolution that would clearly outline a set of specific steps that the Iraqi government must take, with a clear deadline and with a clear authorization for the US and others to use military force if Iraq did not comply.[28] This was a perfectly sensible proposal, and perfectly consistent with the "helpful fixer" tradition in Canadian foreign policy, except that all of the most successful Pearson-era "fixes" came at times when the major powers were actually interested in finding a compromise. In this case, the French and Russians did not want to be locked into anything, so they would not endorse the proposal. But the main opposition came from the Americans, who found Canada's "helpful fixing" profoundly unhelpful. No matter how explicitly the rules for compliance with UN weapons inspections were spelled out, US negotiators argued, Saddam Hussein would always find a way to partially evade them, setting up a whole new round of UN debate about whether or not Iraq's noncompliance was enough to justify the use of force.

Canada-watchers in the State Department wondered what could be done to dissuade the Chrétien government from continuing to undercut the US position at the United Nations. Reports from the embassy in Ottawa suggested that this was mostly just posturing for domestic audiences, and that the prime minister would turn around when the time came for a final decision. Some in Washington were not so sure, however, and there was some talk of putting together some kind of package of positive and/or negative linkages that might shift the Canadian position, much the same as American diplomats were doing with respect to Mexico, Chile, and many other fence-sitting countries. This did not go far, though, because they could not come up with any linkage scenarios that seemed likely to work, and they still hoped that things could be turned around at the UN.[29]

Last Chances

Despite Canada's best diplomatic efforts, the divide in the Security Council widened in early March 2003. Keeping Bush's promise to Blair, the US sponsored a new resolution – in conjunction with Britain and Spain – declaring that Iraq was in "further material breach" of Resolution 1441 and calling for an immediate vote on military intervention. France, Germany, Russia, and China countered with their own joint resolution, calling for weapons inspections to continue with no deadline. As his domestic political position continued to erode, Blair took up the challenge of finding a compromise and proposed his own resolution, which closely resembled the Canadian one but with the deadline set for 17 March.

Canada welcomed Britain's new flexibility and tried to put pressure on the US to do the same. Chrétien appeared on an American current events program and argued that the US had already achieved its main objective by effectively containing Iraq. The president should not push for war without UN authorization, he warned, because it would only increase international mistrust and resentment of the US, and might set dangerous new precedents that the US might come to regret. National Security Adviser Condoleezza Rice was the next guest on the show, and she was clearly irritated by the prime minister's comments. "The US believes that regime change *is* necessary," Rice insisted, "because [Saddam] is *not* going to disarm."[30] It was fairly obvious at this point that the Bush administration did not much appreciate the Canadian government's advice and assistance, but that didn't stop Ottawa from trying again, as Heinbecker offered a new compromise proposal with a later deadline. Again, the plan was rejected by the US, France, and Russia. Blair then managed to convince Bush to accept the idea of a new compromise resolution with a deadline of 24 March, but again the French and Russians said no.

By this point, it was quite clear that there would be no compromise, and the US went back to saying that no additional resolution was necessary. On 16 March, Bush issued an ultimatum: the Security Council had twenty-four hours to approve the resolution it had sponsored with Britain and Spain. When the deadline passed, the resolution was formally withdrawn and there could no longer be any doubt that war was inevitable. In Ottawa, the prime minister quickly conferred with Cabinet and reaffirmed that Canada would not support military intervention without formal UN authorization. The decision was announced in the House of Commons that afternoon. The State Department's reaction was that the US was "disappointed" not to have Canadian support, but this regret was tempered with appreciation for Canada's contributions to the wider fight against terrorism.[31] Nevertheless, warnings about frustration and resentment in Washington and speculation about possible American retaliation erupted almost immediately. Three days later, the war began, with a ferocious air strike on Baghdad designed to "decapitate" the Iraqi leadership and to spread "shock and awe" across the Middle East.

"It Wasn't that They Said No, It Was the Way They Said It"[32]

Given that the main thing the Bush administration hoped to get from Canada on the eve of war with Iraq was an expression of diplomatic support, the Chrétien government's 17 March decision, particularly the way it was conveyed to the US, was difficult to swallow.

Although in retrospect it might seem that the Canadian decision on Iraq was obvious or inevitable, it came as something of a surprise in Washington, and that in itself was a source of irritation. Chrétien was dismissive of this complaint, saying that American officials had known for "more than a year" that Canada was opposed to war without UN authorization.[33] That was true, but – as noted above – the prime minister and his closest advisers had also dropped a number of hints over the preceding weeks that they might be willing to offer support in spite of this opposition, if the US made a strong case for an Iraqi threat and there was a substantial international coalition in favour of military intervention. Past Canadian governments – and even the Chrétien government itself – had been prepared to compromise on multilateralism in the past, and to defy domestic political pressures when necessary, and it was not entirely unreasonable for US officials to expect this to happen again.

If anyone ought to complain about being surprised, Chrétien argued, it should be Canada, since the Bush administration had abruptly forced the issue with its 16 March ultimatum. The Canadian government was thus compelled to make its decision quickly, and to keep it a secret, in order to avoid an embarrassing leak. (To that same end, the decision was kept to just a few Cabinet players, leaving even the most senior civil servants out of the loop.) There must have been a leak anyway, however, because a CNN camera crew was in Ottawa for a live broadcast of the day's parliamentary debate – for the first time ever – on the afternoon that the prime minister officially announced the decision on Iraq.[34]

American officials were surprised and angered by Chrétien's decision not to personally telephone the president to explain the decision before he went public.

> How hard would it be to make that call? ... this is a clear case of wanting to make a big hit with domestic audiences, and not caring much about how it would ... have an impact in Washington ... Frankly, it made many people here angry. Other countries – even Germany – weren't like that. They called ... up front, and they either said "yes" or "no" ... [And the other countries

that rejected the Coalition of the Willing] said "sorry – we want to support you, but we can't."[35]

Bill Graham has since said that he urged Chrétien to phone the president before going public, as a matter of diplomatic courtesy, but was shut down by one of the prime minister's senior advisers.[36] There was apparently a phone call that day, from Minister of International Trade Pierre Pettigrew to Condoleezza Rice; he warned her that the prime minister was about to say no to Iraq, but promised that he would not "make a big fuss" about it.[37]

But of course that was exactly what Chrétien did. Canada's position was proclaimed, as one observer described it, "with scarcely-concealed joy by the prime minister ... to thunderous applause from the Liberal MPs around him."[38] This did not sit well with American officials stung by the inflammatory comments by Parrish and Ducros, and their sense of grievance was intensified a few days later by Dhaliwal's patronizing dismissal of Bush as a "failed statesman." Ambassador Cellucci later reflected that what really aggravated the White House was the fact that "the [Canadian] government said 'we are going to say good things about the President and bad things about Saddam Hussein,'" but then "did the opposite. They pretty much kicked the hell out of the President."[39]

Afterglow and Anxiety

The decision not to formally support the war in Iraq gave the governing Liberals a substantial political boost, and helped strengthen Chrétien's hand as leader of the deeply divided party. Some have argued that the decision was driven in part by the prime minister's search for a powerful "legacy" move in the closing months of his long political career; to the extent that this is so, it seems to have been a clear-cut success. Opinion polls taken in late May showed that a majority of Canadian voters supported the government's decision, and follow-up studies through the summer of 2003 showed that this conviction was powerfully reinforced by the US military's subsequent troubles in bringing law and order to Iraq.[40]

But not everyone agreed at the time, and not everyone thought afterward that Canada's interests were well served by Chrétien's handling of the issue. Immediately after the 17 March decision, critics warned that it would provoke a backlash from the United States that would have devastating effects on Canadian interests, particularly the economy. Several provincial premiers publicly worried about economic repercussions, and Alberta Premier Ralph Klein made a series of press appearances criticizing Ottawa and apologizing to the US for Canada's not having supported it during this hour of need.

These warnings apparently had an effect on the general public in Canada, because support for the government's decision to opt out of Iraq softened noticeably. One poll in early April found that while most Canadians still disagreed with Bush's decision to go to war in Iraq, a substantial majority believed that the Canadian government ought to have given him some kind of diplomatic support anyway.[41] The Chrétien government moved quickly to reassure Canadians that there was nothing to worry about, with Pettigrew predicting that it would still be "business as usual" at the Canada-US border.

Then on 25 March, Ambassador Cellucci gave his highly charged speech to the Economic Club of Toronto, clearly rejecting the idea of business as usual. Thomas d'Aquino, the head of the influential Canadian Council of Chief Executives, told reporters that he was "terribly worried" and that he was sure that "some damage ... [had] been done," but conceded that he had no "significant hard evidence" to back up this assessment.[42]

The prime minister addressed speculation about possible retaliation in a speech on 7 April. "Close friends can disagree at times and still be close friends," he told the House of Commons. "Neither country has ever been in the business of economic retaliation and disagreements on issues of foreign policy. This is not what our relationship is all about." He then dismissed anxiety about linkages as political manipulation, saying that Canada's "friendship with the United States is far stronger than those who scaremonger would have us believe; it is far stronger than some who purport to speak for the business community would have us believe."[43]

As confident as Chrétien appeared to be, however, he evidently recognized that there were limits to how far the United States could be pushed. After Dhaliwal's "failed statesman" comment, the prime minister immediately forced him to recant, and then watched much more carefully over his government than he had in previous months, muzzling criticism of the war and of the Bush administration more generally. He shifted the focus to the future, telling the press that his government hoped the US would win quickly in Iraq, and promising Canadian funding and support for postwar reconstruction.

Still, it was clear that relations between the two countries were strained. In mid-April, the White House announced that the president was cancelling his first official visit to Ottawa, which had been scheduled for 5 May. At the time, US officials said that this was simply a reflection of how busy the president was in managing the war in Iraq, and not a response to Canada's decision. But many in Ottawa were skeptical of these arguments, because the White House used that same block of time to receive an official visit from the prime minister of Australia, John Howard, who was an enthusiastic member of the Coalition of the Willing.[44] Ambassador Cellucci later confirmed that the trip's cancellation really was influenced by the Canadian decision to say no on Iraq.[45] Yet when pressed on whether or not the frustration that led to the cancellation might also lead to direct linkages between substantive issues, the plain-speaking ambassador stated flatly that that had not happened and would not happen. As proof, he pointed to the ongoing talks between Manley and Ridge on border security, in which US officials had been responsive to almost all of Canada's key concerns.[46] When asked the same question a few days later, Secretary of State Powell also offered his assurances that there would be "no consequences."[47]

When Push Comes to Shove: Explaining US Self-Restraint

In the aftermath of 9/11, a number of high-profile observers in Canada argued that, although the United States' new preoccupation with homeland security was a serious problem in terms of near-term access to all-important American markets, there might be a silver lining in that cloud in the sense that Canada might be able to improve its bargaining position on economic issues by offering more extensive cooperation on matters of national security.[48] This "security-for-access" argument was based on some of the core premises of the realist argument about the politics of strategic restraint, which expects the United States to be more forbearing with Canada during periods when security challenges are more intense, and the support of smaller allies more highly valued. Ambassador Cellucci's "security trumps trade" rhetoric was certainly consistent with the realist conception of a hierarchy of national interests, with security always at the top. And, although the Bush administration was generally contemptuous of multilateral institutions, its high-ranking officials frequently acknowledged that the US could not defeat transnational terrorism on its own, and needed the support of other countries. We might therefore expect the US to have been relatively tolerant of trouble from Canada, based on the expectation of support where it really mattered.

The end of the Cold War and the subsequent widening of the military gap between the US and all other states changed the nature of the relationship between the United States and its allies. During the Cold War, the US needed to have steady, long-term relationships with countries holding strategic territory and resources, and relied on second-tier allies to carry a substantial share of the overall alliance burden. After the fall of the Soviet Union, however, the US no longer needed traditional allies to maintain substantial militaries, or to work consistently with it in maintaining a solid strategic front. Because the US found itself shifting from one regional "hot spot" to another, and because the US military totally outclassed all of the forces it confronted, the focus shifted away from maintaining stable multilateral alliances and toward the formation of ad hoc coalitions with regional allies. Because the American public was reserved about the nature and purposes of many of these postwar conflicts – particularly when compared with the extraordinary solidity of the "Cold War consensus" – the political leadership put a higher priority on seeking diplomatic and financial support from other countries, through multilateral institutions when possible, but not necessarily through multilateral institutions.

In the context of America's post-9/11 preoccupation with security issues, and with that nation facing the demands of a two-front war on terror, we might very well expect US officials to have been relatively tolerant of provocations by small allies like Canada. But of course the Canadian challenge with respect to Iraq was not the kind of low-stakes, low politics issue that might be easily swept under the rug. Canada directly challenged the White House on what it saw as the primary national security issue of the day, and did so very publicly, in a way that would be embarrassing for the Bush administration in terms of wider international audiences and also of American voters. If this were all there was to it, the Iraq case would be roughly equivalent to the dispute over nuclear weapons in the early 1960s (see Chapter 3), and it would have been surprising indeed if the US had not turned toward hard linkages as a way of forcing Canada to back down.

It is important to recognize, however, that although the Chrétien government very loudly said no to the war in theory, it also very quietly said yes to the war in practice. That is, while the Canadian government refused to offer direct support – diplomatic or military – for war in Iraq, it offered some *indirect* support, which helped to take away some of the sting for Washington. First, in contrast to some other traditional allies, Canada left in place all of its military officers serving on exchange with the US and Britain, even after war had broken out. Although this was not widely recognized at the time, it meant that a handful of senior Canadian officers were actually serving in the field with American units in the Middle East – some even in Iraq itself – during the heaviest fighting.[49] Second, Canada took command of a multinational naval task force patrolling the Persian Gulf. The task force's primary assignment was to provide support for the NATO intervention in Afghanistan and the broader war on terror, but in practice this inevitably involved extensive coordination with Coalition of the Willing forces operating in Iraq.[50] And third – as noted above – Canada accepted command over NATO forces in Afghanistan, freeing up American soldiers for redeployment to Iraq.

The "we are not there, but we are there" strategy that the Chrétien government followed in Iraq was virtually incoherent as a matter of practical policy. The Canadian commander leading the naval task force in the Persian Gulf, for example, was told that he was to lead patrols looking for terrorists and other "enemy combatants" at the outer edge of Iraqi territorial waters, but that if there was any question that captured vessels or personnel might be Iraqi, then he must phone home for instructions from Ottawa. In military terms, this was simply untenable, and it is hard to believe that American commanders in the region were prepared to put up with it.[51]

Chrétien's hedging of his bets was roundly criticized as hypocritical or just not very well thought out, both by the political opposition in Ottawa and by the American ambassador. On the whole, however, it seems to have worked fairly well as a political solution to the government's diplomatic dilemmas. Canadian officials were able to score a few points in Washington with the argument that their country was "the opposite of Spain" (which had been very supportive of the US in theory but not in practice).[52] But because these commitments were little known and poorly understood at home, it was still possible to assure the public that Canada had no part in the Iraq war.

The crucial element in Chrétien's playing of this two-level game was Afghanistan. Canada had sent a contingent to Kabul in late 2001, but pulled out the following year when the initial mission came to an end and Canada's capacity for overseas deployment was basically used up. As the US geared up for war in Iraq, it began to look for ways to cover the withdrawal of its forces from Afghanistan. Canada seemed like an obvious candidate, and Rumsfeld made a direct approach to McCallum about taking command of the International Security Assistance Force (ISAF) in Kabul. Virtually no one in Ottawa was particularly interested in Afghanistan itself, but the NATO command was seen by many as a way to avoid trouble in Iraq. By putting all of Canada's military eggs in the Afghanistan basket, Chrétien could credibly tell the Americans that he had nothing left for Iraq, and at the same time score points with voters with the argument that Canada was "fighting the real war on terror."[53]

It took some time to secure guarantees of support from the US and Germany, and the grudging acceptance of the Canadian military establishment, but the government moved fairly quickly to get itself ready to go into Afghanistan. On 12 February – a week after Powell's speech to the UN and a week before Heinbecker began to openly pursue a compromise within the Security Council – Foreign Minister Bill Graham announced that Canada would send a battle group and brigade headquarters to Kabul for one year, beginning in August 2003. It would then take command of the ISAF mission in February 2004.[54] This never happened, because some of the European members of NATO wanted to make ISAF a strictly European mission, and Canada eventually ended up with an even more demanding commitment to try to maintain security and promote development in Kandahar province.[55] At the time of the Iraq decision, though, the expectation in Ottawa and in Washington was that Canada would be putting pretty much all that it had into Afghanistan.

There is no question that Canada's substantial commitment in Afghanistan took the edge off the Iraq decision for the Bush administration. In itself, however, this is not a sound explanation for US self-restraint. Canada didn't just say no to war in Iraq; it also publicly questioned the White House's case for intervention, actively campaigned for a compromise solution within the Security Council even in the face of clear US opposition, chose not to warn the US before announcing that it would not support the war, and then delivered the decision in the form of a public rebuke. These moves were problematic not because they directly undercut the US diplomatic and military agenda but rather because of their "demonstration effects" in the international context, and the difficult questions they raised for unconvinced American voters. From a national security standpoint, US self-restraint in this case is less surprising than it was in the Diefenbaker-Kennedy dispute over nuclear weapons, because the practical impact on US plans was marginal and because Canada was just one of many countries refusing to go along with those plans. There is nevertheless still a puzzle to be solved here. Given the signals from Ottawa that the Chrétien government might not support the war – and the certainty that it was actively working against the Bush administration's diplomatic position at the UN – why didn't the United States pursue hard linkages in order to force Canada to back down?

It is much more difficult to say for sure in this case than in the previous ones, but – based on interviews, media reports, and some circumstantial evidence – it seems fairly clear that the United States was *not* restrained because of any reflexive adherence to overarching norms about how Canada-US bargaining was supposed to work. Once it became clear that Canada was going to pursue a diplomatic compromise despite US disapproval, some American officials began to consider hard linkages as a way to bring Canada back into line.[56] In contrast to the dispute over the National Energy Program (NEP) (see Chapter 5), there was apparently no direction from the White House to look into linkages as part of a larger diplomatic strategy; officials in various departments just "kicked around" various policy changes and scenarios.[57] To the extent that they were rather circumspect in trying to identify and evaluate linkage options, it was apparently because they still hoped Chrétien would make a last-minute reversal, without any arm-twisting.

US officials have since talked about their frustration over Canada's handling of the Iraq issue in terms of a set of tacit expectations about how the two sides would handle their disagreement. One layer of these expectations has to do with what US officials expected that Canada *would* do. Canada, like Britain and Australia, was generally expected to be a supporter in Iraq, in diplomatic terms if not in military terms, because its basic values and international interests were supposed to be similar to those of the United States, and – for some at least – simply because Canada had (supposedly) always been there for the US before. The other layer had to do with expectations about what Canada would *not* do. Because Canadians understood America's special international and domestic political challenges, and because they had too much at stake to want to poison the bilateral relationship, the

Canadian government would not do anything to seriously undercut the Bush administration diplomatically, in the context of the Security Council debates, or politically, in the context of the upcoming midterm elections. As tensions mounted in February and March 2003, US officials reluctantly abandoned their expectations about what Canada would do, but still held on to their expectations about what Canada would not do. Thus when the Chrétien government confounded those expectations on 17 March, many in Washington were surprised and angered.

In the closing weeks of 2002, the Bush administration had adopted a "war room" approach to the building of the Coalition of the Willing, with officials closely monitoring the positions of various key countries and trying to develop a package of incentives and threats to secure or hold on to the diplomatic support of reluctant partners. Particular attention was given to France and Russia as major powers that opposed the push to war, to Mexico and Chile as potential swing votes in the Security Council that might be turned by US pressure, and to Turkey and Saudi Arabia as regional powers whose practical support would be critical to any military intervention in Iraq. Canada was none of these things, and it got only a small share of the White House's attention during this period. To the extent that Canada was talked about, it was talked about in much the same way as others that the administration was frustrated with but still hoped to bring on side. In the course of these conversations, officials from different agencies – including the State Department – talked about the damage that might be done on both sides of the border if the relationship were to deteriorate, and wondered aloud why the Canadians would run such a risk. Some talked openly about which bilateral issues might be platforms for US pressure, and about the costs that might be imposed on Canada by specific policy changes or disruptions. Although, as I will explain below, each of the various scenarios for hard linkages was ultimately dismissed, very few seemed to think it improper to consider these kinds of strong-arm tactics with respect to Canada, or to think that relations with Canada ought to be handled separately, and differently, from those with other small countries such as Mexico or Chile.

Just as there was not much evidence of a norm guiding US attitudes toward Canada in this dispute, so there was not much evidence of US decisions having been "managed" by a network of like-minded officials, as they had been back in the early Cold War decades. Relevant officials in Washington did of course have their own personal and professional networks, running within and across various government agencies, and they did talk to one another across interdepartmental fence lines about the "problem" with Canada. But there wasn't the same kind of cohesion that there had been in the past. Where before there had been a very tight cluster of overlapping networks in Washington, closely linked with their Canadian counterparts, now there were many very small and highly fragmented networks, most of which had virtually no contact with Canadian officials beyond their direct, working-level contacts. The major exception to this is in the relationship between the Canadian and American militaries, where network relationships are still relatively extensive and robust, and where there is often substantial agreement on both the content of shared priorities and on the principles and practicalities for the management of relevant policy issues. In this case, those close military-to-military connections probably had mixed effects on the bilateral crisis, in the sense that they heightened the surprise and resentment in the White House after the 17 March decision, but also helped to settle things down in the context of subsequent defence cooperation in Afghanistan and elsewhere.

Most of the monitoring of the Canadian position during the diplomatic frictions over Iraq was done by the embassy in Ottawa and by US military officers talking informally with their Canadian counterparts. Their impression was that the general public in Canada was opposed to war, that Chrétien was likely to play into the public's mistrust of the Bush administration, but that ultimately the Canadian government would probably be supportive of the American position. They picked up on and reported the various ways in which the prime minister and some of his key ministers had left the door open for a role in Iraq, and they passed on their Canadian military contacts' interest in making a direct contribution to the war itself. Canada-watchers in the State Department, who were more attuned to what was happening within the Liberal party and the foreign affairs ministry, were not so confident, but they did not predict or effectively prepare the White House for Chrétien's provocative announcement.

In fact, the situation at the end of 2002 was somewhat similar to that at the end of 1962, when American officials believed that the Diefenbaker government was inclined to accept nuclear weapons but was held back by opposition from party backbenchers and nongovernment activists, and that it was only a matter of time before the prime minister was in a position to turn things around. In both cases, it was the sudden dashing of these unfounded expectations that caused great indignation and resentment in Washington – probably much more than there would have been if Canada had moved more quickly and clearly to a firm rejection.

Personal relations between Chrétien and Bush did not help, but they probably mattered less than some observers evidently believe. Chrétien had established a habit of distance from the White House way back in 1993, as part of his effort to differentiate himself from his "continentalist" predecessor. Bush was not particularly interested in Canada or in Chrétien himself, but he had had no trouble in getting along with the plain-speaking, pragmatic prime minister. The strong negative reaction to Canada's Iraq decision was something that erupted spontaneously all over Washington, with no particular encouragement from the White House. Although working-level officials continued to take care of the day-to-day management of the bilateral relationship, communication between the political leaderships almost immediately went from infrequent to virtually nonexistent. And officials at the Canadian embassy in Washington were told in no uncertain terms that Canadian issues had moved to the bottom of the White House's priority list.

When we look at the period immediately *after* 17 March, there are a number of reasons to expect the US not to have resorted to hard linkages to punish Canada or to compel it to reverse itself. First and foremost, American officials recognized that it was simply too late. There was little that the Canadians could say or do after this point to undo the damage that had been done to the administration's efforts to build support for war. And the Canadian government's basic position on the war had been effectively locked in by Chrétien's splashy public announcement. Given the extent and intensity of public opposition to the war in the general public and among the party rank and file, it would have been politically impossible for Chrétien to reverse himself by openly endorsing the Coalition of the Willing or sending ground troops to Iraq.

Hard linkages after this point could serve no purpose but revenge, or possibly the demonstration of resolve to deter future challenges. But while many in Washington entertained idle thoughts of hitting back, few saw any reason to try to punish Canada in order to make it more compliant in the future. Most in Washington tended to see the Iraq decision as something driven by the prime minister and his closest supporters, and it was well known that Chrétien would soon be compelled to hand over the reins to Paul Martin, who was seen to be committed to a more cooperative approach to managing the bilateral relationship.[58] Equally important, the White House's sense of grievance was partially offset by the Canadian government's concurrent decisions to leave exchange officers in place, to lead the naval task force in the Persian Gulf, and to take on a larger commitment in Afghanistan.

When we look at the period *before* 17 March, there are reasons to think that the US might be somewhat forbearing with Canada, but it is still not obvious why American officials did not resort to hard linkages in order to discourage Canada from pushing ahead with its diplomatic challenge at the UN, or perhaps to encourage it to offer some direct support for the Coalition of the Willing. The main reason for US self-restraint during this period was the mixed signals coming from Ottawa, and the resulting uncertainty about whether Canada might ultimately come on side for Iraq even without having its arms twisted. Because linkages always carry some risk of backfiring, US officials would naturally be inclined to avoid them while they still had reason to expect that the Canadians would turn things around. By the beginning of January 2003, however, the number of government statements suggesting that Canada would insist on UN authorization was far out-weighing the number of statements suggesting otherwise. And by early February, Heinbecker's campaigning at the UN had such a high profile, and was so directly and implacably challenging to the American position there, that this in itself might have been a basis for hard linkages.

Based on what we know so far about American decision-making during this crisis, it appears that the United States' reluctance to bargain aggressively with Canada was not due to a recognition of any special obligation to bargain differently with Canada than with other countries, but rather to US officials' realization that, for all of the possible hard linkage scenarios, the expected benefits were clearly outweighed by countervailing costs or risks.

As explained in Chapter 2, Keohane and Nye argued that ever-expanding economic interdependence between the two countries – despite the profound asymmetry of that interdependence – would generate new bureaucratic and societal coalitions that would resist having their interests traded off for those of others, and thereby raise the political costs associated with pursuing hard linkages. But while these developments have indeed created new political obstacles to hard linkages, the disruptions that have come with economic integration have also tended to solidify some interest groups' determination to deflect the costs of adjustment onto foreigners (e.g., steel, softwood lumber, agriculture), and may therefore also have created new incentives to pursue linkages. The confluence of these cross-cutting pressures on US policymakers has driven them to talk tough and to actually look for hard linkage options, but also makes it less likely that they will actually find them. The net result is a mixture of anxiety, confusion, and frustration.

Ambassador Cellucci's speech of 25 March was the major trigger for speculation about US recourse to hard linkages in the dispute over Iraq. The speech itself was actually a fairly balanced one, emphasizing the established bases for continuing cooperation and saying only that Americans were "disappointed and upset." The really provocative part of the evening was not the speech but Cellucci's media scrum afterward. When reporters asked what the ambassador had in mind in his oblique reference to potential "consequences" following from the Iraq decision, he would say only that they would have to "wait and see."[59] One could interpret this as meaning that the White House had a plan to play rough with Canada but that the ambassador wasn't going to share it, or as meaning that someone else would decide what those consequences would be. This is consistent with a broader ambiguity running through the speech as a whole. Strictly speaking, it refers to the mood of Americans in general – rather than the White House in particular – and seems to imply that it is private interests in the US (importers, investors, etc.) that are likely to take out their frustrations on Canada. The ambassador almost certainly wanted to warn the members of the Economic Club about this, but he probably also expected to leave Canadians wondering about whether the White House might be planning to facilitate these private acts of revenge or to orchestrate its own hard linkages. Certainly, there were many in Canada who heard this as well, or – in some cases – instead.[60]

Over the next few weeks, however, various US officials and other well-placed elites went out of their way to reassure Canadians that there would be no retaliation. Cellucci himself reflected that "it [was] pretty clear that the decision was a disappointment and some of the stuff around it was not helpful. But at the working level – government to government – things [were] going very well."[61] Even more striking than the number of these reassurances is the consistency with which they explained US self-restraint in terms of the economic costs of disruption within such an extensively interdependent relationship. This is reflected, for example, in the remarks of Pentagon strategist Richard Perle, nicknamed the "Prince of Darkness" for his past opposition to arms control and not known for his responsiveness to allies' sensitivities: "Our economies are intertwined, and even if people wanted to be punitive – and I don't know anyone who does – when you have an economic relationship like that existing between us, it's like setting off a munition within your own lethal radius." Responding to the puzzled looks of those in the audience put off by the out-of-place military metaphor, he quickly clarified: "It could damage us as well."[62]

Because there was so much speculation by politicians and journalists about actual or potential linkages in March and April 2003, it is not difficult to identify the most prominent bases for hard linkages in this case. In the next section, I will look more closely at bilateral bargaining on four concurrent disputes: reconstruction contracts, border security, lumber, and beef. For each of these, I will show that hard linkages were not a factor in the process or the outcome of the relevant dispute, but soft linkages by US government agencies or members of Congress, and in some cases "private" retaliation by nongovernment actors, did come into play.[63]

Identifying and Evaluating Linkage Scenarios

As many critics of the war have emphasized, the Bush administration put a lot of thought into the planning and prosecution of the war itself, but virtually none into planning for postwar security and reconstruction.[64] Even without any advance planning, it was obvious that the invasion would utterly devastate the physical infrastructure of the country, just as the first war in Iraq had done. The one exception to this was of course the oil facilities, which US officials made plans to protect, based on their expectation that oil revenues would be absolutely crucial to Iraq's postwar recovery and development. The US not only failed to develop robust operational plans for postwar security and reconstruction but also failed to come up with a diplomatic strategy for sharing the burdens (and the profits) involved in the reconstruction effort. There were two main issues to think through: reconstruction aid and the allocation of reconstruction contracts.

In the 1991 war with Iraq, the US aggressively lobbied traditional allies and trade partners for financial assistance to help cover the costs of the war, and was rewarded for its efforts with substantial contributions from Germany, Japan, and others. Given the lack of attention to these issues in early 2003, one might have assumed that the US planned to pay the whole bill, not only for the war but also for postwar reconstruction. As it became clear that war was imminent and that there would be no multilateral coalition to match that of 1991, questions were raised in the US about what the war would cost and who would pay for it. The White House, determined to deflect anticipated Congressional and public criticism, hinted that postwar Iraqi oil revenues would not only pay for the country's reconstruction but might also pay some US bills for the war itself. Just prior to the outbreak of war, the US began to signal that it would be inclined to pursue postwar reconstruction through the UN, a shift that was welcomed by Canada and other critics of America's tough stand in the Security Council.

As part of his effort to mollify the Bush administration immediately after Canada refused to support the war, Chrétien made an unsolicited offer of financial assistance to help pay for Iraq's reconstruction. US officials acknowledged this commitment, but – given the high level of tension between the two governments at this point – there was no outpouring of appreciation. Nothing more was said about the question of reconstruction aid until it became entangled with the controversy surrounding reconstruction contracts.

Even before the war began, there was a great deal of hype – especially, but not only, in the US – about the lucrative reconstruction contracts that the White House would give out once the war was over, and some conspiracy theories went so far as to speculate that the war itself was driven by the White House's desire to satisfy powerful engineering firms such as Halliburton and Bechtel. When the time came to hand out the first of the reconstruction contracts, in December 2003, the Defense Department announced that only "coalition nations" would be allowed to bid on them, provoking outrage in excluded countries. Canada actually had few firms big enough to bid on any of the major contracts, but being formally excluded tended to vindicate critics of the decision to stay out of the war. The Chrétien government was angered by the Pentagon's announcement, particularly because it came immediately after a visit from State Department officials asking Canada to help with Iraq's reconstruction by forgiving some of its Saddam-era debts.[65] Deputy Prime Minister John Manley called the decision "quite shocking," and said that it was "difficult to explain to Canadian taxpayers why they are paying for reconstruction if Canadian companies are excluded from the contracts."[66]

The US relented a couple of weeks later, expressing appreciation for Canada's help in the wider war on terror and its contributions to Iraq's reconstruction. At the January 2004 Summit of the Americas meeting in Monterrey, President Bush announced that Canadian firms would be allowed to subcontract for work on the original round of reconstruction projects, and that they would be permitted to bid directly for the (smaller) second round of contracts.[67] Soon afterward, newly installed Prime Minister Martin announced that Canada would forgive about $750 million in Iraqi debts.

At the same time, Canadian defence contractors worried that the Iraq decision would undercut their efforts to win new contracts in Washington, even where those deals had nothing to do with Iraq. In April 2003, Derek Burney, the president of the flight simulation equipment and training supplier CAE (and former Mulroney chief of staff), told reporters he was worried that ongoing delays in the consideration of his company's bids might be a sign that American suppliers were looking for ways to avoid contracting with Canadian firms.[68]

Following the provisions of the Defence Production Sharing Agreement, Canadian firms had historically been treated as "domestic" suppliers for the purposes of defence procurement and supply, and were therefore exempt from the Buy American Act. In June, the House of Representatives considered a bill that would toughen the act and remove the Canadian exemption. Subsequent debate of the bill made it clear that most of the Congressional anger that prompted the bill in the first place was reserved for France and Germany, with no explicit criticism of Canada and no clear justification of the proposed removal of the Canadian exemption. There was no ignoring the fact that this provision had been included in the first place, however, and there were many troubling references to the danger involved in relying on suppliers "who might not be with you when the time comes to enter the battle." If the bill were to become law, the removal of the exemption would have had a devastating effect on the defence production industry, which was concentrated in Ontario and Quebec, and on high-tech and heavy manufacturing more generally.

The Canadian government lobbied relevant members of the House directly, to try to prevent removal of the exemption. Support came from the Defense Department, partly out of concern about the threat to Canada's long-term capacity for defence production, but mostly for fear of disruptive effects on ongoing US defence projects that relied on Canadian suppliers.[69] Additional pressure came from the major European producers, who threatened a direct challenge at the World Trade Organization (WTO). The bill was suddenly withdrawn just before it came to a vote. Some of the credit goes to the White House, but it seems that members of Congress had already achieved their main aim; each could claim credit for showing toughness with disloyal allies, each could avoid blame for the bill's overall "failure," and all knew that the legislation would not have stood up to WTO scrutiny.

The fact that Canada held on to its exemption might be seen as special treatment, but the way the US handled the issue is really an indication of how far things had moved away from the old special relationship. Canada was lumped in with all the other candidates for Congressional retaliation, and in fact was specifically singled out for rough treatment in the proposed removal of the established Canadian exemption to the Buy American Act. This shows that coercive linkages were definitely on the table for at least some people in Washington, and that these people were not held back by any particular normative compunctions but rather by straightforward domestic political obstacles and international legal restrictions.

Many corporate executives in the US were angered by Canada's withholding of support in Iraq, and were inclined to try to act on that frustration by avoiding Canadian suppliers and investments. A survey of business executives in the US, which was much talked about by Canadian industry lobbyists, found that nearly 50 percent of Americans said that they planned to look for alternatives to Canadian products and services because of their frustration over Iraq.[70] It is hard to say how many actually acted on these impulses, since shareholders would tend to insist on trade with Canada where that was good for the company's bottom line. Canadian firms probably did lose out on some contracting opportunities, at least at the margin, but there is no evidence to suggest that the White House did anything to orchestrate or even encourage these private forms of retaliation.[71]

Another set of issues that represented a potential basis for hard linkages came out of the evolution of US border-control policies. There was, as mentioned above, a clear divergence of priorities between the two countries after 9/11, with the US focusing on putting up walls to prevent further terrorist attacks and Canada focusing on opening doors to maintain access to the American market. The executive branch was inclined to work out some kind of compromise with Canada, and was therefore quick to negotiate the Smart Border Accord and push ahead with its implementation. Congress, on the other hand, was determined to tighten things up, and therefore persisted with its plan to implement Section 110 of the Illegal Immigration Reform and Immigrant Responsibility Act, which called for an automated system to record entry and exit at all border posts. Many of Section 110's main supporters were determined not to allow special exemptions for Canada, particularly after 9/11, based on the perceived inadequacy of its border facilities and the laxity of its immigration and refugee policies. The Chrétien government had been pouring diplomatic resources into fighting for some kind of blunting of Section 110, and had been rewarded with a series of last-minute postponements, but a number of observers worried that the Iraq decision would aggravate those in the US who had supported the Canadian case and lead to total defeat.

There is no evidence to support a direct, overt linkage between Iraq and US border-control policies. This was affirmed by the US Under Secretary for Border and Transportation Security, not long after the outbreak of war in Iraq: "In terms of our overall partnership, and in particular the border issues, there has been no slowdown of our communications, of our completion of the smart border accord that has been signed by both our countries."[72] The White House was not inclined to expend much political capital to support Canada with respect to the Section 110 initiative, but that was also the case before the confrontation over Iraq. The whole issue of border security is profoundly politicized, originally because of the association with illegal immigration and then later because of the public's insistence on tough border controls to prevent another terrorist attack.

These issues were, however, an important site for soft linkages, as the Iraq decision powerfully reinforced individual legislators' perceptions of Canada as an unreliable ally in the War on Terror, which redoubled their determination to impose strong controls on the Canada-US border. There is no evidence to suggest that the White House actively intervened to undercut the Canadian position vis-à-vis Section 110, but neither did it intervene to help. To the extent that there have been shifts in the US position on these issues over the last few years, they have been driven mostly by shifting coalitions in Congress and by underlying struggles between various domestic interest groups that stand to win or lose from one policy formula or another. The overall pattern, just as it was before 2003, has been a series of ostensibly firm commitments to go ahead with the legislation, followed by a last-minute postponement.[73]

The third and final set of issues to consider comprises various kinds of actual or anticipated restrictions on imports from Canada. This was actually the most commonly cited potential linkage scenario in the lead-up to, and immediately after, the 17 March decision. Most of the speculation at that time referred to trade restrictions in general, but some of it referred to specific sectors or commodities, and a small number of observers referred more generally to greater US resistance to calls for further, post-NAFTA regional integration.[74] To the extent that the relevant politicians and pundits were explicit about this, a few were worried about a vengeful White House making devastating hard linkages, but most were actually mainly concerned about potential soft linkages driven by Congress. Thomas d'Aquino fretted that members of Congress would hold a grudge over Iraq, that this would severely reduce their receptiveness to Canadian arguments in various trade disputes, and that this represented a historic crisis for Canada. J.L. Granatstein, in his alarmist "Empire Strikes Back" article, similarly explains the political problem in terms of the prospect that an aggrieved White House would not be prepared "to moderate the excesses of Congress," especially on trade and investment issues.[75]

As in many of the major disputes since the early 1960s, the most prominent scenario for hard linkages was ongoing US restrictions on imports of Canadian softwood lumber. The previous bilateral settlement (the Canada-US Softwood Lumber Agreement of 1996) had expired in 2001, and – as in each of the previous rounds of the dispute – the Commerce Department again formally condemned the Canadian provinces' stumpage fees regime as a subsidy in violation of US fair trade laws and imposed punishing countervailing and anti-dumping duties. Negotiators came very close to an agreement in December 2002, even while tensions over Iraq were nearing the boiling point. This potential settlement failed, but this seems to have been mostly due to resistance by domestic players on both sides rather than vindictiveness on the part of the US executive branch. Negotiations were effectively suspended through most of the spring of 2003, as the political leadership in both countries had their eyes firmly fixed on what was happening in Iraq and at the UN Security Council. Not long after Ambassador Cellucci declared that bilateral relations were "back to normal," high-level negotiations resumed in earnest, and there was fairly rapid and substantial progress.[76]

The two sides came to a tentative agreement in late July, but neither government could put together enough domestic political support to make a deal and ratify it. Instead, they continued to push ahead with international legal challenges, with Canada achieving partial victories in a series of NAFTA and WTO challenges running from the summer of 2003 to the spring of 2006, before losing an important WTO case in April 2006. Throughout this protracted fight, there was nothing to suggest that the White House had actively intervened to direct the Commerce Department to be tougher with Canada, or that it had manipulated concurrent Congressional debate on these issues. But it does seem clear that there was a soft linkage, which took the form of malign neglect on the part of the Bush administration.

In previous rounds, the White House had consistently stayed aloof in the early phases of the dispute, but then intervened after the two sides had reached an impasse, and brokered a political compromise that set up limited import restrictions but left the underlying legal dispute unresolved. A similar impasse had been reached by the end of 2002, and, while US negotiators were prepared to meet with their Canadian counterparts, it was clear that the White House was not prepared to give the issue much attention (given other, obviously more pressing concerns), nor to expend scarce political capital in trying to broker a new settlement. At the time, American negotiators publicly denied that Iraq (and later the missile defence dispute) prejudiced the US attitude toward Canada on this issue, but in retrospect, off the record, some were prepared to admit that "these things are never hermetically-sealed."[77] The White House, in other words, held a grudge, and it coloured the administration's approach to the lumber issue.

"We don't need Iraq or missile defence to convince us that the way Canada runs the lumber industry amounts to a subsidy. We think it does, and the NAFTA panels agree," reflected another US diplomat. "Of course we prefer to have a political settlement. But going out and getting a settlement can be risky for us. So we have to feel like there is a good reason to take that risk."[78] That reason apparently came along in early 2006, when Stephen Harper's Conservatives replaced Paul Martin's Liberals, because in April of that year the two governments finally reached a deal. The deal itself has since been severely criticized by political opponents and some lumber producers, but at the time it was widely seen as a favour done by the Bush administration in support of what it hoped would be a more cooperative Canadian government.

Another prominent bilateral trade dispute that attracted speculation about possible linkages was the United States' imposition of restrictions on imports of Canadian beef and cattle. In May 2003, Canadian inspectors found a case of "mad cow disease" (bovine spongiform encephalopathy, or BSE) in a single cow from Alberta. The US immediately banned all imports from Canada, with devastating effects on the Canadian ranching industry. Later that summer, the US began to allow imports of finished beef, but maintained the ban on live cattle.

Because the beef dispute did not erupt until two months after the start of the Iraq war, the question of linkage here refers to the possibility that US officials were especially strict or inflexible in applying the import ban, in retaliation for Canada's handling of the dispute over Iraq. The opposition parties certainly thought so, and used the beef ban to criticize Chrétien's handling of Canada-US relations. The Conservatives took the lead here, because they drew most of their political support from beef-exporting western provinces, where most voters were already very critical of the Iraq decision and of the Chrétien government more generally. Harper argued that the beef ban was "strictly a political problem," which had been brought about by the Liberal government's "mismanagement" of the bilateral relationship over the previous year.[79]

But there were in fact many other reasons for the United States to be tough with Canada when it came to BSE, regardless of the Iraq issue.[80] Both Canada and the US had taken aggressively risk-averse stances on BSE in the late 1990s, to reassure their own consumers and their main export markets overseas. Both had previously banned imports from other countries based on the detection of a single infected animal, and in that sense the US was simply following established policy precedents. At the same time, American officials were deeply concerned about maintaining access for their own beef products in Japan, which had been even more risk-averse about BSE, and which made a ban on Canadian beef a precondition for continuing American access to the Japanese market. Once the US ban was in place, moreover, there was tremendous pressure on American regulators to keep it there, as hard-pressed US producers saw it as an opportunity to shelter themselves from Canadian competition.

There is no evidence to support the idea that the White House employed, or even seriously considered employing, the beef ban as the basis for a hard linkage to force changes to Canadian policies in other issue areas. The decision to impose the ban in the first place occurred automatically, as US food safety regulators followed standard procedures established during the 1990s. The Department of Agriculture and relevant members of Congress stubbornly defended the ban against Canadian diplomatic and legal challenges, but they were primarily motivated by protectionist pressure from US producers, not political pressure from the Bush administration. There are signs that there may have been soft linkages at work in this case, although their effects were rather marginal and hard to pin down.

Working-level officials in the US were initially receptive to Canadian calls for the negotiation of a set of common standards and procedures that would allow for the reopening of the border to Canadian beef and cattle, but then abruptly backed away, leaving the Canadians with no one to talk to. This apparent reversal might be explained in part by grudges over Iraq, but it was probably mostly due to growing pressure from Congress, which was responding to protectionist forces at home, and to the inflexibility of Japanese negotiators. Again, the White House did nothing to push for a tougher stance against Canadian beef, but neither did it try to intervene on Canada's behalf.[81]

In the closing months of 2003, with the Bush administration trying to set a positive tone in anticipation of Paul Martin's taking over from Jean Chrétien, there was a diplomatic breakthrough and the US announced that it would relax the rules for Canadian cattle and reopen the border. But then a case of BSE was found in the US, which was quickly traced back to Canada, and the negotiations went back to square one. A new deal struck in December 2004 has subsequently been up and down through the US court system, and the issue is still not completely resolved.

Epilogue: "Things Will Never Be the Same"

When Paul Martin replaced Jean Chrétien as prime minister in December 2003, he promised to repair the bilateral relationship, just as Brian Mulroney had promised after Pierre Trudeau left office in 1983. Martin was personally committed to this goal, but was immediately confronted with a series of difficult obstacles. The Liberal party was deeply divided by his long-running rivalry with Chrétien, and dogged by allegations of corruption stemming from the Chrétien-era "sponsorship scandal."[82] The country's economy was doing well, but regional and sectoral interests harboured grudges over the lumber and beef disputes and there was widespread anxiety about further US protectionism. The Bush administration, while welcoming Chrétien's replacement, was cautious about Martin's initial advances. Then Martin was weakened by the results of the June 2004 election, in which the Liberals lost their parliamentary majority and had to rely on ad hoc coalition building to pass legislation and remain in power.

The new prime minister made a number of moves to patch things up with the White House, including some important contributions to Iraq's reconstruction (election monitoring, training of police officers) and a renewal of the much-appreciated Canadian commitment to Afghanistan. The Bush administration made an effort to reciprocate, starting with a visit by the president in November 2004. Bush disarmed a skeptical audience at his stop in Halifax, by "thank[ing] the Canadian people who came out to wave – with all five fingers – for their hospitality," but then provoked Martin with an impromptu call for Canada to join the United States in pursuing a ballistic missile defence (BMD) program.

Missile defence was an issue that had been haunting the bilateral relationship in one form or another for nearly twenty years, and had risen to the top of the agenda since 9/11. Canadian officials had been involved in negotiations with the US on missile defence for several years, and – as the system itself got closer to activation and the US continued to build up its Northern Command (US NORTHCOM) command centre – it got harder and harder to put off making a final decision. Martin himself was well known to be supportive of Canadian involvement in one form or another, mostly as a way to reinforce the bilateral defence relationship, and he sent signals to the Bush administration that he would try to prepare the skeptical Canadian public for an eventual decision to participate. But opposition to missile defence was widespread within the Liberal party, particularly in the politically pivotal province of Quebec. Much as Diefenbaker had done forty years earlier, Martin tried to put off a decision, anxious to avoid caving in to the US and fearing a fatal split within his party. Eventually, however, the pressure became so intense and immediate that the prime minister felt compelled to avoid a showdown with the youth wing in Quebec by publicly disavowing involvement in the US missile defence program.[83] The decision was announced in February 2005 without warning to anyone in Washington, as with Chrétien's decision on Iraq, and again this caused surprise and irritation in the White House. This time, however, the decision was offered with some deference to the American position, and the Martin government again made a number of quiet moves to temper its formal nonsupport with some informal support (i.e., continuing participation of Canadian personnel at NORAD headquarters in missile tracking that would be essential to the BMD system).

Still, there was severe tension between the political leaders in the two countries, and more speculation about American retaliation.[84] Martin's domestic political position eventually got so shaky that he decided to resort to veiled anti-Americanism in fighting the January 2006 election. The Bush administration's frustration and resentment was so intense at this point that the new ambassador, David Wilkins, publicly rebuked Martin, and Canadians more generally. "It may be smart election-year politics to thump your chest and constantly criticize your friend and your number one trading partner," said the ambassador. "But it's a slippery slope, and all of us should hope that it doesn't have a lasting effect on the relationship."[85]

It's hard to say for sure whether or not the tensions over Iraq and missile defence have had lasting effects on the bilateral relationship. Certainly they seemed to have important effects on the Bush administration's view of Canada, and therefore on the management of the relationship. As in the high-level disputes described in the previous chapters, the top political leadership's antipathy for their Canadian counterparts, and therefore for Canadian issues, does seem to have trickled down to lower levels in the executive branch. Working-level officials still worked hard on the day-to-day management of the many thousands of issues of common concern, and in that sense it was business as usual. But the withholding of White House attention and support made it harder for those officials to make the case for policies that put long-term shared interests ahead of short-term parochial ones, when dealing with Congress, with "domestic" agencies and subnational governments, and with various nongovernment actors such as business associations and advocacy groups. Some issues were effectively put on hold, and that delay in itself seriously damaged Canadian interests, as in the trade disputes over lumber and beef. In some cases, as in the division of labour between NORAD and US NORTHCOM, the lack of engagement with Canadian officials meant that US agencies made important decisions without taking Canadian interests and priorities into account, and sometimes made those decisions in ways that were contrary to Canadian interests, even where it would have cost the US little or nothing to do otherwise.

This is not to say that Canada could not, or should not, have broken with the US on these issues. That it *could* do so is clear enough from the fact that it did, and from the fact that there was no attempt to use hard linkages to deter the Canadian challenge and no direct retaliation afterward. It was not that the Bush administration was unwilling to bargain aggressively with Canada, as indicated by the tough talk from Washington and US officials' low-key efforts to explore linkage options. It appears, rather, that the US government was *unable* to pursue hard linkages, or, more specifically, was unable to find a way to do so that had a reasonable prospect of actually shifting Canadian policy without triggering unacceptably high risks or costs for the White House. (This is less significant in the Iraq dispute than it was in the nuclear weapons and Arctic waters disputes, because some of the actions taken by the Chrétien government, such as the commitment to Afghanistan, made the Canadian decision easier for the White House to swallow, and thus lowered the threshold of costs and risks that the US was willing to accept in order to force Canada to change course.)

The most striking feature of this dispute, as in that over the NEP, was the quiet consensus among American officials that the costs involved in making hard linkages were too high all the way across the broad range of "available" bilateral issues. And, as in the NEP dispute, the main reasons for this were the extraordinary breadth and depth of economic interdependence between the two countries, which generated domestic coalitions in the US with an interest in blocking linkages, and the fragmentation of political power in the American system, which provides those coalitions with various avenues for influencing policy outcomes and bargaining priorities. The main thing that has changed since the days of the NEP is the overlaying of the formal institutional structures of the Canada-US and North American free trade agreements, which tend to reinforce these long-established obstacles through greater transparency, oversight, and, ultimately, legal sanction.

Although the US was clearly held back from pursuing hard linkages in this case, the confrontation over the Iraq war also highlights the other ways in which the US can react to provocative Canadian policies, and these soft linkages can also have important effects on Canadian interests. The Bush administration did not use its leverage on border security or trade issues to twist Canada's arm and force it to change its stand on Iraq, but it also chose not to use it in order to protect and promote Canadian interests (recognizing that such interests are generally compatible with broader US national interests) in the way that it normally would.

Whether or not Canada *should* have broken with the US on these issues, recognizing the likelihood that it would suffer the kinds of indirect costs outlined above, is another matter. Disagreement always comes at some cost, even with friends. The question is therefore how the government of the day weighs the international and domestic benefits of disagreeing with the United States against the probable indirect costs and the limited but ever-present risk that those costs will cascade into something much more serious. The Harper government clearly chose a different path, and its close collaboration with the US on a variety of issues have been evidently earned a measure of goodwill in Washington – at least with the Bush Administration. This seems to have been reflected in the quick resolution of the softwood lumber and beef disputes, and possibly also in the postponement of post-9/11 identity-documentation rules for travellers crossing the Canada-US border (the Western Hemisphere Travel Initiative). Yet, just as we ought to carefully weigh the benefits of going our own way against the likely costs, both direct and indirect, so we should also be objective and careful in weighing the benefits of working closely with the US against the likely costs of such cooperation.

7
Diplomatic Culture: Exceptions, Rules, and Exceptions to the Rule

The two main purposes of this book are to rejuvenate and reformulate an old interpretation of Canada-US relations, and – based on this account of one exceptional relationship – to encourage a new way of thinking about international bargaining more generally.

In the early Cold War decades, the conventional wisdom was that Canada and the United States had a special relationship, rooted in common values and governed by shared norms and practices. Most international relations specialists took this at face value and therefore tended to see it as an odd little anomaly that had little to tell us about the way the rest of the world works. Keohane and Nye's *Power and Interdependence,* in conjunction with a handful of related studies, reaffirmed this reading of Canada-US relations as exceptional, but made the case that it was the exceptional features of the relationship that made it interesting and important for international relations theory.[1]

At the same time that Keohane and Nye were making this argument, more and more scholars and practitioners in Canada were arguing that there was nothing special about the Canada-US relationship, and that perhaps there never had been. In fact, one of the main themes running through the scholarly literature on Canada-US relations during the 1970s was an impulse to disabuse readers of their special relationship "delusions," and this impulse is still seen in much of the literature today.[2] Since then many academic specialists on Canada-US relations, seeking to be taken seriously by colleagues and practitioners, have evidently felt compelled to emphasize the importance of power and interests, and to avoid any reference to culture and ideas.

Of course, politicians in both countries still tend to talk about the relationship as though there were nothing but friendship and fair play, and the news media often just pass this on to their audiences without a second thought. There is therefore an ongoing need for those studying the bilateral relationship, and particularly those writing for undergraduates and general audiences, to spend some time tearing down platitudes and clichés.[3] It would be a mistake, however, to let this kind of healthy skepticism obscure what once was – and in some ways still is – genuinely exceptional about the relationship. Alliance politics and economic interdependence *did* play important roles in shaping Canada-US relations during the 1950s and 1960s, but that is only part of the story. We cannot understand the process and outcomes of bilateral bargaining during this period without reference to the "management" of the agenda by a transgovernmental network, and to the distinctive diplomatic culture that held the network together.

It is equally important to recognize and understand the way things have changed over the last forty years. There have been, for example, some calls recently for Canadian policy-makers to try to restore the special relationship by rebuilding ties with the top levels of the executive branch in Washington, or by working more closely with the US on strategic and diplomatic issues. These are not necessarily bad ideas, but they must be anchored in a recognition of the way that the old bases for influence have broken down, and of the fact that there can be no "turning back the clock" to the way things once were.

A Distinctive Diplomatic Culture

Relations between Canada and the United States were exceptional during the early Cold War decades, but not in the sense that the relationship was governed by principle while other international relationships were governed by power. Relations between states are always governed by some mixture of principles *and* power, and the challenge for researchers is to understand how principles and power interact within the context of a particular relationship. Every established relationship between states generates some stable understandings about how those states will relate to one another – that is, some kind of diplomatic culture – even if it is nothing more than mutual recognition that everything is ad hoc or that there are few limits on what can be said and done. The form that these norms take will generally reflect underlying power relationships, but the norms themselves can also have "steering" and constraining effects on the exercise of power.

In the postwar Canada-US relationship, the core principle was "partnership." This concept had different connotations for the two governments, as both sides understood that it was not a partnership of equals, but these different expectations were generally compatible and mutually reinforcing. In the early postwar years, as Canada slipped from the comfortable embrace of "Mother England" into a new orbit around the United States, Canadian policy-makers sought assurances from Washington that the US would not try to exploit the growing interdependence between the two countries by making linkages between unrelated issues. The American policy-makers who worked most closely with Canadians were inclined to give those assurances, because they recognized how important they were to making it politically possible for Canadian policy-makers to support further integration, and because that kind of self-restraint resonated with their own concept of the kind of international actor the United States was supposed to be. They also recognized that preventing or derailing linkages would reinforce their own capacity to "manage" the bilateral relationship. This interest in avoiding politicization was shared by officials on both sides of the border, and they developed a sense of common purpose based on tacit agreement that the bilateral agenda should be approached as a set of "technical" problems, to be sorted out through quiet diplomacy and mutual restraint.

The diplomatic culture governing Canada-US relations overlapped with those for at least two other, wider communities of states, in terms of both the countries involved and some of the specific bargaining norms. Thomas Risse and others have argued that relations between the US and its Western European allies were governed by a set of specific bargaining norms based on acceptance of special obligations between democracies: consultation, transparency, non-use of force, and a general preference for "integrative" problem-solving governed by formal rules.[4] And Stéphane Roussel has argued that this same sense of trust and mutual obligation between democracies made it possible for Canada and the United States to overcome historic animosities and eventually come together to form a distinct "security community."[5] Roussel is undoubtedly right that mutual recognition as democracies, and the belief that this created special obligations for consultation and self-restraint, played an important part in shaping the distinctive diplomatic culture governing Canada-US relations. But this cannot account for some of the specific norms and practices governing the bilateral relationship, particularly the emphasis on "technical" problem-solving and the strong norm against issue linkages.

Others have argued that there is – or there once was – a distinctive diplomatic culture linking the United States to the other members of the "Anglosphere": Britain, Canada, Australia, and New Zealand.[6] Among the bargaining norms associated with the Anglosphere community are expectations of continuous consultation, quiet diplomacy, and close military and diplomatic support. This sense of community and mutual obligation among "English-speaking peoples" was popular and influential in both Canada and the US during the early postwar years; few openly espouse it in Canada today but it still has a certain popularity in the US, particularly among conservatives. Again, it is useful to see the Canada-US relationship as anchored in this larger community of states, in the sense that it can help us understand some of the broad contours of the bilateral diplomatic culture and its similarity to that between the US and other western allies, but it is important to note that there are subtle but important differences between the expectations that Canada and the US have of each other compared with those linking the US and Britain or the US and Australia.

Diplomatic Culture as an Integral Component of Bargaining Theory

Diplomats everywhere are generally reluctant to pursue overt, direct linkages – as noted in Chapter 1 – because they are inherently provocative and could trigger a spiral that might make everyone worse off. Even profoundly mistrustful adversaries like the US and the Soviet Union, which routinely expected each other to be ruthless and unprincipled in high-stakes disputes, consistently reacted with outrage to each other's more overt linkages (even when there was no audience to perform for). In practice, of course, diplomats have been prepared to pursue hard linkages in a wide variety of different circumstances, and they are generally understood to be an ordinary feature of international bargaining.

The United States, whose self-image as an international actor is predicated on a special commitment to make the exercise of raw power consistent with principles and laws, has been relatively cautious and discreet about the pursuit of coercive linkages,[7] but there is no doubt that it has been prepared to make at least some kinds of linkages against some kinds of states. The Eisenhower administration's use of monetary leverage to force Britain's withdrawal in the Suez crisis makes it clear, moreover, that the US has been prepared to pursue coercive linkages even in disputes with some of its closest allies.

Since bargaining theory is concerned with describing and explaining practice rather than principle, and since linkage is seen almost everywhere in international politics, virtually all of the work that has been done in this area has taken linkage as a given.[8] Particular linkage options may be ruled out, it is observed, but only because they don't offer the right mix of effectiveness and risk, are blocked by domestic interests, or cannot be credibly signalled to the other side. The Canada-US experience during the early Cold War years suggests, however, that linkages may be ruled out on normative criteria as well – that is, according to the "logic of appropriateness" rather than the "logic of consequences."[9]

In some relationships, certain kinds of linkages may be ruled out on normative grounds, as in the Association of Southeast Asian Nations member states' shared commitment to avoid challenging one another's national sovereignty.[10] In postwar Canada-US bargaining, coercive linkages were ruled out per se, because – as described in Chapter 1 – linkage itself was seen to have a special meaning. On one hand, resort to hard linkages was recognized as a "trigger" for Canadian apprehensions about vulnerability, which might set off a spiral of mutually damaging retractions and dislocations. On the other hand, resort to linkage vis-à-vis Canada was contrary to American officials' ideas about the nature and purposes of the United States as an international actor in general, and the nature of its relationship with Canada in particular.

Of course, the Canada-US relationship is not a hard case for the proposition that norms matter, at least sometimes, in bilateral bargaining. One might argue that if we were going to find that bargaining norms make a clear difference anywhere, then it would be in a relationship such as that between Canada and the US. That may be so, but there have been a number of bilateral disputes between the two countries that do constitute hard tests for the argument about bargaining norms advanced here. My research was designed to respond to skepticism surrounding the empirical underpinnings of past constructivist work on the role of norms and ideas in foreign policy, by focusing on cases where the norm-driven account's expectations clearly diverge from those of prominent alternatives that emphasize straightforward rationalist-materialist conceptions of power and interests (i.e., realism, domestic coalition politics).[11] These case studies resemble past constructivist research in that they look for a basic fit between expectations and observed outcomes. The study as a whole, however, goes further than most first-generation constructivist research by identifying and evaluating counterfactual scenarios that were not pursued or, in some cases, not even considered, and by looking more closely at what key decision-makers said (or did not say) about the reasons for their choices.

Anchoring Diplomatic Cultures in Political Structures

"Ideas," as Thomas Risse once argued, "do not float freely"; their impact on policy outcomes depends on their being carried into the political arena by domestic actors who have the capacity to set the agenda and translate ideas into action.[12] The historical cases considered here help to highlight both the agency of the actors who subscribed to and advocated for the postwar diplomatic culture, and the structural features that enabled – and later disabled – their influence on policy outcomes.

The origins, perpetuation, and activation of the diplomatic culture that governed postwar Canada-US bargaining resonate with established theory and research highlighting the importance of transnational and transgovernmental networks as "carriers" of international norms. As in that work, the members of the transgovernmental network here derived their influence over the policy agenda not from control over material resources or placement at the top of formal institutional hierarchies but rather from their control over information and their credibility as expert "managers" of the bilateral relationship.[13] Their capacity to effectively manage the bilateral relationship vindicates E.E. Schattschneider's oft-quoted remark that "the definition of alternatives is the supreme instrument of power."[14]

The rise and fall of the network and norms over the last sixty years supports past theory and research on the importance of domestic political structures in making or breaking opportunities for transnational and transgovernmental networks' ideas to influence policy outcomes.[15] The American officials tied into the transgovernmental network were well positioned to shape the bargaining agenda in the 1950s and 1960s, because the relatively hierarchical and coherent governing structures of the early Cold War "imperial presidency" facilitated a bigger-picture perspective on foreign-policy making and granted special licence for State Department and other likeminded officials to manage particular relationships according to broader agendas and principles. The further fragmentation of foreign-policy making in the United States in the 1970s created space for conflicting ideas and priorities to force their way onto the agenda, making it harder to predict which ideas and priorities would prevail in any given debate over bargaining strategies. It was not that the American officials who worked most closely with Canadians changed their minds about how to manage the relationship, as I emphasized in Chapter 1, but rather that their voices were drowned out by a variety of new players with very different ways of thinking about American interests and about how to approach relations with Canada.

The importance of these bargaining norms to Canada-US relations during the 1950s and 1960s, and the intriguing connections between the Canada-US experience and those of other communities of states (i.e., the transatlantic alliance of democratic states; the Anglosphere), suggests the value of comparative research on diplomatic cultures as phenomena in world politics, which could extend and refine some of the very broad generalizations advanced here. There is already a substantial literature on "strategic cultures," which is concerned with the way that particular states relate to the rest of the world, and with the emergence of more or less universal diplomatic orders governing relations between states in different historical eras.[16] A focus on diplomatic cultures would draw out the way in which there are stable patterns of diplomatic practice that are specific to certain groups of states, explore the domestic political and inter-state institutional contexts that make them possible, and relate them to patterns of diplomatic outcomes. A substantial body of relevant work is already out there, in the aforementioned studies on the democratic peace and the Anglosphere; in theory and research on regional cooperation in Europe, Asia, and other parts of the world; and in work on the evolution of rules and procedures in various international organizations, such as the United Nations and the World Trade Organization.[17] The main challenge now is to try to bring these disparate bodies of literature together, and develop theoretical tools to identify and explain patterns of similarity and difference across different relationships, in different times and places.

A New Look at an Old Argument

Of course, this study is also concerned with understanding the Canada-US relationship in its own right. I have argued that Canada-US relations were governed during the 1950s and 1960s by a distinctive diplomatic culture, including a shared norm against coercive issue linkage. This is not, as noted in Chapter 1, an entirely new interpretation. The argument that Canada-US relations have been governed by a special set of bargaining norms has been prominent – and controversial – since the 1940s, if not earlier.[18] But it has never been carefully specified or empirically tested before. Some of those who originally argued that there was a special relationship have since lamented its passing, but without offering a clear explanation of what changed and why. The second part of my argument is that the salience of the postwar diplomatic culture deteriorated in the 1970s because the transgovernmental network that "carried" it was effectively displaced by other actors seeking to influence the bargaining agenda, particularly in the United States. This disruption was brought about by the further fragmentation of the institutional structure of foreign-policy making that followed the Vietnam War and Watergate.

This bigger-picture interpretation of Canada-US bargaining over the last sixty years can give us new perspective on some of the most controversial bilateral disputes of the postwar era. The four cases examined here were chosen mainly because they are hard cases for the diplomatic-culture interpretation, but they are also interesting episodes in themselves, with plenty of intrigue and room for speculation and second-guessing. These are cases that we tend to return to over and over, because we know intuitively that they are the ones where the relationship was pushed to its limits and all of the big questions about Canada-US relations are in play: power and strategy, tensions between international and domestic politics, personal character and moral crises, and the scope and nature of national autonomy.

There are two most common interpretations of the dispute over nuclear weapons in the early 1960s. Those that disagree with Prime Minister John Diefenbaker's decision tend to see this as a made-in-Canada diplomatic disaster, emphasizing the prime minister's failure to keep his Cabinet under control and his reckless provocation of the White House, and implying that he basically got what he deserved in the end. Those that think Diefenbaker was right tend to see it as a story about US bullying, usually as one example among many. Both interpretations are partly right. Traditionally, we have tended to focus on the way that the dispute became politicized and personalized after January 1963, when many of the established rules of the game were thrown aside. This was the main lesson drawn in the immediate aftermath, as the Merchant-Heeney report reaffirmed the old way of doing things, based on quiet diplomacy and technical problem-solving by bureaucratic professionals.[19] What we tend to lose sight of, is that bilateral bargaining up to the end of 1962 consistently reflected strict adherence to postwar bargaining norms, and – as explained in Chapter 3 – the US exercised remarkable self-restraint during the potentially explosive period between the Cuban Missile Crisis and Lester Pearson's January 1963 reversal. The archival records show that American officials not only never pursued coercive linkages but didn't even recognize them as options. They did violate some of the other core norms from the diplomatic culture, most notably the practice of quiet diplomacy, but in their minds this was justified because Diefenbaker had already crossed that line.

There are also two main interpretations of the Arctic waters dispute. At the time, many observers were sharply critical of Pierre Trudeau's handling of the issue, arguing that it was contrary to the core principles of Canadian diplomacy: close collaboration with the US, quiet diplomacy, multilateralism, and respect for international law (i.e., in contrast to the International Court of Justice reservation). Many more observers, however, welcomed his assertive diplomacy as the precursor to a new diplomacy that put national interests first, even where this meant breaking with the US or international institutions. (Left and right could agree here, because they both saw the national interest the same way on this particular issue.) In the US, most saw Trudeau as having a number of issue-specific bargaining advantages in this case, and having played them for all they were worth. The US could have made coercive linkages to force Canada to back down, and some American officials wanted to do so. But the remnants of the postwar transgovernmental network intervened effectively to derail calls for linkage and keep the US on the negotiating track until after it was too late. This left a sour taste in the mouths of many Americans, with respect not only to the Trudeau government but also to the postwar diplomatic culture itself. The Nixon administration clearly held a grudge afterward, which tended to undercut the Canadian bargaining position in concurrent and subsequent negotiations.

The main debate in the National Energy Program (NEP) dispute roughly parallels that over the Arctic waters case. Some saw Trudeau as too reckless in pushing ahead with the NEP in spite of the predictable American reaction. Others believe that the strategy was sound but that the government was forced to back down under intense US pressure. Again, both are partly right. The core premise of the NEP was sound, but the plan itself was poorly worked out, particularly in its failure to anticipate US legal and diplomatic challenges. It is striking how aggressively the United States reacted to the NEP, and how quickly American officials turned to consider linkages. This can be explained in part by the Reagan administration's visceral reaction to the NEP on ideological grounds, but it also reflects the way that the fragmentation of the American system created opportunities for interest groups adversely affected by Canadian policy to pressure policy-makers for more aggressive bargaining. We can also see here the way that the institutional fragmentation of US foreign-policy making led to a fragmentation of US diplomacy, with many different voices pushing for different objectives and different strategies, making a settlement more difficult and increasing the sense of uncertainty and anxiety in Canada.

Three different stories are told about the diplomatic tensions surrounding the US push to war in Iraq. Some say that the Chrétien government heroically stood by its multilateralist principles and managed to get away with it, and others that Jean Chrétien recklessly provoked the US for domestic political gain. A third group would probably argue that it doesn't really matter what the prime minister's motivation was, because his government had already taken Iraq off the table by making a substantial new commitment to Afghanistan "instead," and there was little opportunity for the US to consider coercive linkages, given the ambiguity surrounding the Canadian position right up to the last minute. There is some truth to this third reading, and it does undercut the case somewhat as a test of the bases for US self-restraint. But there were evidently some in the US who wanted to force the issue with Canada over diplomatic support for the Coalition of the Willing, and to consider issue linkages as a way to compel Canada to change course. Just as in the NEP case, however, the advocates of linkage in the US were unable to work out a viable scenario, mainly because of anticipated counterpressure from domestic interests that would be hurt by the disruption.

When we look at the broad pattern in the four cases, the main thing that stands out is that the US did not actually make effective issue linkages in *any* of these high-stakes disputes. On closer examination, however, it is evident that the reasons for US restraint varied over time. In the two earlier confrontations – over nuclear weapons and Arctic waters – American officials would not pursue linkages, even though some viable scenarios were evidently available. In the two later disputes, they were prepared to pursue linkages but found that they could not do so, primarily because of anticipated domestic political opposition.

The pattern is therefore consistent with the basic expectations of the diplomatic-culture interpretation advanced here, but this in itself is not enough to confirm the argument, because the pattern is also consistent with the general expectations of two main theoretical rivals.

Realists would expect the US to be less forbearing with Canada beginning at some point in the mid or late 1960s, because Cold War tensions were subsiding and Canada's perceived value as a strategic and diplomatic supporter was deteriorating. They would probably also expect the US to become more tolerant in the early 1980s, as the Cold War intensified again, but that would appear to be contradicted by the Reagan administration's aggressive response to the NEP. The bigger problem for the realist interpretation, however, is the two earlier cases – nuclear weapons and Arctic waters. If realists are serious about major powers having a hierarchy of interests, with security always at the top, then we should expect a general US inclination to be forbearing with Canada in the 1950s and 1960s. But we should also expect that inclination to be set aside – and issue linkages to be pursued as necessary – in cases where

Canadian policies directly challenge core US national security priorities, especially where those challenges have demonstration effects for other states.

The basic pattern is also compatible with an alternative conception of the implications of growing economic interdependence. Whereas Keohane and Nye argued that deeper interdependence would tighten the constraints on the exercise of US power, others have argued that – in combination with America's growing vulnerability to international economic dislocations and the further fragmentation of the American political system – interdependence has actually become a catalyst for more aggressive bargaining, including pressure for coercive issue linkages. Since these developments hit home for US policy-makers in the late 1960s and early 1970s, the timing matches up quite well with such policy-makers' new inclination to pursue linkages across the four cases. This is an important part of what happened, but, while it may help us to identify necessary conditions for US self-restraint in the 1950s and 1960s, it has little or nothing to say about sufficient conditions.

The only interpretation that appears unable to explain changing US attitudes over time is Keohane and Nye's argument that growing interdependence would strengthen the Canadian bargaining position. Interdependence grew rapidly in the 1960s and again in the 1990s, yet the US seemed more and more inclined to bargain aggressively with Canada after the early 1970s. Looking more closely at the NEP and Iraq cases, it is clear that the main reason for US restraint was the proliferation of the kinds of blocking coalitions that Keohane and Nye had in mind. But this does not account for US restraint during the period that Keohane and Nye actually studied, because American policy-makers chose not to pursue coercive linkages against Canada in the nuclear weapons and Arctic waters disputes, in spite of the fact that some viable linkage options were clearly within reach. Keohane and Nye's argument conflated the effects of norms and transnational coalitions, but the pattern in these four cases appears to indicate that they should be considered separately. To put it simply, norms did most of the work in the 1950s and 1960s, and coalitions have done most of the work since then. One kind of bilateral bargaining relationship gave way to another, transforming the diplomatic challenges for policy-makers and negotiators on both sides of the border and subtly shifting the dynamics of power and influence, and thus the foundations of Canadian autonomy.

Past and Future

This is primarily a study about the way Canada-US relations used to be. It describes and explains what was genuinely exceptional about the special relationship during the early Cold War decades, and it shows how the relationship changed after the early 1970s. But history is not just for history books. Past decisions explain our present dilemmas and set the guideposts for our future choices. A better understanding of the breakdown of the postwar diplomatic culture can help us account for Canada's switch to a very different approach to influencing US policy in the 1970s and for the surprising turn toward continental integration in the 1980s. And a better understanding of what made the relationship a special one in the 1950s and 1960s, and the reasons why this changed, can help us to properly evaluate more recent proposals for new approaches (some of which are really about going back to old approaches).

In the 1980s and 1990s, there were three main phases in the Canadian effort to adapt to the fragmentation of foreign-policy making in the United States: a new caution about initiating bilateral disputes and a new inclination to look for ways to avoid future disputes; an effort to engage more directly with some of the new players on the US foreign-policy landscape, and to access the American political system in much the same way as US domestic interests; and finally a new interest in economic integration and in building formal institutions.

The Mulroney government is often described as "continentalist." There is certainly an element of truth in this, if by it we mean an inclination to see many of the problems on the policy agenda as problems shared with the United States, and a willingness to try to tackle some of those problems through formal institutional commitments on a continental scale. It is less clear, however, if we mean "continentalist" in the common pejorative way, referring to Brian Mulroney's supposed willingness to sacrifice policy autonomy in order to secure greater access and influence in Washington.[20]

The Mulroney government challenged the US more often than many recognize (e.g., South Africa, Strategic Defense Initiative, Arctic waters, broadcasting and publishing), and Trudeau and Chrétien pursued fewer challenges than we might think. In fact, the nature and outcomes of bilateral bargaining in the 1980s do not look much different from those in the 1970s or the 1990s, *and* the pattern for each of these decades looks more similar to the pattern for the others than to that for the 1960s. There have of course been some important differences from one government to another, but overall the pattern appears to be that, since the early 1970s, the Canadian government has initiated fewer policy changes that could be expected to provoke the United States, is less likely to persist in the face of clear US opposition, and tends not to get away with as many of these challenges as it once did.

Critics of the Chrétien government often characterized it as one that frequently and recklessly challenged the United States. Chrétien launched quite a few provocations at the US, but most were trivial and were barely noticed in Washington.[21] Only one of them really tested American self-restraint – the decision not to support the US in Iraq – and that one seems to have been driven by a variety of unusual circumstances that encouraged Chrétien not to worry too much about the American response, including the strength of public opposition to the war, particularly in Quebec, and his own impending retirement. When we look more broadly at the long sweep of Chrétien's time in power, we see that there were actually very few bilateral disputes – far fewer than under the ostensibly continentalist Lester Pearson – and, whereas most of the bilateral disputes in the 1960s were initiated by Canada, almost all of those in the 1990s were initiated by the United States.

Canada's first genuinely strategic effort to cope with the transformation of the bilateral relationship was a shift toward new strategies for accessing and influencing the policy-making process in the United States. The first signs of trouble were the Nixon administration's decision not to exempt Canada from its aggressive balance of payments measures in August 1971, and Nixon's subsequent pronouncement that the special relationship was dead. But most people in Ottawa tended to attribute these troubling developments to Nixon and his advisers, and were optimistic that things would get back to normal once new players took the stage in Washington. A few years later, it became apparent that things had changed more profoundly and more permanently, with the eruption of open conflict between the White House and Congress over foreign-policy making.

The Canadian government continued, as it had always done, to focus its diplomatic energies on the State Department, and where possible on the White House, but it also began to make an effort to keep track of what was happening in Congress, and to try to cultivate contacts there. After the failure of the East Coast fisheries agreement and the confrontation over the NEP, this diversification of Canadian diplomatic efforts was radically accelerated, with new funding for the embassy in Washington and new efforts to build ad hoc transnational alliances with US firms, unions, and other organized interest groups.[22]

Canadian officials also relaxed their long-standing reservations about public diplomacy and began to pursue more aggressive efforts to reach relevant government and nongovernment audiences in the US, by hiring Washington insiders and by initiating coordinated public relations campaigns. And they became increasingly inclined to pursue direct legal engagement in the US, by supporting Canadian interests fighting their way through American courts and by actively engaging with quasi-judicial entities such as the US International Trade Commission.

Recognizing that the direct channel for influence that it had enjoyed during the early Cold War years had broken down, Canada felt compelled to throw itself head-first into the more complex workings of post-Watergate Washington, and essentially to play the game there much like any other "special interest" group. But as Mulroney and Ambassador Allan Gotlieb discovered, this was much easier said than done, and many in Ottawa grew frustrated with the results.[23] There was a growing consensus that something new would need to be done in order to make Canada's diplomatic engagement with Washington more predictable and effective.

The other part of Canada's adaptation was a turn toward formal, integrative institution building as a way to secure new restraints on the exercise of American power. US officials had proposed free trade agreements and other broad integrative initiatives in the past, but had always been politely but firmly turned down by cautious Canadian politicians. George Ball later referred to this resistance to integration, and subsequent efforts to direct and contain the growth of economic interdependence, as a "rearguard action against the inevitable." One of the things that encouraged Canadian politicians to carry on that struggle through the 1950s and 1960s – and to be fairly assured that they could continue to do so in the future – was the confidence that the diplomatic culture gave them in the limits that the US would set on the exercise of its own power, and in their capacity to find their way along the edges of those limits. Once it became clear that the old, informal system of bilateral dispute resolution had broken down, however, Canadian elites became increasingly inclined to look to formal integration as the only way to restore a measure of predictability and to protect their issue-specific advantages.

Of course, many factors played into the Mulroney government's leap of faith to bilateral free trade in the mid-1980s.[24] Canadian officials, like their American counterparts, saw a regional trade agreement as a way to insulate their country from the dislocations caused by – and possibly also a means to force a breakthrough in – the ongoing stalemate in the multilateral trade regime. At the same time, the greater mobility of capital and the globalization of production were seen to put pressure on all economies to strip away barriers to trade and investment, and to try to bring regulations and taxes into line with those of regional powerhouse economies. These changes were embraced, moreover, by Mulroney's Progressive Conservative government, which was caught up in the larger ideological turn to the right that was sweeping through the advanced industrial countries at that time. Formal trade liberalization agreements, they hoped, would help lock in domestic market reforms in Canada.

Underlying all of these concurrent developments, however, was a growing apprehension about the unpredictable and arbitrary exercise of American power. In the early stages of the CUSFTA negotiations, the main Canadian aim was to secure some kind of legal or institutional restraint on the arbitrary exercise of US "trade remedy" laws, and this continued to be a key priority for Canadian negotiators. By the end of the process, many Canadian officials and influential business leaders had come to think about the agreement as a "grand bargain" in which each side agreed to give up a measure of autonomy: Canada would make substantial concessions on unconventional trade issues that American negotiators cared about (trade in services, cultural subsidies, etc.), in exchange for some kind of legal mechanism that would set limits on the exercise of US anti-dumping and countervailing duties.

One of the most striking things about Canada's turn toward formal integration in the 1980s is the way it essentially reverses the logic of the first-generation theories of regional integration, from the 1960s. Neofunctionalists such as Ernst Haas argued that increasingly dense webs of "transactions" between modern economies would stitch together new networks of governmental and nongovernmental elites, foster mutual identification between societies, tame diplomatic conflicts, and create self-perpetuating momentum for further regional integration.[25] This way of thinking was deeply embedded in Keohane and Nye's interpretation of Canada-US bargaining. There is no question that the need to work together to resolve policy frictions fostered the emergence of the postwar transgovernmental network that managed bilateral relations. But it was transgovernmental cooperation that was predicated on the *avoidance* of formal integration wherever possible, with policy-makers on both sides preferring to stick with informal, ad hoc co-management of the bilateral agenda.[26] When deepening interdependence began to impose serious costs on powerful interest groups in the United States, they pushed hard to have adjustment costs dumped on other countries, and those pressures contributed to the further fragmentation of US foreign-policy making.[27] It was only after the transgovernmental network had been displaced, and established practices for informal co-management had clearly broken down, that Canadian elites were prepared to think seriously about formal institution building, mostly as a defensive strategy to try to hold on to traditional markets, rather than as a way to resolve new policy problems.

What Next?

Some Canadians – and perhaps some Canadian policy-makers as well – thought at the time that the CUSFTA would finally settle the new mechanics of the bilateral relationship. Twenty years later, however, and with the CUSFTA rolled into the more complex NAFTA agreement, many Canadians – and more than a few Canadian policy-makers – are still anxious about the way their relationship with the United States works.[28]

One kind of reaction to the more complex Canada-US landscape today is to just learn to live with it. On one hand, there are new pressures within the US that push the American government to be aggressive and parochial with Canada from time to time. Sometimes it will be possible to defuse those pressures through the kind of transnational lobbying pursued by Gotlieb's embassy in the 1980s; at other times, Canada will have no choice but to bend, by changing its own policies to fit those of the United States. On the other hand, the proliferation of blocking coalitions in the United States – now reinforced by the institutional constraints implied by the free trade regime – means that the White House will have a hard time making linkages against Canada, just as it did in the NEP and Iraq cases reviewed here. With both of these developments in mind, Canada's best strategy would presumably be to try to keep track of all of the shifting political alliances and institutional venues inside the Washington Beltway, take advantage of transnational alliances wherever possible, and live very carefully on the margins of what it can get away with.[29]

There are some signs that this was exactly the way that the Chrétien government approached the bilateral relationship during the 1990s and early 2000s. Jean Chrétien and Paul Martin both played up their efforts to rejuvenate the Washington embassy and play the transnational coalition-building game, following the model set down by Allan Gotlieb in the 1980s.[30] Both went ahead with foreign-policy challenges that they knew would provoke a strong reaction in the White House – Chrétien in Iraq and Martin on ballistic missile defence (BMD). Both knew that there were serious diplomatic and political risks involved, but both also seemed fairly confident that – as long as they didn't push too far – the US would be either unwilling or unable to pursue direct, overt linkages.[31] Chrétien even had the nerve to experiment with making linkage threats of his own, hinting that Canada would make its position on natural gas exports to the US conditional on a satisfactory outcome to the ongoing trade dispute over softwood lumber.[32]

Critics of the Iraq and BMD decisions worried at first about the prospect of hard linkages, but when those did not materialize, began to worry about soft linkages instead. The latter fears were not unwarranted, as I explained in the discussion of the Iraq dispute in Chapter 6. The evidence suggests that Bush administration officials did hold a grudge over Iraq, and were therefore less inclined to be responsive to Canadian requests on issues such as lumber, beef, and post-9/11 border security measures.

One could therefore argue that the outcome of the Iraq dispute supports what has long been said by proponents of greater foreign-policy independence: Canada can get away with directly challenging the US from time to time, as long as it is willing to pay a price indirectly.[33] The problem with this argument, and with Chrétien's approach to the bilateral relationship, is that the price to be paid through soft linkages will always be hard to assess, and may turn out to be far higher than Canada can afford. During the early Cold War, Canadian diplomats almost always had a pretty good sense of what the US would accept, and how serious American reaction to a provocative Canadian policy initiative might be. But in the more fragmented American system today, it is virtually impossible to guess where the line in the sand might be, and because no one in Washington is in a position to coordinate these things, the accumulation of many small grudges held by different bureaucratic and legislative players might add up to a tsunami of bilateral disruptions.

Canadian governments may nevertheless be more – rather than less – inclined to test the limits, because, while triggering a hard linkage is certain to cause serious domestic political trouble, it is much easier to avoid blame for provoking soft linkages, since by definition they are harder to identify and almost impossible to trace back to the original provocation. Opportunistic politicians might therefore be tempted to initiate bilateral disputes in order to score political points at home, particularly where they are facing an election or some other domestic political crisis.

This brings us to a second type of Canadian strategy for coping with the new bilateral relationship. A number of observers have argued for trying to recreate the special relationship by collaborating more closely with the US on national security issues, and/or by strengthening personal ties between prime minister and president.[34] Many proponents of this kind of argument are less concerned about testing the limits of Canada's autonomy and more concerned with Canada's maintaining its ability to influence policy outcomes in the US, and are therefore more concerned with soft linkages than with hard ones. Most people taking this position were critical of Chrétien's approach, but not all of them are Conservatives. Many of Martin's supporters also subscribed to this way of thinking, and strongly encouraged him to try to recreate the old spirit of partnership.[35]

But Canadian efforts to pursue influence in Washington, through collaboration and quiet diplomacy, were successful during the early Cold War decades for the same reason that the postwar diplomatic culture was also so salient then: authority over foreign-policy goals and bargaining strategies was relatively concentrated and hierarchically organized, so the political leadership was in a position to make sweeping, cross-issue trade-offs, even where the interests of some domestic interests would be compromised in the process.[36] Lyndon Johnson, for example, was able to tip the political balance in support of the Auto Pact in 1965 – in spite of strong opposition from US autoworkers and other interest groups – in part as an expression of thanks for the Pearson government's contribution of peacekeeping troops in Cyprus.[37] But the same fragmentation of power that displaced the postwar diplomatic culture also seriously undercut the White House's capacity to make *cooperative* linkages.

Some have argued that there was a new concentration of power after 9/11, effectively restoring the "imperial presidency"[38] and opening up new opportunities for Canada to trade support on security issues for influence in Washington. There is no question that Congress was temporarily paralyzed and that power shifted back toward the White House immediately after 9/11. But the structural changes of the 1970s were only partially offset, and for the most part only within certain areas directly related to certain aspects of national security (e.g., borders, defence contracting). The Bush administration's failure to secure a renewal of fast-track negotiating authority in 2007, and the Obama administration's inability to prevent the attachment of protectionist "Buy American" provisions to its economic stimulus package in early 2009, are among the many signs that power remains fragmented, raising serious questions about the executive branch's capacity to make broad, cross-issue trade-offs.

A third kind of argument that has recently been made about how to cope with the new bilateral relationship is based on a recognition that neither of the preceding proposals can be counted on to prevent linkages and contain American power. It is basically an extension of the logic behind the free trade negotiations, outlined above: ad hoc bargaining is not working out for Canada, so Canada needs to try to take bargaining out of the equation by entangling the US in formal institutions.

It wasn't long after the CUSFTA was signed and ratified that the first complaints were heard about the dispute resolution mechanism. In some of the early decisions, the panels ruled against US policies, and those policies were changed accordingly. But in the high-stakes softwood lumber dispute, the US lumber lobby – with tacit support from the Commerce Department – overrode the system by throwing up challenge after challenge, battering their Canadian competitors with countervailing and anti-dumping duties until they accepted "voluntary" export restraint agreements. Even some of the CUSFTA's strongest supporters have therefore argued that the CUSFTA/NAFTA regime needs to be strengthened, in order to set more effective limits on US trade remedy laws and to deal with issues that were left aside, like regulations, investment codes, and taxes.[39] A number of proposals have been offered over the last ten years or so, for an improved NAFTA, a common "security perimeter," a customs union, or a "North American community of laws."[40]

The most immediate problem with all of these "deep integration" proposals is that the United States has far less to gain from them than Canada does, and its general lack of interest is likely to be reinforced by the severe recession that erupted in the fall of 2008. A few commentators suggested in the immediate aftermath of 9/11 that it might be possible to capture the attention of American policy-makers by offering greater support on homeland security issues.[41] But the Bush administration – and indeed virtually everyone in the United States – expected this sort of cooperation and support from Canada anyway, and the last thing they wanted to do in the first years after 9/11 was to "streamline" the border. Others have argued that Ottawa might draw in the US by pushing for a much more ambitious legal and regulatory harmonization, going beyond what has been pursued since 2005 in the Security and Prosperity Partnership of North America, as a way to improve efficiencies and increase the region's competitiveness in world markets.[42] There are some in Washington who would like to pursue this agenda, but it is not enough to win the attention of a new administration that is hard-pressed by two wars and a global economic meltdown.

Even if the stars do suddenly align themselves for further integration in the near future, we should not be too confident that this will fix all our problems. The CUSFTA dispute resolution mechanism was seen by many as an extraordinary diplomatic coup for Canada, and it did dampen the application of US trade remedy laws, but the ease with which the lumber lobby smashed its way through the process suggests that even formal integration cannot completely contain US power and parochialism.

It may be that going farther down the road of formal integration is the best way – perhaps the only way – to hold on to a measure of Canadian autonomy in the face of an increasingly complex and unpredictable bargaining relationship with the United States. If that is so, then it is an extraordinary historical development, one that would have been fantastic and deeply troubling to the Canadian policy-makers who helped cultivate the postwar diplomatic culture just a couple of generations ago. Nothing is certain about where we might go from here, except perhaps that there is no going back.

Notes

Chapter 1: The Social Foundations of the Special Relationship

1 David Haglund, "The US-Canada Relationship: How 'Special' Is America's Longest Unbroken Alliance?" in *America's Special Relationships*, ed. John Dumbrell and Axel Schäfer (London: Routledge, 2009).

2 K.J. Holsti, "Canada and the United States," in *Conflict in World Politics*, ed. Steven Spiegel and Kenneth Waltz (Cambridge: Winthrop, 1971), 71.

3 Allan E. Gotlieb, "Canada-US Relations: The Rules of the Game," *SAIS Review* 2 (Summer 1982): 172-87.

4 A.D.P. Heeney and Livingston T. Merchant, *Canada and the United States: Principles for Partnership* (Ottawa: Queen's Printer, 1965).

5 For example, Patrick Lennox, *At Home and Abroad: The Canada-US Relationship and Canada's Place in the World* (Vancouver: UBC Press, 2009).

6 The quote is from Arnold Wolfers, *Collaboration and Discord* (Baltimore: The Johns Hopkins University Press, 1962), 97. The dismissal is most plain in David A. Baldwin, "The Myths of the Special Relationship," *International Studies Quarterly* 12 (June 1968): 127-51.

7 Stephen Clarkson, *Uncle Sam and Us: Globalization, Neoconservatism and the Canadian State* (Toronto: University of Toronto Press, 2002).

8 Gotlieb, "The Rules of the Game," 182-83.

9 For example, Pauline Jewett, "The Menace Is the Message," in *An Independent Foreign Policy for Canada?* ed. Stephen Clarkson (Toronto: McClelland and Stewart, 1968).

10 A.F.W. Plumptre, "Tit for Tat," in Clarkson, *An Independent Foreign Policy for Canada?*

11 Ibid., 45.

12 Brian Bow, "Rethinking 'Retaliation' in Canada-US Relations," in *An Independent Foreign Policy for Canada? Challenges and Choices for the Future*, ed. Brian Bow and Patrick Lennox (Toronto: University of Toronto Press, 2008).

13 Sean M. Shore, "No Fences Make Good Neighbors: The Development of the Canadian-US Security Community, 1871-1940," in *Security Communities*, ed. Emanuel Adler and Michael N. Barnett (Cambridge, UK: Cambridge University Press, 1998).

14 Norman Hillmer and J.L. Granatstein, *Empire to Umpire: Canada and the World to the 1990s* (Toronto: Copp Clark Longman, 1994), ch. 1.

15 R.D. Cuff and J.L. Granatstein, *Ties that Bind: Canada-US Cooperation during Wartime* (Toronto: Samuel Stevens, 1977), 37.

16 Ibid., ch. 5.

17 John Herd Thompson and Stephen J. Randall, *Canada and the United States: Ambivalent Allies*, 3rd ed. (Athens: University of Georgia Press, 2002), ch. 6.

18 Cuff and Granatstein, *Ties that Bind*, ch. 5.

19 Joseph T. Jockel, *No Boundaries Upstairs: Canada, the United States, and the Origins of North American Air Defence, 1945-58* (Vancouver: UBC Press, 1987).

20 R.D. Cuff and J.L. Granatstein, *American Dollars, Canadian Prosperity: Canadian-American Economic Relations, 1945-50* (Toronto: Samuel Stevens, 1978); Robert Bothwell and David Kilbourn, *C.D. Howe: A Biography* (Toronto: McClelland and Stewart, 1978), esp. chs. 3-4.

21 James C. Bennett, *The Anglosphere Challenge: Why the English-Speaking Nations Will Lead the Way in the Twenty-First Century* (New York: Rowman and Littlefield, 2007).

22 Alex Danchev, "On Specialness," *International Affairs* 72, 4 (1996): 703-10; John Dumbrell, *A Special Relationship: Anglo-American Relations from the Cold War to Iraq* (Basingstoke, UK: Palgrave Macmillan, 2006).

23 The following characterization of the larger "diplomatic culture" is based on interviews with former Canadian and American officials, and on the descriptions in Holsti, "Canada and the United States"; Gotlieb, "The Rules of the Game," esp. 183-84; and Denis Stairs, "The Political Culture of Canadian Foreign Policy," *Canadian Journal of Political Science* 15 (December 1982): 667-90.

24 The distinction is spelled out clearly in John S. Odell, *Negotiating the World Economy* (Ithaca, NY: Cornell University Press, 2002), esp. 2 and ch. 2.

25 K.J. Holsti and Thomas Allen Levy, "Bilateral Institutions and Transgovernmental Relations between Canada and the United States," in *Canada and the United States: Transnational and Transgovernmental Relations*, ed. Annette Baker Fox, Alfred O. Hero, and Joseph Nye (New York: Columbia University Press, 1976).

26 Edelgard Mahant and Graeme S. Mount, *Invisible and Inaudible in Washington: American Policies toward Canada* (Vancouver: UBC Press, 1999), ch. 1.

27 "Never Play Leapfrog with a Unicorn," *National Post*, 9 April 2001, 18.

28 James W. Davis, *Threats and Promises: The Pursuit of International Influence* (Baltimore: The Johns Hopkins University Press, 2000), 13.

29 Rick Atkinson and Barton Gellman, "Iraq Trying to Shelter Jets in Iran, US Says," *Washington Post*, 29 January 1991, A1.

30 Jonathan Kirshner, *Currency and Coercion: The Political Economy of International Monetary Power* (Princeton, NJ: Princeton University Press, 1997), 63-82.

31 I.M. Destler, *Managing an Alliance: The Politics of US-Japanese Relations* (Washington, DC: Brookings Institution, 1976), 23-45.

32 Donald L. Wyman, "Dependence and Conflict: US Relations with Mexico, 1920-1975," in *Diplomatic Dispute: US Conflict with Iran, Japan, and Mexico*, ed. Robert L. Paarlberg et al. (Cambridge, MA: Harvard University Center for International Affairs, 1978), esp. 87.

33 Shore, "No Fences Make Good Neighbors," 353-56.

34 Robert Bothwell and John Kirton, "'A Sweet Little Country': American Attitudes toward Canada, 1925 to 1963," *Queen's Quarterly* 90 (Winter 1983): 1079.

35 J. Legere, "Memorandum for the President: Canadian Chronology," 13 February 1963, John F. Kennedy Presidential Library, JFK National Security Files.

36 Paul Martin, *A Very Public Life. Vol. 2, So Many Worlds* (Toronto: Deneau, 1985), esp. 195-98.

37 US Embassy in Ottawa to State Department, 14 March 1955, in *Foreign Relations of the United States, 1955-57*, vol. 15 (Washington, DC: United States Government Printing Office, 1990), 698.

38 For example, Denis Stairs, "Liberalism and the Triumph of Efficiency in Canada-US Relations," *ISUMA* 1, 1 (Spring 2000): 13.

39 Leonard Legault interview, Ottawa, 21 June 2001.

40 Don Page, "The Representation of China in the United Nations: Canadian Perspectives and Initiatives, 1949-1971," in *Reluctant Adversaries: Canada and the People's Republic of China*, ed. Paul M. Evans and Michael B. Frolic (Toronto: University of Toronto Press, 1991).

41 Robert Bothwell, "Canada-United States Relations: Options for the 1970s," *International Journal* 58 (Winter 2002-3): 65-88.

42 Roger F. Swanson, "The Ford Interlude and the US-Canada Relationship," *American Review of Canadian Studies* 8 (Spring 1978): 3-17.

43 Thomas E. Cronin, "A Resurgent Congress and the Imperial Presidency," *Political Science Quarterly* 95 (Summer 1980): 209-37; Charles F. Doran and Joel J. Sokolsky, *Canada and*

Congress: Lobbying in Washington (Halifax: Dalhousie University Centre for Foreign Policy Studies, 1985).

44 Peter C. Dobell, "Negotiating with the United States," *International Journal* 36, 1 (Winter 1980-81): 20-21; Stephen Sandelius and Charles R. Foster, "Economic Shift to Sunbelt Reflected in Foreign Policy," *International Perspectives* (May/June 1981): 11-14.

45 Vladimir Toumanoff interview, Washington, DC, 28 June 2002.

46 Two important examples are: Kenneth A. Oye, "The Domain of Choice: International Constraints and Carter Administration Foreign Policy," in *Eagle Entangled: US Foreign Policy in a Complex World*, ed. Kenneth Oye, Donald Rothchild, and Robert J. Lieber (New York: Longman, 1979), esp. 13-17; Arthur A. Stein, "The Politics of Linkage," *World Politics* 33 (October 1980): 62-81.

47 There have also been applications of social psychology experiments that show that coercive linkages are inherently provocative, and therefore risky, because they draw the target's attention away from the issue at hand and toward questions of power and vulnerability: Morton Deutsch and Robert M. Krauss, "The Effect of Threat upon Interpersonal Bargaining," *Journal of Abnormal and Social Psychology* 6 (1960): 181-89.

48 John M. Owen, "How Liberalism Produces Democratic Peace," *International Security* 19, 2 (1994): 87-124; Michael N. Barnett, *Dialogues in Arab Politics: Negotiations in Regional Order* (New York: Columbia University Press, 2000), chs. 1, 7; Amitav Acharya, *The Quest for Identity: The International Relations of Southeast Asia* (Oxford: Oxford University Press, 2000), ch. 1.

49 Peter J. Katzenstein, Robert O. Keohane, and Stephen D. Krasner, "International Organization and the Study of World Politics," *International Organization* 52, 4 (Autumn 1998): 671-72.

50 James Fearon and Alexander Wendt, "Rationalism vs. Constructivism: A Skeptical View," in *Handbook of International Relations*, ed. Walter Carlsnaes, Thomas Risse, and Beth A. Simmons (London: Sage, 2002).

51 Andrew Moravcsik, "Is Something Rotten in the State of Denmark? Constructivism and European Integration," *Journal of European Public Policy* 6, 4 (1999): 669-81. See also Stephen G. Brooks and William C. Wohlforth, "Power, Globalization, and the End of the Cold War: Re-evaluating a Landmark Case for Ideas," *International Security* 25, 3 (2000-1): 5-53.

52 Robert O. Keohane, and Joseph S. Nye Jr., *Power and Interdependence: World Politics in Transition* (Boston: Little, Brown, 1977).

53 Arthur Andrew, *The Rise and Fall of a Middle Power: Canadian Diplomacy from King to Mulroney* (Toronto: Lorimer, 1993); Andrew Cohen, *While Canada Slept: How We Lost Our Place in the World* (Toronto: McClelland and Stewart, 2004).

54 For example, John W. Holmes, *Life with Uncle: The Canadian-American Relationship* (Toronto: University of Toronto Press, 1981), 61-76.

55 Adam Chapnick, "The Golden Age: A Canadian Foreign Policy Paradox," *International Journal* 64, 1 (Winter 2008-9): 205-22.

Chapter 2: Power, Interdependence, and Ideas

1 Robert O. Keohane and Joseph S. Nye Jr., *Power and Interdependence: World Politics in Transition* (Boston: Little, Brown, 1977), ch. 7.

2 For an extended discussion of the pattern of bilateral disputes and their outcomes, from 1950-2000, with supporting graphs and citations, see my dissertation: Brian Bow, "The Missing Link: Bargaining Norms, Transgovernmental Networks, and Canada-US Relations," PhD dissertation, Cornell University, 2003.

3 Brian Bow, "Parties and Partisanship in Canadian Defence Policy," *International Journal* 64, 1 (Winter 2008-9): 67-88.

4 Robert O. Keohane and Joseph S. Nye Jr., *"Power and Interdependence* Revisited," *International Organization* 41 (Summer 1987): 728.

5 William Mark Habeeb, *Power and Tactics in International Negotiation* (Baltimore: The Johns Hopkins University Press, 1988), esp. chs. 2-3.

6 Hans J. Morgenthau, *Politics among Nations*, 3rd ed. (New York: Knopf, 1973), 185; Thomas Risse-Kappen, *Cooperation among Democracies: The European Influence on US Foreign Policy* (Princeton, NJ: Princeton University Press, 1997), ch. 2.

7 Andrew Cohen, *While Canada Slept: How We Lost Our Place in the World* (Toronto: McClelland and Stewart, 2003); John J. Noble, "Canada-US Relations in the Post-Iraq War Era: Stop the Drift towards Irrelevance," *Policy Options* 24 (May 2003): 19-24.

8 The phrase "strategic restraint" is borrowed, and the general theoretical argument is adapted, from G. John Ikenberry, *After Victory: Institutions, Strategic Restraint and the Rebuilding of Order after Major Wars* (Princeton, NJ: Princeton University Press, 2000).

9 The reintensification of the Cold War confrontation began after the Soviet invasion of Afghanistan in 1979. The initial defence spending increases took place under Pierre Trudeau's Liberals, and were continued (for a few years) by Brian Mulroney's Conservatives: Brian Bow, "Parties and Partisanship in Canadian Defence Policy," *International Journal* 64, 1 (Winter 2008-9): 67-88.

10 Allan Gotlieb, *I'll Be with You in a Minute, Mr. Ambassador: The Education of a Canadian Diplomat in Washington* (Toronto: University of Toronto Press, 1989), esp. ch. 2.

11 This hunch is echoed in Charles Doran, *Forgotten Partnership: US-Canada Relations Today* (New York: The Johns Hopkins University Press, 1984), 49.

12 The United States is still far less trade-dependent – at about 12 percent of GDP – than most Organisation for Economic Co-operation and Development (OECD) countries, but trade with Canada matters much more to the US today, and is much more likely to directly affect the livelihoods of larger numbers of Americans today than it was in the mid-1960s. A little over forty years later (twenty of those under free trade), the share of American exports going to Canada has gone up to nearly 20 percent of the US total. Meanwhile, sales to the US have come to represent a staggering 85 percent of Canada's total exports.

13 Doran, *Forgotten Partnership*, 22-24.

14 Donald Barry, "The Politics of 'Exceptionalism': Canada and the United States as a Distinctive International Relationship," *Dalhousie Review* 60 (Spring 1980): 125-26.

15 R. Harrison Wagner, "Economic Interdependence, Bargaining Power and Political Influence," *International Organization* 42 (Summer 1988): 461-83.

16 C. Robert Dickerman, "Transgovernmental Challenge and Response in Scandinavia and North America," *International Organization* 30 (Spring 1979): 213-40; Bengt Sundelius, "Coping with Transnationalism in Northern Europe," *West European Politics* 3 (May 1980): 219-29.

17 For a slightly different but essentially compatible framing of this trade-off, see Doran, *Forgotten Partnership*, 22.

18 G. John Ikenberry, "An Institutional Approach to American Foreign Economic Policy," *International Organization* 42 (Winter 1988): 219-43.

19 One notable exception is Allan Gotlieb, "Canada-US Relations: The Rules of the Game," *SAIS Review* 2 (Summer 1982): 177-87, and *I'll Be with You in a Minute*, esp. ch. 2.

20 Keohane and Nye, *Power and Interdependence*, 182.

21 For example, A.E. Safarian, "The Web of Repercussions," in *An Independent Foreign Policy for Canada?* ed. Stephen Clarkson (Toronto: McClelland and Stewart, 1968).

22 Denis Stairs, "Liberalism and the Triumph of Efficiency in Canada-US Relations," *ISUMA* 1, 1 (Spring 2000): 13.

23 Peter C. Dobell, "Negotiating with the United States," *International Journal* 36, 1 (Winter 1980-81): 24.

24 Lawrence Martin, *The Presidents and the Prime Ministers* (Toronto: Doubleday, 1982), 10-12.

25 These tests are predicated on the logic of "congruence testing," which involves getting more theoretical leverage out of a small number of cases by increasing the number of expectations derived from the theory that can be checked against observations "within" the case: Alexander L. George and Andrew Bennett, *Case Studies and Theory Development in the Social Sciences* (Cambridge, MA: MIT Press, 2005), ch. 9.

26 Ideally, counterfactual thought experiments are based on fully developed deductive theories that clearly specify particular choices or outcomes, given relevant conditions: Philip Tetlock and Aaron Belkin, "Counterfactual Thought Experiments in World Politics," in *Counterfactual Thought Experiments in World Politics,* ed. Philip Tetlock and Aaron Belkin (Princeton, NJ: Princeton University Press, 1996). Since there are few, if any, such theories in international

relations, it seems appropriate to follow less restrictive standards of "reasonableness": Richard Ned Lebow, "What's So Different about a Counterfactual?" *World Politics* 52 (July 2000): 577-85.

27 R. Harrison Wagner, "Economic Interdependence, Bargaining Power, and Political Influence," *International Organization* 42 (Summer 1988): 470-71.

28 David A. Baldwin, "Interdependence and Power: A Conceptual Analysis," *International Organization* 34 (Autumn 1980): 471-506.

29 Keohane and Nye, *Power and Interdependence,* 16-17.

30 James D. Fearon, "Signaling Foreign Policy Interests: Tying Hands vs. Sinking Costs," *Journal of Conflict Resolution* 41 (February 1997): 68-90.

31 For similar attention to "norm talk," for similar purposes, see Nina Tannenwald, "The Nuclear Taboo: The United States and the Normative Basis of Nuclear Non-Use," *International Organization* 53 (Summer 1999): 433-68.

Chapter 3: Nuclear Weapons, 1959-63

1 Jocelyn Ghent-Mallet, "Deploying Nuclear Weapons," in *Canadian Foreign Policy: Selected Cases,* ed. Don Munton and John Kirton (Scarborough, ON: Prentice Hall, 1992), 102.

2 Canada also procured the CF-104 Starfighter, which was deployed for "strike-reconnaissance" in Europe, and the Honest John short-range artillery rocket, for use by Canadian Army troops in West Germany.

3 Don Munton has questioned the conventional wisdom that these systems technically "required" nuclear weapons: "Going Fission: Tales and Truths about Canada's Nuclear Weapons," *International Journal* 51 (Summer 1996): 514-20. This is an important matter in evaluating Diefenbaker's decision to hold out for conventional alternatives. For the purposes of this study, however, the important points are: (1) There was a virtual consensus at the time among military planners in both countries that – mainly because of the inaccuracy of the missiles – these weapons needed to be nuclear-armed in order to make an "effective" contribution to continental defence; and (2) The Kennedy administration made that assessment the basis for its bargaining position.

4 Ghent-Mallet, "Deploying Nuclear Weapons," 102.

5 H. Basil Robinson, *Diefenbaker's World: A Populist in Foreign Affairs* (Toronto: University of Toronto Press, 1989), 4, 11, 48, 151-56.

6 For a general argument that places this decision to delay in broader, comparative perspective, see Brian Bow, "Defence Dilemmas: Continental Defence Cooperation from Bomarc to BMD," *Canadian Foreign Policy* 15, 1 (Winter 2008-9).

7 Ghent-Mallet, "Deploying Nuclear Weapons," 102. For a recent alternative reading of news media views on the issue, see Mark Eaton, "Canadian Editorial Opinion and the 1963 Nuclear Weapon Acquisition Debate," *American Review of Canadian Studies* 35, 4 (Winter 2005): 641-66.

8 Don Munton and R.B. Byers, "Canadian Defence, Nuclear Arms, and Public Opinion: Consensus and Controversy," paper presented to the Annual Meeting of the Canadian Political Science Association, Vancouver, 1983.

9 Robinson, *Diefenbaker's World,* 15-17.

10 For a more extensive account of the tensions surrounding the Rostow memo, see ibid., 206-8, 269-70.

11 Ibid., 195-96, 204-6.

12 Ottawa Embassy to State Department, 24 May 1961, John F. Kennedy Presidential Library [JFK Library], JFK National Security Files.

13 For the US side, ibid. For the Canadian side, Basil Robinson interview, Ottawa, 31 May 2001.

14 Ottawa Embassy to State Department, 12 October 1961, JFK Library, JFK National Security Files.

15 Ghent-Mallet, "Deploying Nuclear Weapons," 103; Ottawa Embassy to State Department, 11 April 1962, JFK Library, JFK National Security Files.

16 Ottawa Embassy to State Department, 8 May 1962, JFK Library, JFK National Security Files. See also Legere, "Memorandum for the President: Canadian Chronology," 13 February 1963, JFK Library, JFK National Security Files.

17 Jocelyn Ghent-Mallet and Don Munton, "Confronting Kennedy and the Missiles in Cuba," in Munton and Kirton, *Canadian Foreign Policy;* Robinson, *Diefenbaker's World,* 284-95.

18 Knowlton Nash, *Kennedy and Diefenbaker: Fear and Loathing across the Undefended Border* (Toronto: McClelland and Stewart, 1990), 206.

19 Ghent-Mallet, "Deploying Nuclear Weapons," 102.

20 Robinson, *Diefenbaker's World,* 298.

21 Legere, "Memorandum for the President: Canadian Chronology."

22 State Department to Ottawa Embassy, 10 January 1963, JFK Library, JFK National Security Files; Ottawa Embassy to State Department, 11 January 1963, JFK Library, JFK National Security Files.

23 Ghent-Mallet, "Deploying Nuclear Weapons," 104-5; Peyton V. Lyon, *Canada in World Affairs. Vol. 12, 1961-63* (Toronto: Oxford University Press, 1968), 136.

24 Ottawa Embassy to State Department, 2 January 1963, JFK Library, JFK National Security Files.

25 John A. Munro and Alex I. Inglis, eds., *Mike: Memoirs of the Right Honourable Lester B. Pearson,* vol. 3 (Toronto: University of Toronto Press, 1975), 69-75.

26 The text of Hellyer's memo is reproduced in Peter C. Newman, *The Distemper of Our Times* (Toronto: McClelland and Stewart, 1968), 426-29.

27 Denis Smith, *Gentle Patriot: A Political Biography of Walter Gordon* (Edmonton: Hurtig, 1973), 119. See also Howard H. Lentner, "Foreign Policy Decision-Making: The Case of Canada and Nuclear Weapons," *World Politics* 29 (October 1976): 29-66.

28 John G. Diefenbaker, *One Canada: Memoirs of the Right Honourable John G. Diefenbaker,* vol. 3 (Toronto: Macmillan, 1977), 104.

29 Ottawa Embassy to State Department, 27 January 1963, JFK Library, JFK National Security Files.

30 Butterworth took credit for the press release, and explained the rationale behind it, in a 1974 interview: Ghent-Mallet, "Deploying Nuclear Weapons," fn. 45. Confirmed in Ball to Tyler, 28 January 1963, 1:00 p.m., JFK Library, George Ball Files, Memoranda of Telephone Conversations.

31 Nash, *Kennedy and Diefenbaker,* 253; Ball to Bundy, 31 January 1963, 10:00 a.m., and Ball to JFK, 31 January 1963, 7:30 p.m., both in JFK Library, George Ball Files, Memoranda of Telephone Conversations.

32 A CTV poll taken on 10 February found that 67 percent of Canadians disapproved of Diefenbaker's handling of the nuclear weapons issue, and only 39 percent thought the State Department's 30 January press release was "undue interference in Canadian affairs": Ottawa Embassy to State Department, n.d., JFK Library, JFK National Security Files.

33 Donald M. Fleming, *So Very Near: The Political Memoirs of the Honourable Donald M. Fleming,* vol. 2 (Toronto: McClelland and Stewart, 1985), ch. 5.

34 Robinson, *Diefenbaker's World,* 308.

35 Nash, *Kennedy and Diefenbaker,* 256. See also Ghent-Mallet, "Deploying Nuclear Weapons," 111-12.

36 See, for example, Ball to Bundy, 7 February 1963, 12:20 p.m., JFK Library, George Ball Files, Memoranda of Telephone Conversations.

37 Nash, *Kennedy and Diefenbaker,* 254.

38 Edward Kolodziej, *French International Policy under de Gaulle and Pompidou: The Politics of Grandeur* (Ithaca, NY: Cornell University Press, 1974), 69-86.

39 Frank Costigliola, *France and the United States: The Cold Alliance since World War Two* (New York: Twayne Publishing, 1992), 138, 145, 140-41.

40 Rusk to Gavin, 5 May 1961, *Foreign Relations of the United States [FRUS], 1961-63,* vol. 13 (Washington, DC: US Government Printing Office, 1992), 654-56. See also Robert S. Norris, Andrew S. Burrows, and Richard W. Fieldhouse, *Nuclear Weapons Databook. Vol. 5, British, French, and Chinese Nuclear Weapons* (Boulder, CO: Westview Press, 1994), ch. 4, esp. 190, n. 49; Eileen Shanahan, "Washington Hopeful of Averting Tariff War with Europeans," *New York Times,* 8 August 1963, 1, 32; "US Raises Duties as a Retaliation for Chicken Levy," *New York Times,* 5 December 1963, 1, 30; Kolodziej, *French International Policy,* 81.

41 See, for example, Rusk to Gavin, 21 May 1961, *FRUS,* 670.

42 State Department to Ottawa Embassy, 10 January 1963, JFK Library, JFK National Security Files.
43 Charles Lynch, "Secret US Paper – Ace Up PM's Sleeve," *Vancouver Province*, 27 March 1963, 1.
44 David Cox, "Canada and NORAD, 1958-1978: A Cautionary Retrospective," *Aurora Papers* 1 (Winter 1985): 26-33.
45 Kelly, "In Support of Proposals to Amend the Oil Import Program," n.d., JFK Library, Myer Feldman Files, Box 23.
46 State Department to Ottawa Embassy, 23 November 1963, JFK Library, JFK National Security Files.
47 Washington Embassy to External Affairs, 23 April 1963, National Archives of Canada [NAC], RG 25, vol. 5662, file 14405-U-16-40, pt. 4.
48 Thomas W. Zeiler, *American Trade and Power in the 1960s* (New York: Columbia University Press, 1962), 90-99.
49 Ibid., 54-56, 65-66. See also Bundy to Bundy, Rostow, Johnson, "Subject: Possible Canadian Quotas," 25 May 1962, JFK Library, JFK National Security Files.
50 Nash, *Kennedy and Diefenbaker*, 11.
51 Basil Robinson interview, Ottawa, 31 May 2001.
52 This pattern is reflected in a State Department report on the "resumption of communication" after the spring 1963 election: Legere to Bundy, "Subject: Follow-up with Canadians on Hyannis Port," n.d., JFK Library, White House Staff Files, Myer Feldman.
53 Basil Robinson interview, Ottawa, 31 May 2001.
54 Robinson, *Diefenbaker's World*, 35, 314-15.
55 Basil Robinson interview, Ottawa, 31 May 2001.
56 See, for example, Robinson, *Diefenbaker's World*, 203-9; Memorandum of Conversation, "President's Trip to Ottawa, May 16-18, 1961," 17 May 1961, JFK Library, JFK National Security Files.
57 Basil Robinson interview, Ottawa, 31 May 2001.
58 State Department, "Guidelines for Policy and Operations: Canada," March 1962, JFK Library, JFK National Security Files, 9.
59 Legere to Bundy, "Foreign Relations Committee Hearing on Canada," 1 February 1963, JFK Library, JFK National Security Files; Legere, "Memorandum for the President: Canadian Chronology," 13 February 1963, JFK Library, JFK National Security Files.
60 "Meeting between the President of the United States and the Prime Minister of Canada ... at Hyannis Port, Mass. – May 10-11, 1963 – Final Report," n.d., NAC, RG 25, ser. A-4, vol. 9788.
61 Greg Donaghy, *Tolerant Allies: Canada and the United States, 1963-1968* (Montreal and Kingston: McGill-Queen's University Press, 2002), 16-21.
62 A.D.P. Heeney and Livingston T. Merchant, *Canada-United States Relations: Principles for Partnership* (Ottawa: Queen's Printer, 1965).
63 Ghent-Mallet, "Deploying Nuclear Weapons," 113-14.
64 For a more detailed treatment of the Pearson-Kennedy/Johnson period, see Donaghy, *Tolerant Allies*.
65 This skeptical reflex was reflected in a series of left-nationalist academic studies warning of Canada's slide toward political subordination and/or absorption: e.g., George Grant, *Lament for a Nation: The Defeat of Canadian Nationalism* (Ottawa: Carleton University Press, 1965).
66 John Hilliker and Don Barry, *Canada's Department of External Affairs*, vol. 2 (Montreal and Kingston: McGill-Queen's University Press, 1995), 250-56.
67 I.M. Destler, *Presidents, Bureaucrats, and Foreign Policy* (Princeton, NJ: Princeton University Press, 1972), ch. 5.
68 Generally, see, for example, Thomas M. Franck and Edward Weisband, *Foreign Policy by Congress* (New York: Oxford University Press, 1979), 6-8.

Chapter 4: Arctic Waters, 1969-71

1 Ted Lee interview, Ottawa, 11 June 2001.
2 Ann L. Hollick, "Canadian-American Relations: Law of the Sea," *International Organization* 28 (Autumn 1974): 755-80.

3   Christopher J. Kirkey, "The Arctic Waters Pollution Prevention Initiatives: Canada's Response to an American Challenge," *International Journal of Canadian Studies* 13 (1996): 55.
4   Gerald Stoner interview, Ottawa, 22 July 2001.
5   Edgar J. Dosman, *The National Interest: The Politics of Northern Development, 1968-75* (Toronto: McClelland and Stewart, 1975), 46-48.
6   John J. Kirton and Don Munton, "The *Manhattan* Voyages and Their Aftermath," in *The Politics of the Northwest Passage*, ed. Franklyn Griffiths (Montreal and Kingston: McGill-Queen's University Press, 1987), 75-76.
7   Abraham Rotstein, "Canada: The New Nationalism," *Foreign Affairs* 55 (October 1976): 101.
8   US Embassy reports referred to a current of "blatant anti-US jingoism" and argued that the Canadian press was "erratic" and "more interested in controversy and confrontation than sense or accuracy": Ottawa Embassy to Secretary of State, 21 February 1970, US National Archives and Records Administration [USNARA], RG 59, Subject-Numeric Files 1970-73, Box 2162, Political and Defense.
9   In fact, a plurality of respondents to one poll believed that Canada "own[ed]" the North Pole: Kirton and Munton, "The *Manhattan* Voyages," 86.
10 Gordon Robertson interview, Ottawa, 18 June 2001; Mitchell Sharp interview, Ottawa, 14 June 2001.
11 Thorgrimsson, "Notes for Suggested Changes to Memorandum to Cabinet on Ratification of the Shelf Convention and Possible Adoption of 12-Mile Territorial Sea, Forthcoming Meeting with External Affairs," 25 July 1969, National Archives of Canada [NAC], RG 21, vol. 198. On EMR's general opposition to the AWPPA and the ICJ reservation, see Crosby to McNabb and Isbister, 31 March 1970, NAC, RG 21, vol. 216.
12 Ivan L. Head and Pierre Trudeau, *The Canadian Way: Shaping Canada's Foreign Policy, 1968-84* (Toronto: McClelland and Stewart, 1995), 40-41.
13 The multilateral diplomacy that followed the Canadian decision to go ahead with the AWPPA legislation is described in Kirton and Munton, "The *Manhattan* Voyages," 93-96, and Roger D. McConchie and Robert S. Reid, "Canadian Foreign Policy and International Straits," in *Canadian Foreign Policy and the Law of the Sea*, ed. Barbara Johnson and Mark Zacher (Vancouver: UBC Press, 1977), 173-74.
14 R. Michael M'Gonigle and Mark Zacher, "Canadian Foreign Policy and the Control of Marine Pollution," in Johnson and Zacher, *Canadian Foreign Policy and the Law of the Sea*, 113-17.
15 For example: Rogers to Hickel (draft), 31 December 1969, USNARA, RG 59, Subject-Numeric Files 1967-69, Box 2927; Ottawa Embassy to Secretary of State, "Arctic Sovereignty: Embassy Advises against Public Confrontation with GOC," 23 February 1970, USNARA, RG 59, Subject-Numeric Files 1970-73, Box 2163, Political and Defense.
16 Kirton and Munton, "The *Manhattan* Voyages," 85.
17 The Cabinet debates over the ICJ reservation are laid out in detail in Kirton and Munton, "The *Manhattan* Voyages," 89-90, and Head and Trudeau, *The Canadian Way*, 53-54. Details were confirmed in interviews with former Canadian officials.
18 Volpe to Rogers, 14 March 1970, USNARA, RG 59, Subject-Numeric Files 1970-73, Box 2911, Science.
19 Head and Trudeau, *The Canadian Way*, 46-48; Ivan Head interview, Vancouver, 3 July 2001.
20 There is no archival record of this call. Head and Trudeau say that it was an ordinary, businesslike one, but Dosman describes it as aggressive and threatening, with an implied coercive linkage to ongoing negotiations on oil. Cf. Head and Trudeau, *The Canadian Way*, 52, and Dosman, *The National Interest*, 58.
21 "Canadian Legislation on the Arctic," State Department Memorandum of Conversation, 20 March 1970 (two parts), USNARA, RG 59, Subject-Numeric Files 1970-73, Box 2911, Science.
22 Johnson to Nixon, "Memorandum for the President, Canadian Legislation on the Arctic," 21 March 1970, USNARA, RG 59, Subject-Numeric Files 1970-73, Box 2911, Science.
23 Memorandum of Conversation, "Imminent Canadian Legislation on Arctic Pollution, Territorial Sea and Fisheries," 7 April 1970, USNARA, RG 59, Subject-Numeric Files 1970-73, Box 2163, Political and Defense.

24 The account of this conversation, and the circumstances surrounding it, is based on Head and Trudeau, *The Canadian Way*, 54-56, and Ivan Head interview, Vancouver, 3 July 2001. Later reports, citing unidentified sources, said that Nixon, enraged by Canadian inflexibility, had refused the call: John Best, "Nixon Was So Angry He Refused Trudeau's Call," *Globe and Mail*, 25 August 1973, 7.

25 Canada, House of Commons, *Debates*, 16 April 1970, 5941.

26 Leonard Legault interview, Ottawa, 21 May 2001.

27 State Department Press Release 121, 15 April 1970.

28 Rome Embassy to Secretary of Defense 1857, 16 April 1970, USNARA, RG 59, Subject-Numeric Files 1970-73, Box 2911, Science. Eliot to Kissinger, attachment ("Subject: Canadian Arctic Legislation"), 14 April 1970, USNARA, RG 59, Subject-Numeric Files 1970-73, Box 2911, Science. See also Canada, House of Commons, *Debates*, "Appendix 'A,'" 15 April 1970, 5823-24.

29 Peter Towe interview, Ottawa, 14 May 2001.

30 Ann Hollick interview, Washington, DC, 10 February 2003; Bernard Oxman correspondence, 18 February 2003.

31 Ottawa Embassy to Secretary of State, 26 August 1970, USNARA, RG 59, Subject-Numeric Files 1970-73, Box 2911, Science.

32 Mitchell Sharp, "A Ship and Sovereignty in the North," *Globe and Mail*, 18 September 1969, 7.

33 Robert Russo, "Latest Nixon Tapes Show Contempt for Trudeau," *Globe and Mail*, 18 March 2002, A2.

34 Mitchell Sharp interview, Ottawa, 14 June 2001.

35 The following examples are from McConchie and Reid, "Canadian Foreign Policy and International Straits," 178.

36 Dosman, *The National Interest*, 58.

37 Washington Embassy to External Affairs, 19 February 1970, NAC, RG 20, vol. 1637; "Canada-US Oil Discussion," Cabinet Minutes/Conclusions, 12 February 1970, NAC, RG 2, series A-5a, vol. 6359.

38 United States Cabinet Task Force on Oil Import Control (USCTFOIC), *The Oil Import Question: A Report on the Relationship of Oil Imports and the National Security* (Washington, DC: US Government Printing Office, 1970), 94, 105-6.

39 Ritchie, "Interdepartmental Oil Committee – January 13, 1970," 14 January 1970, NAC, RG 20, vol. 1637; Clark to Warren, 9 February 1970, NAC, RG 20, vol. 1637.

40 Dosman, *The National Interest*, 58.

41 On the US side: USCTFOIC, *The Oil Import Question*, 94. On the Canadian side: Kirton and Munton, "The *Manhattan* Voyages," 85-86, 93. Energy Minister J.J. Greene attacked this interpretation, arguing that the 10 March move was just a predictable response to the rapid growth of Canada's share of the US oil market, but added that the abrupt shift to very tight, mandatory controls was "arbitrary" and a "mistake": "'Canada Can't Moan Over Oil Cuts' – Greene," *Ottawa Citizen*, 11 March 1970, 1, 21.

42 Ritchie, "Interdepartmental Oil Committee"; Clark to Schwarzmann, "Canada/US Oil Discussions," 2 February 1970, NAC, RG 20, vol. 1637.

43 Memorandum of Conversation, "Talks on US-Canadian Oil Policy," 10-11 February 1970, USNARA, RG 59, Subject-Numeric Files 1970-73, Box 1494, Economic.

44 "Oil Negotiations with the US," Cabinet Minutes/Conclusions, 26 February 1970, NAC, RG 2, series A-5a, vol. 6359.

45 Rowland Evans and Robert Novak, "Mitchell, Heeding Oilmen's Pleas, Killed Move to Ease Import Quotas," *Washington Post*, 12 January 1970, 22.

46 Treasury Secretary John Connally included the termination of the Auto Pact in the initial drafts of the larger package of radical balance of payments measures that were introduced in August 1971, but it was "rescued" by last-minute intervention of the State Department: J.L. Granatstein and Robert Bothwell, *Pirouette: Pierre Trudeau and Foreign Policy* (Toronto: University of Toronto Press, 1990), 64-65.

47 John J. Kirton, "The Consequences of Integration: The Case of the Defence Production Sharing Agreements," in *Continental Community? Independence and Integration in North America*, ed. Andrew W. Axline et al. (Toronto: McClelland and Stewart, 1974).

48   Arthur Andrew, *The Rise and Fall of a Middle Power: Canadian Diplomacy from King to Mulroney* (Toronto: James Lorimer, 1993), 103-8.
49   Kim Richard Nossal, "The PM and the SSEA in Canada's Foreign Policy: Dividing the Territory, 1968-1994," *International Journal* 50 (Winter 1994-95): 189-208.
50   Leonard Legault interview, Ottawa, 21 May 2001.
51   Henry Kissinger, *White House Years* (New York: Little, Brown, 1978), 28-31, 40-41, 717.
52   Vladimir Toumanoff interview, Washington, DC, 28 June 2002.
53   J. Alan Beesley interview, Victoria, 5 July 2001.
54   Rogers to Hickel (draft), 31 December 1969, USNARA, RG 59, Subject-Numeric Files 1967-69, Box 2927, Science; Ottawa Embassy to Secretary of State, "Arctic Sovereignty: Embassy Advises Against Public Confrontation with GOC," 23 February 1970, USNARA, RG 59, Subject-Numeric Files 1970-73, Box 2163, Political and Defense.
55   Former US official interview. See also: Ottawa Embassy to Secretary of State, "Arctic Claims," 10 December 1969, USNARA, RG 59, Subject-Numeric Files 1967-69, Box 2927, Science.
56   Vladimir Toumanoff interview, Washington, DC, 28 June 2002.
57   Ted Lee interview, Ottawa, 11 July 2001.
58   Johnson to Nixon, "Memorandum for the President, Canadian Legislation on the Arctic," 21 March 1970, USNARA, RG 59, Subject-Numeric Files 1970-73, Box 2911, Science. It is also reflected in the conduct of the critical March 1970 meetings, as mentioned in Chapter 1. At the 20 March meeting, the question of the economic implications of the anticipated Canadian legislation was raised, in very general terms, and Johnson remarked that he thought that a unilateral claim would have a "destabilizing effect." The Canadian negotiators pounced on this, demanding a full explanation. Johnson hastily clarified, saying that the US would of course not do anything to actively block investment in the Canadian Arctic, but that he expected that prospective investors might be put off by a unilateral claim that was under legal challenge: Part 1 of "Canadian Legislation on the Arctic," State Department Memorandum of Conversation, 20 March 1970, USNARA, RG 59, Subject-Numeric Files 1970-73, Box 2911, Science.
59   See, for example, Johnson to Stevenson, "Ottawa Talks," 8 March 1970, USNARA, RG 59, Subject-Numeric Files 1970-73, Box 2911, Science.
60   Ottawa Embassy to Secretary of State, "Arctic Claims," 1 February 1970, USNARA, RG 59, Subject-Numeric Files 1970-73, Box 2911, Science; Johnson to Nixon, "Memorandum for the President, Canadian Legislation on the Arctic," 21 March 1970, USNARA, RG 59, Subject-Numeric Files 1970-73, Box 2911, Science; Rogers to Hickel (draft), 31 December 1969, USNARA, RG 59, Subject-Numeric Files 1967-69, Box 2927, Science; Stevenson to Rogers, "Law of the Sea," 4 November 1969, USNARA, RG 59, Subject-Numeric Files 1967-69, Box 2927, Science.
61   Senior Canadian official interview, May 2001.
62   For a concise account of the dispute and its resolution, see Granatstein and Bothwell, *Pirouette*, 64-70.
63   Roger Frank Swanson, "The Ford Interlude and the US-Canada Relationship," *American Review of Canadian Studies* 8 (Spring 1978): 3-17.
64   Donald K. Alpert and Robert L. Monahan, "Bill C-58 and the American Congress: The Politics of Retaliation," *Canadian Public Policy* 4 (1979): 184-92.
65   John Herd Thompson and Stephen J. Randall, *Canada and the United States: Ambivalent Allies*, 3rd ed. (Athens: University of Georgia Press, 2002), 258-63.
66   Allan E. Gotlieb, *I'll Be with You in a Minute, Mr. Ambassador: The Education of a Canadian Diplomat in Washington* (Toronto: University of Toronto Press, 1991), esp. chs. 1-2.

Chapter 5: Oil and Gas, 1980-83

1   Kenneth North, "Canadian Oil and Gas – Surplus or Shortage?" in *Energy Policy: The Global Challenge*, ed. Peter Nemetz (Ottawa: Institute for Research on Public Policy, 1980), 49-68.
2   Energy, Mines and Resources Canada (EMR), *The National Energy Program* (Ottawa: Supply and Services Canada, 1980), 7.

3   Charles F. Doran, *Forgotten Partnership? US-Canada Relations Today* (Baltimore: The Johns Hopkins University Press, 1984), 214-15.
4   David Leyton-Brown, *Weathering the Storm: Canadian-US Relations, 1980-83* (Toronto and Washington, DC: Canadian-American Committee, 1985), 23.
5   Doran, *Forgotten Partnership?* 212-13.
6   For example, Glen Toner and François Bregha, "The Political Economy of Energy," in *Canadian Politics in the 1980s*, ed. Michael S. Whittington and Glen Williams (Toronto: Methuen, 1981).
7   Doran, *Forgotten Partnership?* 226-30.
8   Thomas A. Hockin, "Canada's 'Mass Legitimate' Parties and Their Implications for Party Leaders," in *Apex of Power*, 2nd ed., ed. Thomas A. Hockin (Scarborough, ON: Prentice Hall, 1977), 70-85.
9   Stephen Clarkson, *Canada and the Reagan Challenge* (Toronto: Lorimer, 1982), 297-98. The first External Affairs official to see the NEP was the minister, Mark MacGuigan, who received an advance copy just hours before its formal announcement: Robert Bothwell, *Canada and the United States: The Politics of Partnership* (New York: Twayne Publishers, 1992), 130.
10 On the US reaction: Leyton-Brown, *Weathering the Storm*, 26. For the argument that US officials were not surprised by the NEP, see Edward F. Wonder, "Canada-US Energy Relations," in *The United States and Canada: Dependence and Divergence*, ed. the Atlantic Council Working Group on US and Canada (Cambridge, MA: Ballinger, 1982), 80. For the argument that they were, but should not have been, see Clarkson, *Canada and the Reagan Challenge*, 56-57, 60-68.
11 Henry Giniger, "Canadian Oil Plans Bring US Objection," *New York Times*, 9 November 1980, 17. "National treatment" refers to the expectation that governments will not impose regulations that impose burdens on foreign investors but not on their "local" competitors.
12 Edward F. Wonder, "The US Government Response to the Canadian National Energy Program" (468-92), and Roy McLaren, "Canadian Views on the US Government Reaction to the National Energy Program" (492-94), both in *Canadian Public Policy* 8 (Supplement, 1982).
13 Leyton-Brown, *Weathering the Storm*, 29-30.
14 Clarkson, *Canada and the Reagan Challenge*, ch. 2.
15 Leyton-Brown, *Weathering the Storm*, 32-33.
16 Wonder, "The US Government Response," 487-90.
17 Former US Embassy official interview, July 2002.
18 Clarkson, *Canada and the Reagan Challenge*, 29.
19 Former Canadian official interview, June 2001.
20 Wonder, "The US Government Response," 485.
21 Clarkson, *Canada and the Reagan Challenge*, 30.
22 Peter Towe interview, Ottawa, 14 May 2001.
23 Clarkson, *Canada and the Reagan Challenge*, 31.
24 Leyton-Brown, *Weathering the Storm*, 29.
25 James Akins interview, Washington, DC, 22 June 2002, and Peter Towe interview, Ottawa, 14 May 2001, respectively.
26 "Welcoming Mr. Trudeau," *Wall Street Journal*, 9 July 1981, 29.
27 Clarkson, *Canada and the Reagan Challenge*, 33.
28 Henry Giniger, "Canada Acts to Curb American Acquisitions," *New York Times*, 30 July 1981, D1; Leyton-Brown, *Weathering the Storm*, 37.
29 For the three reported threats that follow: Robert Stephens, "Trade Trouble: Protectionist Policies Fuel US Resentment," *Globe and Mail*, 15 July 1981, A2; Hyman Solomon, "US Steps Up Its Drive to 'Punish' Us," *Financial Post*, 22 August 1981, A1; Art Pine and Frederick Rose, "Neighborly Feud," *Wall Street Journal*, 6 August 1981, A10; John Honderich, "How Reagan Might Lower the Boom on Us: Energy Policy and FIRA Have Americans in a Rage," *Toronto Star*, 29 August 1981, A1.
30 Allan Gotlieb interview, Toronto, 23 May 2001.
31 Clarkson, *Canada and the Reagan Challenge*, 34; Wonder, "The US Government Response," 491; Leyton-Brown, *Weathering the Storm*, 36.

32 Harald B. Malmgren, "Storm Flags Up for Canadian Business," *World Business Outlook* 3 (1981): 4-5; Leyton-Brown, ibid., 36. These linkage scenarios are examined in detail below.
33 Leyton-Brown, ibid., 28-29.
34 Peter Towe interview, Ottawa, 14 May 2001.
35 David Shribman, "Canada-US Irritants Rub Both Ways," *New York Times,* 29 November 1981, E6.
36 Clarkson, *Canada and the Reagan Challenge,* 38.
37 Ibid., 38.
38 Henry Giniger, "Canada Ties: Relations with US are 'Full of Tensions,'" *New York Times,* 21 September 1981, A11.
39 Myer Rashish, "North American Economic Relations," *Department of State Bulletin* 81 (November 1981): 24-28.
40 Clarkson, *Canada and the Reagan Challenge,* 39.
41 Ibid., 39-40.
42 Giniger, "Canada Ties: Relations with US are 'Full of Tensions.'"
43 Clarkson, *Canada and the Reagan Challenge,* 35, 36.
44 Peter Towe interview, Ottawa, 14 May 2001.
45 Washington Embassy to External Affairs, 5 December 1981, National Archives of Canada [NAC], RG 25, vol. 9774; Wonder, "The US Government Response," 486.
46 Henry Giniger, "Energy Bill Passes Test in Canada," *New York Times,* 10 December 1981, D1.
47 Gotlieb to Brock, 12/16/81, 16 December 1981, NAC, RG 25, vol. 9774; Allan Gotlieb interview, Toronto, 23 May 2001.
48 Clarkson, *Canada and the Reagan Challenge,* 40.
49 Jennifer Lewington, "Energy Projects Hurt by Disputes," *Globe and Mail,* 28 December 1981, A8; Anthony McCallum, "Oil Companies Shifting Funds to Frontier," *Globe and Mail,* 4 January 1982, A4.
50 Herb Gray interview, Ottawa, 20 June 2001.
51 Henry Giniger, "Canada's New Budget is Assailed," *New York Times,* 30 June 1982, D1; Herb Gray interview, ibid.
52 John F. Helliwell, Mary MacGregor, and André Plourde, "The National Energy Program Meets Falling World Oil Prices," *Canadian Public Policy* 9 (Summer 1983): 284-96.
53 Robert D. Putnam, "Diplomacy and Domestic Politics: The Logic of Two-Level Games," *International Organization* 42 (Summer 1988): 427-60.
54 A poll taken in the spring of 1981, sponsored by the Canadian Petroleum Association, found that 84 percent of Canadians supported the NEP's goal of 50 percent Canadian control by 1990: *Nickle's Daily Oil Bulletin,* 15 September 1981.
55 Lauren S. McKinsey, "Détente in Canada's Energy War," *American Review of Canadian Studies* 12 (Summer 1982): 98-119, esp. 104.
56 For analysis of winners and losers in the September 1981 agreement, see John F. Helliwell and Robert D. McRae, "Resolving the Energy Conflict: From the National Energy Program to the Energy Agreements," *Canadian Public Policy* 8 (Winter 1982): 14-23; McKinsey, ibid., 107-8.
57 Clarkson, *Canada and the Reagan Challenge,* 36-42.
58 The fact that American officials were most aggressive in publicly attacking the NEP in the weeks immediately leading up to the Canadian cruise missile decision suggests that the two issues were being kept at arms' length – that is, that there was no underlying positive linkage in play.
59 Former US official interview, July 2002.
60 Wonder, "The US Government Response," 490. Confirmed in interviews with former Canadian officials, May and June 2001.
61 James Akins interview, Washington, DC, 22 June 2002.
62 Wonder, "The US Government Response," 486; Clarkson, *Canada and the Reagan Challenge,* 30.
63 Roy MacLaren, "Canadian Views on the US Government Reaction to the National Energy Program," *Canadian Public Policy* 8, supplement (Summer 1982): 493-97.

64 Wonder, "The US Government Response," 486.
65 Ibid., 485.
66 Washington Embassy to External Affairs, 5 December 1981, NAC, RG 25, vol. 9774.
67 Clarkson, *Canada and the Reagan Challenge*, 33.
68 Peter Towe interview, Ottawa, 14 May 2001.
69 Wonder, "The US Government Response," 492; former US official interview, July 2002.
70 Peter Towe interview, Ottawa, 14 May 2001; Donald Barry, "The US Senate and the Collapse of the East Coast Fisheries Agreement," *Dalhousie Review* 62 (Autumn 1982): 495-503.
71 Clarkson, *Canada and the Reagan Challenge*, 26.
72 Former Canadian official interview, June 2001.
73 Allan Gotlieb interview, Toronto, 23 May 2001.
74 Peter Towe interview, Ottawa, 14 May 2001.
75 Former US official interview, July 2002.
76 Wonder, "The US Government Response," 491. As an example of press coverage, see John Carson-Parker, "Stop Worrying about the Canadian Invasion," *Fortune*, 19 October 1981, 200.
77 Former Canadian official interview, June 2001.
78 Leyton-Brown, *Weathering the Storm*, 21.
79 When Brian Mulroney's Conservatives were elected in 1984, they said that they were going to kill off the NEP and FIRA, but by that time there was really virtually nothing left to strip away.
80 Stephen Clarkson, "Canada-US Relations and the Changing of the Guard in Ottawa," in *Canada among Nations 1984*, ed. Brian W. Tomlin and Maureen Appel Molot (Toronto: Lorimer, 1985), 150.
81 Allan E. Gotlieb, *I'll Be with You in a Minute, Mr. Ambassador: The Political Education of a Canadian Diplomat in Washington* (Toronto: University of Toronto Press, 1990). See also Michael Hart, "Of Friends, Interests, Crowbars, and Marriage Vows in Canada-United States Trade Relations," in *Images of Canadianness: Visions on Canada's Politics, Culture, Economics*, ed. Leen D'Haenans (Ottawa: University of Ottawa Press, 1998).
82 G. Bruce Doern and Brian W. Tomlin, *Faith and Fear: The Free Trade Story* (Toronto: Stoddart, 1991), 18-20.
83 Joseph T. Jockel, "Canada and the United States: Still Calm in the 'Remarkable Relationship,'" in *Canada among Nations 1996*, ed. Fen Osler Hampson and Maureen Appel Molot (Ottawa: Carleton University Press, 1996).

Chapter 6: War in Iraq, 2002-4

1 Speech by US ambassador Paul Cellucci to the Economic Club of Toronto, 25 March 2003: US Embassy in Canada, http://canada.usembassy.gov/content/textonly.asp?section= embconsul&document=cellucci_030325.
2 J.L. Granatstein, "The Empire Strikes Back," *National Post*, 26 March 2003, A15.
3 Joan Bryden, "US Won't Hold Grudge on Iraq, PM's Aide Says," *Ottawa Citizen*, 15 March 2003, A4.
4 Granatstein, "The Empire Strikes Back"; Theresa Tedesco, "CEOs March to Washington to Avert Crisis," *National Post*, 7 April 2003, A3; Michael Den Tandt, "Presto! Canada-US Trade Fears Go Up in Smoke," *Globe and Mail*, 8 April 2003, A19.
5 Peter Beaumont et al., "US to Punish German 'Treachery,'" *(London) Observer*, 16 February 2003, 25; Michael Wines, "Putin Again Rejects US Calls for Support of a War," *New York Times*, 1 March 2003, A8; Ed Vulliamy et al., "America the Arm Twister," *(Manchester) Guardian*, 2 March 2003, 51.
6 State Department official interview, Washington, DC, August 2005.
7 David Haglund, "North American Cooperation in an Era of Homeland Security," *Orbis* 47, 4 (Autumn 2004): 676-80.
8 Peter Andreas, "A Tale of Two Borders: The US-Mexico and US-Canada Lines after 9-11," Working Paper 77 (San Diego: Center for Comparative Immigration Studies, University of California at San Diego, 2003), 8.

9 Frank P. Harvey, "The Homeland Security Dilemma: Imagination, Failure and the Escalating Costs of Perfecting Security," *Canadian Journal of Political Science* 40, 2 (June 2007): 283-316.
10 Murray Campbell, "Nation's Grief Turns to Anger," *Globe and Mail,* 19 April 2002, A1, A7.
11 Yuen Foong Khong, "Neoconservatism and the Domestic Sources of American Foreign Policy: The Role of Ideas in Operation Iraqi Freedom," in *Foreign Policy: Theories, Actors and Cases,* ed. Steve Smith, Amelia Hadfield, and Timothy Dunne (Toronto: Oxford University Press, 2008).
12 Joshua Muravchik, "Why We Are Better Off without that UN Resolution," *Wall Street Journal,* 18 March 2003, A20.
13 Emma Brockes, "What Can Eritrea Possibly Do to Help the US in Iraq?" *(Manchester) Guardian,* 20 March 2003, http://www.guardian.co.uk/world/2003/mar/20/iraq.emmabrockes.
14 Janice Gross Stein and Eugene Lang, *The Unexpected War: Canada in Afghanistan* (Toronto: Viking Canada, 2007), 49-50, 68-69.
15 Jason Fekete and Stephen Thorne, "Top-Level General Quits Army in Wake of Afghan Deployment," *National Post,* 15 February 2003, A17.
16 Donald Barry, "Chrétien, Bush and the War in Iraq," *American Review of Canadian Studies* 35, 2 (June 2005): 224; Chris Wattie, "Ottawa Offered to Join Iraq War: Proposal to US to Send 600-800 Soldiers Dropped Suddenly in Favour of Afghan Plan," *National Post,* 27 November 2004, A1.
17 Jeff Sallot, "Chrétien Faces Caucus Revolt over Iraq Crisis," *Globe and Mail,* 11 February 2003, A4.
18 Donald McKenzie, "Canadians Still Leery of Bush Invasion Plan," *National Post,* 9 September 2002, A4; Gloria Galloway, "Canadians Oppose War in Iraq without UN," *Globe and Mail,* 18 January 2003, A10.
19 Interviews with current and former Canadian officials, Ottawa, November 2006. See also: Barry, "Chrétien, Bush and the War in Iraq." For a strong version of the argument that the Canadian government was motivated by its commitment to multilateralism, see Srdjan Vucetic, "Why Did Canada Sit Out the Iraq War? One Constructivist Analysis," *Canadian Foreign Policy* 13, 1 (December 2006): 133-53.
20 Sheldon Alberts, "Powell Urges Canada to Join Iraq Coalition," *National Post,* 15 November 2002, A1.
21 Former Canadian official interview, Ottawa, November 2006.
22 Andrew Richter, "From Trusted Ally to Suspicious Neighbor: Canada-US Relations in a Changing Global Environment," *American Review of Canadian Studies* 35, 3 (Autumn 2005): 477-86.
23 Jan Cienski, "Canada Might Not Wait for UN," *National Post,* 10 January 2003, A1. See also Tim Harper, "Liberal Dissent Brewing in Iraq Crisis," *Toronto Star,* 14 January 2003, A1.
24 Shawn McCarthy and Daniel LeBlanc, "PM Scolds McCallum on Canada's Role in Iraq," *Globe and Mail,* 16 January 2003, A1.
25 Barry, "Chrétien, Bush and the War in Iraq," 222.
26 Interviews with US and Canadian officials, Washington, DC, August 2005, and Ottawa, November 2006. Also compare Barry, "Chrétien, Bush and the War in Iraq," 221, and Stein and Lang, *The Unexpected War,* 61-64.
27 Jeff Sallot, "Proposed Iraq Briefing Had Canada Skeptical," *Globe and Mail,* 12 March 2004, A10.
28 Jeff Sallot, "PM Aims to Broker UN Deal," *Globe and Mail,* 20 February 2003, A8.
29 Interviews with State Department and Department of Homeland Security officials, Washington, DC, August 2005.
30 Barry, "Chrétien, Bush and the War in Iraq," 227.
31 Beth Gorham, "US OK with Canada's Stance," *Halifax Chronicle-Herald,* 26 February 2003, A1.
32 Terry Breese interview, Washington, DC, 24 August 2005.
33 "Canada's Decision No Surprise to Bush: PM," *CBC News Online,* 18 March 2003, http://www.cbc.ca/stories/print/2003/03/18/Iraq.
34 Stein and Lang, *The Unexpected War,* 76-77.

35 State Department official interview, Washington, DC, August 2005.
36 Stein and Lang, *The Unexpected War*, 76.
37 Barry, "Chrétien, Bush and the War in Iraq," 228.
38 Kim Richard Nossal, "Defence Policy and the Atmospherics of Canada-US Relations," *American Review of Canadian Studies* 37, 1 (Spring 2007): 23-34, 24.
39 Sheldon Alberts, "Anti-US Rhetoric Risky, Cellucci Warns," *Globe and Mail*, 1 December 2005, A9.
40 For example, Wallace Immen, "Canadian Public Skeptical of War in Iraq, Poll Shows," *Globe and Mail*, 19 July 2003, A1. Chrétien later reflected, "The Canadian people are very pleased with the decision, and feel very good about it and it was a good occasion, too, to prove our independence": Kevin Ward, "Chrétien: Stance on Iraq was Right," *Halifax Chronicle-Herald*, 31 March 2004, A1.
41 Michael Higgins, "72% Believe Canada Should Have Backed War," *National Post*, 8 April 2003, A1.
42 Theresa Tedesco, "CEOs March to US to Avert Crisis," *National Post*, 7 April 2003, A1.
43 Sheldon Alberts, "PM: War Stance was 'Principled,'" *National Post*, 9 April 2003, A1.
44 Brian Knowlton, "Mexico and Canada Assess the Cost of Having Opposed War in Iraq," *New York Times*, 17 April 2003, A5.
45 "Envoy Links Bush Snub to War Policy," *Toronto Star*, 17 April 2003, A11.
46 Sheldon Alberts, "US Relents on Border Checks," *National Post*, 17 April 2003, A1.
47 "Powell Reassures Canadians on Iraq Dispute," *Agence France-Presse*, 25 April 2003.
48 See, for example, Wendy Dobson, "Shaping the Future of the North American Economic Space: An Agenda for Action," *Border Papers (C.D. Howe Institute)* 162 (April 2002). If anything, the Chrétien government did exactly the opposite, and the big question here is whether it therefore got the opposite result: Michael Hart, "Canada Blew It," *Financial Post*, 12 February 2008, A12.
49 Janice Gross Stein and Eugene Lang, "Our Man in Iraq: Did Canada Really Stay Out of War in Iraq?" *Globe and Mail*, 12 October 2007, A19.
50 This is described in detail in Stein and Lang, *The Unexpected War*, 79-86.
51 Andrew Richter, "From Trusted Ally to Suspicious Neighbor," 484-86.
52 Stein and Lang, *The Unexpected War*, 90. These contributions were appreciated by those in the US who actually paid close attention to what Canada was doing, but they were generally unknown by those who did not deal with Canada on a regular basis or knew little about defence issues (i.e., most members of Congress, some parts of the bureaucracy, the private sector): State Department official interview, August 2005.
53 Stein and Lang, *The Unexpected War*, 65-72.
54 Daniel LeBlanc, "Canada Takes Afghan Mission," *Globe and Mail*, 13 February 2003, A1.
55 For extended analysis of Canada's involvement in Afghanistan, see Stein and Lang, *The Unexpected War*, and Independent Panel on Canada's Future Role in Afghanistan, *Final Report* (Ottawa: Queen's Printer, 2008).
56 Interviews with State Department and Department of Homeland Security officials, Washington, DC, August 2005.
57 State Department official interview, Washington, DC, August 2005.
58 Terry Breese interview, Washington, DC, 24 August 2005.
59 Cellucci later said that he was misquoted, but there is too much consistency across the various reports to think that all of these reporters got the essence of his message wrong.
60 David Olive, "Canada Has Leverage with US," *Hamilton Spectator*, 1 April 2003, B4.
61 Alberts, "US Relents on Border Checks," A1.
62 Sinclair Stewart, "Rift over Iraq Expected to Heal," *Globe and Mail*, 7 April 2003, B1.
63 On the latter, see Diane Francis, "Expect Severe Consequences from Anti-US Stance: Failure to Back US War Effort is Foreign Policy Disaster," *National Post*, 8 April 2003, FP3.
64 For example, James Fallows, *Blind into Baghdad: America's War in Iraq* (New York: Random House, 2006), ch. 3.
65 Anne Dawson, "Canada Will Be Left Out of First Contracts in Iraq: Powell," *National Post*, 26 April 2003, A2.
66 Sheldon Alberts, "US Cuts Canada Out of Iraq Work," *National Post*, 10 December 2003, A1.

67 John Partridge, "US Lets Canada in on Iraq Bidding," *Globe and Mail,* 14 December 2003, A9.
68 Nicholas Van Praet, "CAE Fears Canada's Iraq Stance: Military Contracts Could Be at Risk," *Montreal Gazette,* 8 May 2003, B1.
69 Nathan Hodge, "Fight Brewing over 'Buy American' Legislation," *Defense Week,* 23 June 2003, 9.
70 Les Whittington, "Economy at Risk in US Tiff, Beatty Says," *Toronto Star,* 29 March 2003, A1; Richard Bloom, "Boycott of Canada Unlikely, Poll Finds," *Globe and Mail,* 14 April 2003, A8.
71 Stephen Handelman, "The Big Chill," *Time,* 7 April 2003, 57.
72 Alberts, "US Relents on Border Checks," A1.
73 "Passport Delay Is Good for Us All," *Montreal Gazette,* 27 December 2007, A28.
74 Handelman, "The Big Chill."
75 Bryden, "US Won't Hold Grudge on Iraq"; Granatstein, "The Empire Strikes Back."
76 Interview with Canadian Embassy official, Washington, DC, August 2005.
77 State Department official interview, Washington, DC, August 2005.
78 Former State Department official interview, Washington, DC, August 2005.
79 "Harper Calls for Action on Mad Cow Crisis," *CBC News Online,* 7 September 2004, http://www.cbc.ca/canada/story/2004/09/07/harper_bse040907.html.
80 Kate O'Neill, "How Two Cows Make a Crisis: US-Canada Trade Relations and Mad Cow Disease," *American Review of Canadian Studies* 35, 2 (Summer 2005): 295-319.
81 Former Department of Agriculture official interview, Washington, DC, August 2005.
82 The "sponsorship scandal" refers to the criminal investigation of the alleged misuse of funds from a federal government program designed to bolster support for federalism in the province of Quebec. Several Liberal cabinet members, including the former prime minister were implicated and compelled to testify before a public inquiry.
83 David Rudd, "Muddling Through on Missile Defence: The Politics of Indecision," *Policy Options* 26, 4 (May 2005): 30-34.
84 Brian Laghi, "Martin Charts New Course with US: Public Opinion Made Relationship Frosty despite Early Promises to Turn Down Heat," *Globe and Mail,* 16 December 2005, A1.
85 Daniel LeBlanc and Gloria Galloway, "Washington Scolds Ottawa: US Tired of Canadian Attacks on Environment, Trade Policies," *Globe and Mail,* 14 December 2005, A1.

Chapter 7: Diplomatic Culture

1 Robert O. Keohane and Joseph S. Nye, *Power and Interdependence: World Politics in Transition* (Boston: Little, Brown, 1977), ch. 7. See also Annette Baker Fox, Alfred O. Hero, and Joseph S. Nye, eds., *Canada and the United States: Transnational and Transgovernmental Relations* (New York: Columbia University Press, 1976).
2 In fact, this impulse had been present for some time in the work of James Eayrs, John Holmes, and others. But it really took over as the new conventional wisdom only in the late 1960s and 1970s. See Stephen Clarkson, "The Choice to Be Made," in *An Independent Foreign Policy for Canada?* ed. Stephen Clarkson (Toronto: McClelland and Stewart, 1968).
3 Denis Stairs, "Myths, Morals and Reality in Canadian Foreign Policy," *International Journal* 58 (Spring 2003): 239-56.
4 Thomas Risse-Kappen, *Cooperation among Democracies: The European Influence on US Foreign Policy* (Princeton, NJ: Princeton University Press, 1997).
5 Stéphane Roussel, *The North American Democratic Peace: Absence of War and Security Institution-Building in Canada-US Relations, 1867-1958* (Montreal and Kingston: McGill-Queen's University Press, 2004).
6 James C. Bennett, *The Anglosphere Challenge: Why the English-Speaking Nations Will Lead the Way in the Twenty-First Century* (New York: Rowman and Littlefield, 2007); John Dumbrell, *A Special Relationship: Anglo-American Relations from the Cold War to Iraq* (Basingstoke, UK: Palgrave Macmillan, 2006).
7 Robert W. McElroy, *Morality and American Foreign Policy* (Princeton, NJ: Princeton University Press, 1993); Stephen M. Walt, "Taming American Power," *Foreign Affairs* 84, 5 (September/October 2005): 105-20.

8   John S. Odell has gone so far as to argue that "defining issue linkage as a strategy in itself can confuse analysis by implying that some strategies avoid it": *Negotiating the World Economy* (Ithaca, NY: Cornell University Press, 2000), 37-38. But some bargaining strategies *do* avoid linkage altogether, and one of the main aims of this book has been to show that there was a time when bargaining between the US and Canada reflected a blanket rejection of linkages per se.

9   James G. March and Johan P. Olsen, *Rediscovering Institutions: The Institutional Basis of Politics* (New York: Free Press, 1989), esp. ch. 2.

10 Amitav Acharya, "Do Norms and Identity Matter? Community and Power in Southeast Asia's Regional Order," *The Pacific Review* 18, 1 (March 2005): 95-118.

11 In addition to sources cited on this point in Chapter 1, see also Martha Finnemore and Kathryn Sikkink, "Taking Stock: The Constructivist Research Program in International Relations and Comparative Politics," *Annual Review of Political Science* 4 (2001): 391-416.

12 Thomas Risse-Kappen, "Ideas Do Not Float Freely: Transnational Coalitions, Domestic Structures and the End of the Cold War," *International Organization* 48 (Spring 1994): 185-214.

13 Robert O. Keohane and Joseph S. Nye Jr., "Transgovernmental Relations and World Politics: An Introduction," *World Politics* 27, 1 (October 1974): 39-62; Anne-Marie Slaughter, *A New World Order* (Princeton, NJ: Princeton University Press, 2004).

14 E.E. Schattschneider, *The Semisovereign People: A Realist's View of Democracy in America* (Hinsdale, IL: Dryden Press, 1960), 68.

15 Thomas Risse-Kappen, "Introduction," in *Bringing Transnational Relations Back in*, ed. Thomas Risse-Kappen (Cambridge, UK: Cambridge University Press, 1995); Matthew Evangelista, "The Paradox of State Strength: Transnational Relations, Domestic Structures, and Security Policy in Russia and the Soviet Union," *International Organization* 49, 1 (Winter 1995): 1-38.

16 On strategic cultures, see Alistair Iain Johnston, "Thinking about Strategic Cultures," *International Security* 19, 4 (1995): 32-64. On the idea of (more or less) universal diplomatic cultures, which may evolve over time, see Christian Reus-Smit, "The Constitutional Structure of International Society and the Nature of Fundamental Institutions," *International Organization* 51, 3 (Fall 1997): 555-89.

17 For example: Frank Schimmelfennig, *The EU, NATO and the Integration of Europe* (Cambridge, UK: Cambridge University Press, 2003); Amitav Acharya, *The Quest for Identity: The International Relations of Southeast Asia* (Oxford: Oxford University Press, 2000); Alistair Iain Johnston, "Treating International Institutions as Social Environments," *International Studies Quarterly* 45, 4 (2001): 487-515.

18 As an especially clear-cut example, see K.J. Holsti, "Canada and the United States," in *Conflict in World Politics,* ed. Steven Spiegel and Kenneth Waltz (Cambridge, UK: Winthrop, 1971).

19 A.D.P. Heeney and Livingston T. Merchant, *Canada and the United States: Principles for Partnership* (Ottawa: Queen's Printer, 1965).

20 Nelson Michaud and Kim Richard Nossal, "Diplomatic Departures? Assessing the Conservative Era in Foreign Policy," in *Diplomatic Departures: The Conservative Era in Canadian Foreign Policy, 1984-93,* ed. Nelson Michaud and Kim Richard Nossal (Vancouver: UBC Press, 2001).

21 Joseph T. Jockel, "Canada and the United States: Still Calm in the 'Remarkable Relationship,'" in *Canada among Nations 1996,* ed. Fen Osler Hampson and Maureen Appel Molot (Ottawa: Carleton University Press, 1996); David T. Jones, "Canada and the US in the Chrétien Years: Edging toward Confrontation," *Policy Options* (November 2002): 33-43.

22 Allan Gotlieb, *I'll Be with You in a Minute, Mr. Ambassador: The Education of a Canadian Diplomat in Washington* (Toronto: University of Toronto Press, 1989); Andrew Fenton Cooper, "Playing by New Rules: Allan Gotlieb, Public Diplomacy and the Management of Canada-US Relations," *Fletcher Forum of World Affairs* 14 (1990): 93-109.

23 Allan Gotlieb, *The Washington Diaries, 1981-1989* (New York: Random House, 2006), esp. ch. 2.

24 G. Bruce Doern, and Brian W. Tomlin, *Faith and Fear: The Free Trade Story* (Toronto: Stoddart, 1991).

25 Ernst Haas, *Beyond the Nation State: Functionalism and International Integration* (Palo Alto, CA: Stanford University Press, 1964).

26 K.J. Holsti and Thomas Allen Levy, "Bilateral Institutions and Transgovernmental Relations between Canada and the United States," in Fox et al., *Canada and the United States.*

27 Pietro S. Nivola, "The New Protectionism: US Policy in Historical Perspective," *Political Science Quarterly* 101, 4 (1986): 577-600.

28 See also Brian Bow, "Out of Ideas? Models and Strategies for Canada-US Relations," *International Journal* 62 (Winter 2006-7): 123-44.

29 Robert Wolfe, "See You in Washington? A Pluralist Perspective on North American Institutions," *Choices* 9, 4 (2003).

30 John Higginbotham and Jeff Heynen, "Managing through Networks: The State of Canada-US Relations," in *Canada among Nations 2004: Setting Priorities Straight,* ed. David Carment, Fen Osler Hampson, and Norman Hillmer (Montreal and Kingston: McGill-Queen's University Press, 2005).

31 Donald Barry, "Chrétien, Bush and the War in Iraq," *American Review of Canadian Studies* 35, 2 (June 2005): 215-45.

32 Allan Gotlieb, "Never Play Leapfrog with a Unicorn," *National Post,* 9 April 2001, 18.

33 Clarkson, "The Choice to Be Made."

34 For example, John J. Noble, "Canada-US Relations in the Post-Iraq War Era: Stop the Drift toward Irrelevance," *Policy Options* 24, 5 (May 2003): 19-25.

35 Drew Fagan, "Martin's House Divided on Ties with Bush," *Globe and Mail,* 10 March 2004.

36 Donald Barry, "Managing Canada-US Relations in the Post-9/11 Era: Do We Need a Big Idea?" CSIS Policy Papers on the Americas 14 (Washington, DC: Center for Strategic and International Studies, 2003).

37 Costas Melakopides, *Pragmatic Idealism: Canadian Foreign Policy, 1945-95* (Montreal and Kingston: McGill-Queen's University Press, 1998), 69-70.

38 Andrew Rudalevige, *The New Imperial Presidency?* (Ann Arbor: University of Michigan Press, 2005).

39 Michael Hart and Bill Dymond, *Common Borders, Shared Destinies: Canada, the United States and Deepening Integration* (Ottawa: Centre for Trade Policy and Law, 2001).

40 Wendy Dobson, "Shaping the Future of the North American Economic Space: An Agenda for Action," *Border Papers (C.D. Howe Institute)* 162 (April 2002); Allan Gotlieb, "A North American Community of Law," *The Quarterly: Ideas that Matter* 2, 4 (2003): 25-30.

41 Dobson, ibid.; Michael Hart, "Canada Blew It," *National Post,* 12 February 2008, A12.

42 Michael Hart, "Steer or Drift: Taking Charge of Canada-US Regulatory Convergence," *C.D. Howe Institute Commentary,* 15 March 2006.

Bibliography

Archival Sources
Abbreviations: JFK Library = John F. Kennedy Presidential Library; NAC = National Archives of Canada; USNARA = US National Archives and Records Administration

United States
Ball to Bundy, 31 January 1963, 10:00 a.m., and Ball to JFK, 31 January 1963, 7:30 p.m., both in JFK Library, George Ball Files, Memoranda of Telephone Conversations.
Ball to Bundy, 7 February 1963, 12:20 p.m., JFK Library, George Ball Files, Memoranda of Telephone Conversations.
Ball to Tyler, 28 January 1963, 1:00 p.m., JFK Library, George Ball Files, Memoranda of Telephone Conversations.
Bundy to Bundy, Rostow, and Johnson, "Subject: Possible Canadian Quotas," 25 May 1962, JFK Library, JFK National Security Files.
"Canadian Legislation on the Arctic," State Department Memorandum of Conversation, 20 March 1970 (two parts), USNARA, RG 59, Subject-Numeric Files 1970-73, Box 2911, Science.
Eliot to Kissinger, attachment ("Subject: Canadian Arctic Legislation"), 14 April 1970, USNARA, RG 59, Subject-Numeric Files 1970-73, Box 2911, Science.
Johnson to Nixon, "Memorandum for the President, Canadian Legislation on the Arctic," 21 March 1970, USNARA, RG 59, Subject-Numeric Files 1970-73, Box 2911, Science.
Johnson to Stevenson, "Ottawa Talks," 8 March 1970, USNARA, RG 59, Subject-Numeric Files 1970-73, Box 2911, Science.
Kelly, "In Support of Proposals to Amend the Oil Import Program," n.d., JFK Library, Myer Feldman Files, Box 23.
Legere, "Memorandum for the President: Canadian Chronology," 13 February 1963, JFK Library, JFK National Security Files.
Legere to Bundy, "Foreign Relations Committee Hearing on Canada," 1 February 1963, JFK Library, JFK National Security Files.
Legere to Bundy, "Subject: Follow-up with Canadians on Hyannis Port," n.d., JFK Library, White House Staff Files, Myer Feldman.
Memorandum of Conversation, "Imminent Canadian Legislation on Arctic Pollution, Territorial Sea and Fisheries," 7 April 1970, USNARA, RG 59, Subject-Numeric Files 1970-73, Box 2163, Political and Defense.
Memorandum of Conversation, "President's Trip to Ottawa, May 16-18, 1961," 17 May 1961, JFK Library, JFK National Security Files.
Memorandum of Conversation, "Talks on US-Canadian Oil Policy," 10-11 February 1970, USNARA, RG 59, Subject-Numeric Files 1970-73, Box 1494, Economic.
Ottawa Embassy to Secretary of State, 21 February 1970, USNARA, RG 59, Subject-Numeric Files 1970-73, Box 2162, Political and Defense.

Ottawa Embassy to Secretary of State, 26 August 1970, USNARA, RG 59, Subject-Numeric Files 1970-73, Box 2911, Science.

Ottawa Embassy to Secretary of State, "Arctic Claims," 10 December 1969, USNARA, RG 59, Subject-Numeric Files 1967-69, Box 2927, Science.

Ottawa Embassy to Secretary of State, "Arctic Claims," 1 February 1970, USNARA, RG 59, Subject-Numeric Files 1970-73, Box 2911, Science.

Ottawa Embassy to Secretary of State, "Arctic Sovereignty: Embassy Advises against Public Confrontation with GOC," 23 February 1970, USNARA, RG 59, Subject-Numeric Files 1970-73, Box 2163, Political and Defense.

Ottawa Embassy to State Department, n.d., JFK Library, JFK National Security Files.

Ottawa Embassy to State Department, 24 May 1961, JFK Library, JFK National Security Files.

Ottawa Embassy to State Department, 12 October 1961, JFK Library, JFK National Security Files.

Ottawa Embassy to State Department, 11 April 1962, JFK Library, JFK National Security Files.

Ottawa Embassy to State Department, 8 May 1962, JFK Library, JFK National Security Files.

Ottawa Embassy to State Department, 2 January 1963, JFK Library, JFK National Security Files.

Ottawa Embassy to State Department, 11 January 1963, JFK Library, JFK National Security Files.

Ottawa Embassy to State Department, 27 January 1963, JFK Library, JFK National Security Files.

Rogers to Hickel (draft), 31 December 1969, USNARA, RG 59, Subject-Numeric Files 1967-69, Box 2927, Science.

Rome Embassy to Secretary of Defense 1857, 16 April 1970, USNARA, RG 59, Subject-Numeric Files 1970-73, Box 2911, Science.

State Department, "Guidelines for Policy and Operations: Canada," March 1962, JFK Library, JFK National Security Files.

State Department to Ottawa Embassy, 10 January 1963, JFK Library, JFK National Security Files.

State Department to Ottawa Embassy, 23 November 1963, JFK Library, JFK National Security Files.

Stevenson to Rogers, "Law of the Sea," 4 November 1969, USNARA, RG 59, Subject-Numeric Files 1967-69, Box 2927, Science.

Volpe to Rogers, 14 March 1970, USNARA, RG 59, Subject-Numeric Files 1970-73, Box 2911, Science.

Canada

"Canada-US Oil Discussion," Cabinet Minutes/Conclusions, 12 February 1970, NAC, RG 2, series A-5a, vol. 6359.

Clark to Schwarzmann, "Canada/US Oil Discussions," 2 February 1970, NAC, RG 20, vol. 1637.

Clark to Warren, 9 February 1970, NAC, RG 20, vol. 1637.

Crosby to McNabb and Isbister, 31 March 1970, NAC, RG 21, vol. 216.

Gotlieb to Brock, 16 December 1981, NAC, RG 25, vol. 9774.

"Meeting between the President of the United States and the Prime Minister of Canada ... at Hyannis Port, Mass. – May 10-11, 1963 – Final Report," n.d., NAC, RG 25, ser. A-4, vol. 9788.

"Oil Negotiations with the US," Cabinet Minutes/Conclusions, 26 February 1970, NAC, RG 2, series A-5a, vol. 6359.

Ritchie, "Interdepartmental Oil Committee – January 13, 1970," 14 January 1970, NAC, RG 20, vol. 1637.

Thorgrimsson, "Notes for Suggested Changes to Memorandum to Cabinet on Ratification of the Shelf Convention and Possible Adoption of 12-Mile Territorial Sea, Forthcoming Meeting with External Affairs," 25 July 1969, NAC, RG 21, vol. 198.

Washington Embassy to External Affairs, 23 April 1963, NAC, RG 25, vol. 5662, file 14405-U-16-40, pt. 4.
Washington Embassy to External Affairs, 19 February 1970, NAC, RG 20, vol. 1637.
Washington Embassy to External Affairs, 5 December 1981, NAC, RG 25, vol. 9774.

Books and Articles
Acharya, Amitav. "Do Norms and Identity Matter? Community and Power in Southeast Asia's Regional Order." *Pacific Review* 18, 1 (2005): 95-118.
–. *The Quest for Identity: The International Relations of Southeast Asia*. Oxford: Oxford University Press, 2000.
Alpert, Donald K., and Robert L. Monahan. "Bill C-58 and the American Congress: The Politics of Retaliation." *Canadian Public Policy* 4 (1979): 184-92.
Andreas, Peter. "A Tale of Two Borders: The US-Mexico and US-Canada Lines after 9-11." Working Paper 77. San Diego: Center for Comparative Immigration Studies, University of California at San Diego, 2003.
Andrew, Arthur. *The Rise and Fall of a Middle Power: Canadian Diplomacy from King to Mulroney.* Toronto: Lorimer, 1993.
Baldwin, David A. "Interdependence and Power: A Conceptual Analysis." *International Organization* 34 (Autumn 1980): 471-506.
–. "The Myths of the Special Relationship." *International Studies Quarterly* 12 (June 1968): 127-51.
Barnett, Michael N. *Dialogues in Arab Politics: Negotiations in Regional Order.* New York: Columbia University Press, 2000.
Barry, Donald. "Chrétien, Bush and the War in Iraq." *American Review of Canadian Studies* 35, 2 (June 2005): 215-45.
–. "Managing Canada-US Relations in the Post-9/11 Era: Do We Need a Big Idea?" CSIS Policy Papers on the Americas 14. Washington, DC: Center for Strategic and International Studies, 2003.
–. "The Politics of 'Exceptionalism': Canada and the United States as a Distinctive International Relationship." *Dalhousie Review* 60 (Spring 1980): 125-26.
–. "The US Senate and the Collapse of the East Coast Fisheries Agreement." *Dalhousie Review* 62 (Autumn 1982): 495-503.
Bennett, James C. *The Anglosphere Challenge: Why the English-Speaking Nations Will Lead the Way in the Twenty-First Century.* New York: Rowman and Littlefield, 2007.
Bothwell, Robert. *Canada and the United States: The Politics of Partnership.* New York: Twayne Publishers, 1992.
–. "Canada-United States Relations: Options for the 1970s." *International Journal* 58 (Winter 2002-3): 65-88.
Bothwell, Robert, and David Kilbourn. *C.D. Howe: A Biography.* Toronto: McClelland and Stewart, 1978.
Bothwell, Robert, and John Kirton. "'A Sweet Little Country': American Attitudes toward Canada, 1925 to 1963." *Queen's Quarterly* 90 (Winter 1983): 1078-1102.
Bow, Brian. "Defence Dilemmas: Continental Defence Cooperation from Bomarc to BMD." *Canadian Foreign Policy* 15, 1 (Winter 2008-9): 40-59.
–. "The Missing Link: Bargaining Norms, Transgovernmental Networks, and Canada-US Relations." PhD dissertation, Cornell University, 2003.
–. "Out of Ideas? Models and Strategies for Canada-US Relations." *International Journal* 62 (Winter 2006-7): 123-44.
–. "Parties and Partisanship in Canadian Defence Policy." *International Journal* 64, 1 (Winter 2008-9): 67-88.
–. "Rethinking 'Retaliation' in Canada-US Relations." In *An Independent Foreign Policy for Canada? Challenges and Choices for the Future,* ed. Brian Bow and Patrick Lennox. Toronto: University of Toronto Press, 2008.
Brooks, Stephen G., and William C. Wohlforth. "Power, Globalization, and the End of the Cold War: Re-evaluating a Landmark Case for Ideas." *International Security* 25, 3 (2000-1): 5-53.

Canada. House of Commons. *Debates.* "Appendix 'A,'" 15 April 1970, 5823-24.

–. House of Commons. *Debates.* 16 April 1970, 5941.

Cellucci, Paul. Speech to the Economic Club of Toronto, 25 March 2003. US Embassy in Canada, http://canada.usembassy.gov/content/textonly.asp?section=embconsul& document=cellucci_030325.

Chapnick, Adam. "The Golden Age: A Canadian Foreign Policy Paradox." *International Journal* 64, 1 (Winter 2008-9): 205-21.

Clarkson, Stephen. *Canada and the Reagan Challenge.* Toronto: Lorimer, 1982.

–. "Canada-US Relations and the Changing of the Guard in Ottawa." In *Canada among Nations 1984,* ed. Brian W. Tomlin and Maureen Appel Molot. Toronto: Lorimer, 1985.

–. "The Choice to Be Made." In *An Independent Foreign Policy for Canada?* ed. Stephen Clarkson. Toronto: McClelland and Stewart, 1968.

–. *Uncle Sam and Us: Globalization, Neoconservatism and the Canadian State.* Toronto: University of Toronto Press, 2002.

Cohen, Andrew. *While Canada Slept: How We Lost Our Place in the World.* Toronto: McClelland and Stewart, 2004.

Cooper, Andrew Fenton. "Playing by New Rules: Allan Gotlieb, Public Diplomacy and the Management of Canada-US Relations." *Fletcher Forum of World Affairs* 14 (1990): 93-109.

Costigliola, Frank. *France and the United States: The Cold Alliance since World War Two.* New York: Twayne Publishing, 1992.

Cox, David. "Canada and NORAD, 1958-1978: A Cautionary Retrospective." *Aurora Papers* 1 (Winter 1985): 26-33.

Cronin, Thomas E. "A Resurgent Congress and the Imperial Presidency." *Political Science Quarterly* 95 (Summer 1980): 209-37.

Cuff, R.D., and J.L. Granatstein. *American Dollars, Canadian Prosperity: Canadian-American Economic Relations, 1945-50.* Toronto: Samuel Stevens, 1978.

–. *Ties that Bind: Canada-US Cooperation during Wartime.* Toronto: Samuel Stevens, 1977.

Danchev, Alex. "On Specialness." *International Affairs* 72, 4 (1996): 703-10.

Davis, James W. *Threats and Promises: The Pursuit of International Influence.* Baltimore: The Johns Hopkins University Press, 2000.

Destler, I.M. *Managing an Alliance: The Politics of US-Japanese Relations.* Washington, DC: Brookings Institution, 1976.

–. *Presidents, Bureaucrats, and Foreign Policy.* Princeton, NJ: Princeton University Press, 1972.

Deutsch, Morton, and Robert M. Krauss. "The Effect of Threat upon Interpersonal Bargaining." *Journal of Abnormal and Social Psychology* 6 (1960): 181-89.

Dickerman, C. Robert. "Transgovernmental Challenge and Response in Scandinavia and North America." *International Organization* 30 (Spring 1979): 213-40.

Diefenbaker, John G. *One Canada: Memoirs of the Right Honourable John G. Diefenbaker,* vol. 3. Toronto: Macmillan, 1977.

Dobell, Peter C. "Negotiating with the United States." *International Journal* 36, 1 (Winter 1980-81): 18-40.

Dobson, Wendy. "Shaping the Future of the North American Economic Space: An Agenda for Action." *Border Papers (C.D. Howe Institute) 162.* April 2002.

Doern, G. Bruce, and Brian W. Tomlin. *Faith and Fear: The Free Trade Story.* Toronto: Stoddart, 1991.

Donaghy, Greg. *Tolerant Allies: Canada and the United States, 1963-1968.* Montreal and Kingston: McGill-Queen's University Press, 2002.

Doran, Charles. *Forgotten Partnership? US-Canada Relations Today.* Baltimore: The Johns Hopkins University Press, 1984.

Doran, Charles F., and Joel J. Sokolsky. *Canada and Congress: Lobbying in Washington.* Halifax: Dalhousie University Centre for Foreign Policy Studies, 1985.

Dosman, Edgar J. *The National Interest: The Politics of Northern Development, 1968-75.* Toronto: McClelland and Stewart, 1975.

Dumbrell, John. *A Special Relationship: Anglo-American Relations from the Cold War to Iraq.* Basingstoke, UK: Palgrave Macmillan, 2006.

Eaton, Mark. "Canadian Editorial Opinion and the 1963 Nuclear Weapon Acquisition Debate." *American Review of Canadian Studies* 35, 4 (Winter 2005): 641-66.

Energy, Mines and Resources Canada (EMR). *The National Energy Program.* Ottawa: Supply and Services Canada, 1980.

Evangelista, Matthew. "The Paradox of State Strength: Transnational Relations, Domestic Structures, and Security Policy in Russia and the Soviet Union." *International Organization* 49, 1 (Winter 1995): 1-38.

Fallows, James. *Blind into Baghdad: America's War in Iraq.* New York: Random House, 2006.

Fearon, James D. "Signaling Foreign Policy Interests: Tying Hands vs. Sinking Costs." *Journal of Conflict Resolution* 41 (February 1997): 68-90.

Fearon, James, and Alexander Wendt. "Rationalism vs. Constructivism: A Skeptical View." In *Handbook of International Relations,* ed. Walter Carlsnaes, Thomas Risse, and Beth A. Simmons. London: Sage, 2002.

Finnemore, Martha, and Kathryn Sikkink. "Taking Stock: The Constructivist Research Program in International Relations and Comparative Politics." *Annual Review of Political Science* 4 (2001): 391-416.

Fleming, Donald M. *So Very Near: The Political Memoirs of the Honourable Donald M. Fleming,* vol. 2. Toronto: McClelland and Stewart, 1985.

Foreign Relations of the United States, 1955-57, vol. 15. Washington, DC: US Government Printing Office, 1990.

Foreign Relations of the United States, 1961-63, vol. 13. Washington, DC: US Government Printing Office, 1992.

Fox, Annette Baker, Alfred O. Hero, and Joseph S. Nye, eds. *Canada and the United States: Transnational and Transgovernmental Relations.* New York: Columbia University Press, 1976.

Franck, Thomas M., and Edward Weisband. *Foreign Policy by Congress.* New York: Oxford University Press, 1979.

George, Alexander L., and Andrew Bennett. *Case Studies and Theory Development in the Social Sciences.* Cambridge, MA: MIT Press, 2005.

Ghent-Mallet, Jocelyn. "Deploying Nuclear Weapons." In *Canadian Foreign Policy: Selected Cases,* ed. Don Munton and John Kirton. Scarborough, ON: Prentice Hall, 1992.

Ghent-Mallet, Jocelyn, and Don Munton. "Confronting Kennedy and the Missiles in Cuba." In *Canadian Foreign Policy: Selected Cases,* ed. Don Munton and John Kirton. Scarborough, ON: Prentice Hall, 1992.

Gotlieb, Allan E. "Canada-US Relations: The Rules of the Game." *SAIS Review* 2 (Summer 1982): 172-87.

–. *I'll Be with You in a Minute, Mr. Ambassador: The Education of a Canadian Diplomat in Washington.* Toronto: University of Toronto Press, 1989.

–. "A North American Community of Law." *The Quarterly: Ideas that Matter* 2, 4 (2003): 25-30.

–. *The Washington Diaries, 1981-1989.* New York: Random House, 2006.

Granatstein, J.L., and Robert Bothwell. *Pirouette: Pierre Trudeau and Foreign Policy.* Toronto: University of Toronto Press, 1990.

Grant, George. *Lament for a Nation: The Defeat of Canadian Nationalism.* Ottawa: Carleton University Press, 1965.

Haas, Ernst. *Beyond the Nation State: Functionalism and International Integration.* Palo Alto, CA: Stanford University Press, 1964.

Habeeb, William Mark. *Power and Tactics in International Negotiation.* Baltimore: The Johns Hopkins University Press, 1988.

Haglund, David. "North American Cooperation in an Era of Homeland Security." *Orbis* 47, 4 (Autumn 2004): 675-91.

–. "The US-Canada Relationship: How 'Special' Is America's Longest Unbroken Alliance?" In *America's Special Relationships,* ed. John Dumbrell and Axel Schäfer. London: Routledge, 2009.

Hart, Michael. "Of Friends, Interests, Crowbars, and Marriage Vows in Canada-United States Trade Relations." In *Images of Canadianness: Visions on Canada's Politics, Culture, Economics,* ed. Leen D'Haenans. Ottawa: University of Ottawa Press, 1998.

–. "Steer or Drift: Taking Charge of Canada-US Regulatory Convergence." *C.D. Howe Institute Commentary,* 15 March 2006.

Hart, Michael, and Bill Dymond. *Common Borders, Shared Destinies: Canada, the United States and Deepening Integration.* Ottawa: Centre for Trade Policy and Law, 2001.

Harvey, Frank P. "The Homeland Security Dilemma: Imagination, Failure and the Escalating Costs of Perfecting Security." *Canadian Journal of Political Science* 40, 2 (June 2007): 283-316.

Head, Ivan L., and Pierre Trudeau. *The Canadian Way: Shaping Canada's Foreign Policy, 1968-84.* Toronto: McClelland and Stewart, 1995.

Heeney, A.D.P., and Livingston T. Merchant. *Canada and the United States: Principles for Partnership.* Ottawa: Queen's Printer, 1965.

Helliwell, John F., Mary MacGregor, and André Plourde. "The National Energy Program Meets Falling World Oil Prices." *Canadian Public Policy* 9 (Summer 1983): 284-96.

Helliwell, John F., and Robert D. McRae. "Resolving the Energy Conflict: From the National Energy Program to the Energy Agreements." *Canadian Public Policy* 8 (Winter 1982): 14-23.

Higginbotham, John, and Jeff Heynen. "Managing through Networks: The State of Canada-US Relations." In *Canada among Nations 2004: Setting Priorities Straight,* ed. David Carment, Fen Osler Hampson, and Norman Hillmer. Montreal and Kingston: McGill-Queen's University Press, 2005.

Hilliker, John, and Don Barry. *Canada's Department of External Affairs,* vol. 2. Montreal and Kingston: McGill-Queen's University Press, 1995.

Hillmer, Norman, and J.L. Granatstein. *Empire to Umpire: Canada and the World to the 1990s.* Toronto: Copp Clark Longman, 1994.

Hockin, Thomas A. "Canada's 'Mass Legitimate' Parties and Their Implications for Party Leaders." In *Apex of Power,* 2nd ed., ed. Thomas A. Hockin. Scarborough, ON: Prentice Hall, 1977.

Hollick, Ann L. "Canadian-American Relations: Law of the Sea." *International Organization* 28 (Autumn 1974): 755-80.

Holmes, John W. *Life with Uncle: The Canadian-American Relationship.* Toronto: University of Toronto Press, 1981.

Holsti, K.J. "Canada and the United States." In *Conflict in World Politics,* ed. Steven Spiegel and Kenneth Waltz. Cambridge, UK: Winthrop, 1971.

Holsti, K.J., and Thomas Allen Levy. "Bilateral Institutions and Transgovernmental Relations between Canada and the United States." In *Canada and the United States: Transnational and Transgovernmental Relations,* ed. Annette Baker Fox, Alfred O. Hero and Joseph Nye. New York: Columbia University Press, 1976.

Ikenberry, G. John. *After Victory: Institutions, Strategic Restraint and the Rebuilding of Order after Major Wars.* Princeton, NJ: Princeton University Press, 2000.

–. "An Institutional Approach to American Foreign Economic Policy." *International Organization* 42 (Winter 1988): 219-43.

Independent Panel on Canada's Future Role in Afghanistan. *Final Report.* Ottawa: Queen's Printer, 2008.

Jewett, Pauline. "The Menace Is the Message." In *An Independent Foreign Policy for Canada?* ed. Stephen Clarkson. Toronto: McClelland and Stewart, 1968.

Jockel, Joseph T. "Canada and the United States: Still Calm in the 'Remarkable Relationship.'" In *Canada among Nations 1996,* ed. Fen Osler Hampson and Maureen Appel Molot. Ottawa: Carleton University Press, 1996.

–. *No Boundaries Upstairs: Canada, the United States, and the Origins of North American Air Defence, 1945-58.* Vancouver: UBC Press, 1987.

Johnston, Alistair Iain. "Thinking about Strategic Cultures." *International Security* 19, 4 (October 1995): 32-64.

–. "Treating International Institutions as Social Environments." *International Studies Quarterly* 45, 4 (November 2001): 487-515.

Jones, David T. "Canada and the US in the Chrétien Years: Edging toward Confrontation." *Policy Options* (November 2002): 33-43.

Katzenstein, Peter J., Robert O. Keohane, and Stephen D. Krasner. *"International Organization and the Study of World Politics." International Organization* 52, 4 (Autumn 1998): 645-85.

Keohane, Robert O., and Joseph S. Nye Jr. *Power and Interdependence: World Politics in Transition.* Boston: Little, Brown, 1977.

–. *"Power and Interdependence* Revisited." *International Organization* 41 (Summer 1987): 725-53.

–. "Transgovernmental Relations and World Politics: An Introduction." *World Politics* 27, 1 (October 1974): 39-62.

Khong, Yuen Foong. "Neoconservatism and the Domestic Sources of American Foreign Policy: The Role of Ideas in Operation Iraqi Freedom." In *Foreign Policy: Theories, Actors and Cases*, ed. Steve Smith, Amelia Hadfield, and Timothy Dunne. Toronto: Oxford University Press, 2008.

Kirkey, Christopher J. "The Arctic Waters Pollution Prevention Initiatives: Canada's Response to an American Challenge." *International Journal of Canadian Studies* 13 (1996): 51-59.

Kirshner, Jonathan. *Currency and Coercion: The Political Economy of International Monetary Power.* Princeton, NJ: Princeton University Press, 1997.

Kirton, John J. "The Consequences of Integration: The Case of the Defence Production Sharing Agreements." In *Continental Community? Independence and Integration in North America*, ed. Andrew W. Axline et al. Toronto: McClelland and Stewart, 1974.

Kirton, John J., and Don Munton. "The *Manhattan* Voyages and Their Aftermath." In *The Politics of the Northwest Passage*, ed. Franklyn Griffiths. Montreal and Kingston: McGill-Queen's University Press, 1987.

Kissinger, Henry. *White House Years.* New York: Little, Brown, 1978.

Kolodziej, Edward. *French International Policy under de Gaulle and Pompidou.* Ithaca, NY: Cornell University Press, 1974.

Lebow, Richard Ned. "What's So Different about a Counterfactual?" *World Politics* 52 (July 2000): 550-85.

Lennox, Patrick. *At Home and Abroad: The Canada-US Relationship and Canada's Place in the World.* Vancouver: UBC Press, 2009.

Lentner, Howard H. "Foreign Policy Decision-Making: The Case of Canada and Nuclear Weapons." *World Politics* 29 (October 1976): 29-66.

Leyton-Brown, David. *Weathering the Storm: Canadian-US Relations, 1980-83.* Toronto and Washington, DC: Canadian-American Committee, 1985.

Lyon, Peyton V. *Canada in World Affairs. Vol. 12, 1961-63.* Toronto: Oxford University Press, 1968.

Mahant, Edelgard, and Graeme S. Mount. *Invisible and Inaudible in Washington: American Policies toward Canada.* Vancouver: UBC Press, 1999.

Malmgren, Harald B. "Storm Flags Up for Canadian Business." *World Business Outlook* 3 (1981): 4-5.

March, James G., and Johan P. Olsen. *Rediscovering Institutions: The Institutional Basis of Politics.* New York: Free Press, 1989.

Martin, Lawrence. *The Presidents and the Prime Ministers.* Toronto: Doubleday, 1982.

Martin, Paul. *A Very Public Life. Vol. 2, So Many Worlds.* Toronto: Deneau, 1985.

McConchie, Roger D., and Robert S. Reid. "Canadian Foreign Policy and International Straits." In *Canadian Foreign Policy and the Law of the Sea*, ed. Barbara Johnson and Mark Zacher. Vancouver: UBC Press, 1977.

McElroy, Robert W. *Morality and American Foreign Policy.* Princeton, NJ: Princeton University Press, 1993.

McKinsey, Lauren S. "Détente in Canada's Energy War." *American Review of Canadian Studies* 12 (Summer 1982): 98-119.

McLaren, Roy. "Canadian Views on the US Government Reaction to the National Energy Program." *Canadian Public Policy* 8 (Supplement, 1982): 492-94.

Melakopides, Costas. *Pragmatic Idealism: Canadian Foreign Policy, 1945-95* (Montreal and Kingston: McGill-Queen's University Press, 1998.

M'Gonigle, R. Michael, and Mark Zacher. "Canadian Foreign Policy and the Control of Marine Pollution." In *Canadian Foreign Policy and the Law of the Sea,* ed. Barbara Johnson and Mark Zacher. Vancouver: UBC Press, 1977.

Michaud, Nelson, and Kim Richard Nossal. "Diplomatic Departures? Assessing the Conservative Era in Foreign Policy." In *Diplomatic Departures: The Conservative Era in Canadian Foreign Policy, 1984-93,* ed. Nelson Michaud and Kim Richard Nossal. Vancouver: UBC Press, 2001.

Moravcsik, Andrew. "Is Something Rotten in the State of Denmark? Constructivism and European Integration." *Journal of European Public Policy* 6, 4 (1999): 669-81.

Morgenthau, Hans J. *Politics among Nations,* 3rd ed. New York: Knopf, 1973.

Munro, John A., and Alex I. Inglis, eds. *Mike: Memoirs of the Right Honourable Lester B. Pearson,* vol. 3. Toronto: University of Toronto Press, 1975.

Munton, Don. "Going Fission: Tales and Truths about Canada's Nuclear Weapons." *International Journal* 51 (Summer 1996): 506-28.

Munton, Don, and R.B. Byers. "Canadian Defence, Nuclear Arms, and Public Opinion: Consensus and Controversy." Paper presented to the Annual Meeting of the Canadian Political Science Association, Vancouver, 1983.

Nash, Knowlton. *Kennedy and Diefenbaker: Fear and Loathing across the Undefended Border.* Toronto: McClelland and Stewart, 1990.

Newman, Peter C. *The Distemper of Our Times.* Toronto: McClelland and Stewart, 1968.

Nivola, Pietro S. "The New Protectionism: US Policy in Historical Perspective." *Political Science Quarterly* 101, 4 (Fall 1986): 577-600.

Noble, John J. "Canada-US Relations in the Post-Iraq War Era: Stop the Drift towards Irrelevance," *Policy Options* 24 (May 2003): 19-24.

Norris, Robert S., Robert S. Burrows, and Richard W. Fieldhouse. *Nuclear Weapons Databook. Vol. 5, British, French, and Chinese Nuclear Weapons.* Boulder, CO: Westview Press, 1994.

North, Kenneth. "Canadian Oil and Gas – Surplus or Shortage?" In *Energy Policy: The Global Challenge,* ed. Peter Nemetz. Ottawa: Institute for Research on Public Policy, 1980.

Nossal, Kim Richard. "Defence Policy and the Atmospherics of Canada-US Relations." *American Review of Canadian Studies* 37, 1 (Spring 2007): 23-34.

–. "The PM and the SSEA in Canada's Foreign Policy: Dividing the Territory, 1968-1994." *International Journal* 50 (Winter 1994-95): 189-208.

Odell, John S. *Negotiating the World Economy.* Ithaca, NY: Cornell University Press, 2000.

O'Neill, Kate. "How Two Cows Make a Crisis: US-Canada Trade Relations and Mad Cow Disease." *American Review of Canadian Studies* 35, 2 (Summer 2005): 295-319.

Owen, John M. "How Liberalism Produces Democratic Peace." *International Security* 19, 2 (1994): 87-124.

Oye, Kenneth A. "The Domain of Choice: International Constraints and Carter Administration Foreign Policy." In *Eagle Entangled: US Foreign Policy in a Complex World,* ed. Kenneth Oye, Donald Rothchild, and Robert J. Lieber. New York: Longman, 1979.

Page, Don. "The Representation of China in the United Nations: Canadian Perspectives and Initiatives, 1949-1971." In *Reluctant Adversaries: Canada and the People's Republic of China,* ed. Paul M. Evans and Michael B. Frolic. Toronto: University of Toronto Press, 1991.

Plumptre, A.F.W. "Tit for Tat." In *An Independent Foreign Policy for Canada?* ed. Stephen Clarkson. Toronto: McClelland and Stewart, 1968.

Putnam, Robert D. "Diplomacy and Domestic Politics: The Logic of Two-Level Games." *International Organization* 42 (Summer 1988): 427-60.

Rashish, Myer. "North American Economic Relations." *Department of State Bulletin* 81 (November 1981): 24-28.

Reus-Smit, Christian. "The Constitutional Structure of International Society and the Nature of Fundamental Institutions." *International Organization* 51, 3 (Fall 1997): 555-89.

Richter, Andrew. "From Trusted Ally to Suspicious Neighbor: Canada-US Relations in a Changing Global Environment." *American Review of Canadian Studies* 35, 3 (Autumn 2005): 471-502.

Risse-Kappen, Thomas. *Cooperation among Democracies: The European Influence on US Foreign Policy.* Princeton, NJ: Princeton University Press, 1997.

–. "Ideas Do Not Float Freely: Transnational Coalitions, Domestic Structures and the End of the Cold War." *International Organization* 48 (Spring 1994): 185-214.
–. "Introduction." In *Bringing Transnational Relations Back in*, ed. Thomas Risse-Kappen. Cambridge, UK: Cambridge University Press, 1995.
Robinson, H. Basil. *Diefenbaker's World: A Populist in Foreign Affairs*. Toronto: University of Toronto Press, 1989.
Rotstein, Abraham. "Canada: The New Nationalism." *Foreign Affairs* 55 (October 1976): 97-118.
Roussel, Stéphane. *The North American Democratic Peace: Absence of War and Security Institution-Building in Canada-US Relations, 1867-1958*. Montreal and Kingston: McGill-Queen's University Press, 2004.
Rudalevige, Andrew. *The New Imperial Presidency?* Ann Arbor: University of Michigan Press, 2005.
Rudd, David. "Muddling Through on Missile Defence: The Politics of Indecision." *Policy Options* 26, 4 (May 2005): 30-34.
Safarian, A.E. "The Web of Repercussions." In *An Independent Foreign Policy for Canada?* ed. Stephen Clarkson. Toronto: McClelland and Stewart, 1968.
Sandelius, Stephen, and Charles R. Foster. "Economic Shift to Sunbelt Reflected in Foreign Policy." *International Perspectives* (May/June 1981): 11-14.
Schattschneider, E.E. *The Semisovereign People: A Realist's View of Democracy in America*. Hinsdale, IL: Dryden Press, 1960.
Schimmelfennig, Frank. *The EU, NATO and the Integration of Europe*. Cambridge, UK: Cambridge University Press, 2003.
Shore, Sean M. "No Fences Make Good Neighbors: The Development of the Canadian-US Security Community, 1871-1940." In *Security Communities*, ed. Emanuel Adler and Michael N. Barnett. Cambridge, UK: Cambridge University Press, 1998.
Smith, Denis. *Gentle Patriot: A Political Biography of Walter Gordon*. Edmonton: Hurtig, 1973.
Stairs, Denis. "Liberalism and the Triumph of Efficiency in Canada-US Relations." *ISUMA* 1, 1 (Spring 2000): 11-16.
–. "Myths, Morals and Reality in Canadian Foreign Policy." *International Journal* 58 (Spring 2003): 239-56.
–. "The Political Culture of Canadian Foreign Policy." *Canadian Journal of Political Science* 15 (December 1982): 667-90.
Stein, Arthur A. "The Politics of Linkage." *World Politics* 33 (October 1980): 62-81.
Stein, Janice Gross, and Eugene Lang. *The Unexpected War: Canada in Afghanistan*. Toronto: Viking Canada, 2007.
Sundelius, Bengt. "Coping with Transnationalism in Northern Europe." *West European Politics* 3 (May 1980): 219-29.
Swanson, Roger Frank. "The Ford Interlude and the US-Canada Relationship." *American Review of Canadian Studies* 8 (Spring 1978): 3-17.
Tannenwald, Nina. "The Nuclear Taboo: The United States and the Normative Basis of Nuclear Non-Use." *International Organization* 53 (Summer 1999): 433-68.
Tetlock, Philip, and Aaron Belkin. "Counterfactual Thought Experiments in World Politics." In *Counterfactual Thought Experiments in World Politics*, ed. Philip Tetlock and Aaron Belkin. Princeton, NJ: Princeton University Press, 1996.
Thompson, John Herd, and Stephen J. Randall. *Canada and the United States: Ambivalent Allies*, 3rd ed. Athens: University of Georgia Press, 2002.
Toner, Glen, and François Bregha. "The Political Economy of Energy." In *Canadian Politics in the 1980s*, ed. Michael S. Whittington and Glen Williams. Toronto: Methuen, 1981.
United States Cabinet Task Force on Oil Import Control (USCTFOIC). *The Oil Import Question: A Report on the Relationship of Oil Imports and the National Security*. Washington, DC: US Government Printing Office, 1970.
Vucetic, Srdjan. "Why Did Canada Sit Out the Iraq War? One Constructivist Analysis." *Canadian Foreign Policy* 13, 1 (December 2006): 133-53.
Wagner, R. Harrison. "Economic Interdependence, Bargaining Power, and Political Influence." *International Organization* 42 (Summer 1988): 461-83.

Walt, Stephen M. "Taming American Power." *Foreign Affairs* 84, 5 (September/October 2005): 105-20.

Wolfe, Robert. "See You in Washington? A Pluralist Perspective on North American Institutions." *Choices* 9, 4 (2003).

Wolfers, Arnold. *Collaboration and Discord.* Baltimore: The Johns Hopkins University Press, 1962.

Wonder, Edward F. "Canada-US Energy Relations." In *The United States and Canada: Dependence and Divergence,* ed. the Atlantic Council Working Group on US and Canada. Cambridge, MA: Ballinger, 1982.

–. "The US Government Response to the Canadian National Energy Program." *Canadian Public Policy* 8 (Supplement, 1982): 468-92.

Wyman, Donald L. "Dependence and Conflict: US Relations with Mexico, 1920-1975." In *Diplomatic Dispute: US Conflict with Iran, Japan, and Mexico,* ed. Robert L. Paarlberg et al. Cambridge, MA: Harvard University Center for International Affairs, 1978.

Zeiler, Thomas W. *American Trade and Power in the 1960s.* New York: Columbia University Press, 1962.

News Reports and Opinion Pieces

Alberts, Sheldon. "Anti-US Rhetoric Risky, Cellucci Warns." *Globe and Mail,* 1 December 2005, A9.

–. "PM: War Stance was 'Principled.'" *National Post,* 9 April 2003, A1.

–. "Powell Urges Canada to Join Iraq Coalition." *National Post,* 15 November 2002, A1.

–. "US Cuts Canada Out of Iraq Work." *National Post,* 10 December 2003, A1.

–. "US Relents on Border Checks." *National Post,* 17 April 2003, A1.

Atkinson, Rick, and Barton Gellman. "Iraq Trying to Shelter Jets in Iran, US Says." *Washington Post,* 29 January 1991, A1.

Beaumont, Peter, et al. "US to Punish German 'Treachery.'" *(London) Observer,* 16 February 2003, 25.

Best, John. "Nixon Was So Angry He Refused Trudeau's Call." *Globe and Mail,* 25 August 1973, 7.

Bloom, Richard. "Boycott of Canada Unlikely, Poll Finds." *Globe and Mail,* 14 April 2003, A8.

Brockes, Emma. "What Can Eritrea Possibly Do to Help the US in Iraq?" *(Manchester) Guardian,* 20 March 2003. http://www.guardian.co.uk/world/2003/mar/20/iraq.emmabrockes.

Bryden, Joan. "US Won't Hold Grudge on Iraq, PM's Aide Says." *Ottawa Citizen,* 15 March 2003, A4.

Campbell, Murray. "Nation's Grief Turns to Anger." *Globe and Mail,* 19 April 2002, A1, A7.

"'Canada Can't Moan Over Oil Cuts' – Greene." *Ottawa Citizen,* 11 March 1970, 1, 21.

"Canada's Decision No Surprise to Bush: PM." *CBC News Online,* 18 March 2003. http://www.cbc.ca/stories/print/2003/03/18/Iraq.

Carson-Parker, John. "Stop Worrying about the Canadian Invasion." *Fortune,* 19 October 1981, 200.

Cienski, Jan. "Canada Might Not Wait for UN." *National Post,* 10 January 2003, A1.

Dawson, Anne. "Canada Will Be Left Out of First Contracts in Iraq: Powell." *National Post,* 26 April 2003, A2.

Den Tandt, Michael. "Presto! Canada-US Trade Fears Go Up in Smoke." *Globe and Mail,* 8 April 2003, A19.

"Envoy Links Bush Snub to War Policy." *Toronto Star,* 17 April 2003, A11.

Evans, Rowland, and Robert Novak. "Mitchell, Heeding Oilmen's Pleas, Killed Move to Ease Import Quotas." *Washington Post,* 12 January 1970, 22.

Fagan, Drew. "Martin's House Divided on Ties with Bush." *Globe and Mail,* 10 March 2004, A5.

Fekete, Jason, and Stephen Thorne. "Top-Level General Quits Army in Wake of Afghan Deployment." *National Post,* 15 February 2003, A17.

Francis, Diane. "Expect Severe Consequences from Anti-US Stance: Failure to Back US War Effort Is Foreign Policy Disaster." *National Post,* 8 April 2003, FP3.

Galloway, Gloria. "Canadians Oppose War in Iraq without UN." *Globe and Mail*, 18 January 2003, A10.

Giniger, Henry. "Canada Acts to Curb American Acquisitions." *New York Times*, 30 July 1981, D1.

–. "Canada Ties: Relations with US are 'Full of Tensions.'" *New York Times*, 21 September 1981, A11.

–. "Canada's New Budget is Assailed." *New York Times*, 30 June 1982, D1.

–. "Canadian Oil Plans Bring US Objection." *New York Times*, 9 November 1980, 17.

–. "Energy Bill Passes Test in Canada." *New York Times*, 10 December 1981, D1.

Gorham, Beth. "US OK with Canada's Stance." *Halifax Chronicle-Herald*, 26 February 2003, A1.

Gotlieb, Allan E. "Never Play Leapfrog with a Unicorn." *National Post*, 9 April 2001, 18.

Granatstein, J.L. "The Empire Strikes Back." *National Post*, 26 March 2003, A15.

Handelman, Stephen. "The Big Chill." *Time*, 7 April 2003, 57.

Harper, Tim. "Liberal Dissent Brewing in Iraq Crisis." *Toronto Star*, 14 January 2003, A1.

"Harper Calls for Action on Mad Cow Crisis." *CBC News Online*, 7 September 2007. http://www.cbc.ca/canada/story/2004/09/07/harper_bse040907.html.

Hart, Michael. "Canada Blew It." *Financial Post*, 12 February 2008, A12.

Higgins, Michael. "72% Believe Canada Should Have Backed War." *National Post*, 8 April 2003, A1.

Hodge, Nathan. "Fight Brewing over 'Buy American' Legislation." *Defense Week*, 23 June 2003, 9.

Honderich, John. "How Reagan Might Lower the Boom on Us: Energy Policy and FIRA Have Americans in a Rage." *Toronto Star*, 29 August 1981, A1.

Immen, Wallace. "Canadian Public Skeptical of War in Iraq, Poll Shows." *Globe and Mail*, 19 July 2003, A1.

Knowlton, Brian. "Mexico and Canada Assess the Cost of Having Opposed War in Iraq." *New York Times*, 17 April 2003, A5.

Laghi, Brian. "Martin Charts New Course with US: Public Opinion Made Relationship Frosty despite Early Promises to Turn Down Heat." *Globe and Mail*, 16 December 2005, A1.

LeBlanc, Daniel. "Canada Takes Afghan Mission." *Globe and Mail*, 13 February 2003, A1.

LeBlanc, Daniel, and Gloria Galloway. "Washington Scolds Ottawa: US Tired of Canadian Attacks on Environment, Trade Policies." *Globe and Mail*, 14 December 2005, A1.

Lewington, Jennifer. "Energy Projects Hurt by Disputes." *Globe and Mail*, 28 December 1981, A8.

Lynch, Charles. "Secret US Paper – Ace Up PM's Sleeve." *Vancouver Province*, 27 March 1963, 1.

McCallum, Anthony. "Oil Companies Shifting Funds to Frontier." *Globe and Mail*, 4 January 1982, A4.

McCarthy, Shawn, and Daniel LeBlanc. "PM Scolds McCallum on Canada's Role in Iraq." *Globe and Mail*, 16 January 2003, A1.

McKenzie, Donald. "Canadians Still Leery of Bush Invasion Plan." *National Post*, 9 September 2002, A4.

Muravchik, Joshua. "Why We Are Better Off without that UN Resolution." *Wall Street Journal*, 18 March 2003, A20.

Nickle's Daily Oil Bulletin, 15 September 1981.

Olive, David. "Canada Has Leverage with US." *Hamilton Spectator*, 1 April 2003, B4.

Partridge, John. "US Lets Canada in on Iraq Bidding." *Globe and Mail*, 14 December 2003, A9.

"Passport Delay Is Good for Us All." *Montreal Gazette*, 27 December 2007, A28.

Pine, Art, and Frederick Rose. "Neighborly Feud." *Wall Street Journal*, 6 August 1981, A10.

"Powell Reassures Canadians on Iraq Dispute." *Agence France-Presse*, 25 April 2003.

Russo, Robert. "Latest Nixon Tapes Show Contempt for Trudeau." *Globe and Mail*, 18 March 2002, A2.

Sallot, Jeff. "Chrétien Faces Caucus Revolt over Iraq Crisis." *Globe and Mail*, 11 February 2003, A4.

–. "PM Aims to Broker UN Deal." *Globe and Mail,* 20 February 2003, A8.

–. "Proposed Iraq Briefing Had Canada Skeptical." *Globe and Mail,* 12 March 2004, A10.

Shanahan, Eileen. "Washington Hopeful of Averting Tariff War with Europeans." *New York Times,* 8 August 1963, 1, 32.

Sharp, Mitchell. "A Ship and Sovereignty in the North." *Globe and Mail,* 18 September 1969, 7.

Shribman, David. "Canada-US Irritants Rub Both Ways." *New York Times,* 29 November 1981, E6.

Solomon, Hyman. "US Steps Up Its Drive to 'Punish' Us." *Financial Post,* 22 August 1981, A1.

Stein, Janice Gross, and Eugene Lang. "Our Man in Iraq: Did Canada Really Stay Out of War in Iraq?" *Globe and Mail,* 12 October 2007, A19.

Stephens, Robert. "Trade Trouble: Protectionist Policies Fuel US Resentment." *Globe and Mail,* 15 July 1981, A2.

Stewart, Sinclair. "Rift over Iraq Expected to Heal." *Globe and Mail,* 7 April 2003, B1.

Tedesco, Theresa. "CEOs March to Washington to Avert Crisis." *National Post,* 7 April 2003, A3.

"US Raises Duties as a Retaliation for Chicken Levy." *New York Times,* 5 December 1963, 1, 30.

Van Praet, Nicholas. "CAE Fears Canada's Iraq Stance: Military Contracts Could Be at Risk." *Montreal Gazette,* 8 May 2003, B1.

Vulliamy, Ed, et al. "America the Arm Twister." *(Manchester) Guardian,* 2 March 2003, 51.

Ward, Kevin. "Chrétien: Stance on Iraq Was Right." *Halifax Chronicle-Herald,* 31 March 2004, A1.

Wattie, Chris. "Ottawa Offered to Join Iraq War: Proposal to US to Send 600-800 Soldiers Dropped Suddenly in Favour of Afghan Plan," *National Post,* 27 November 2004, A1.

"Welcoming Mr. Trudeau." *Wall Street Journal,* 9 July 1981, 29.

Whittington, Les. "Economy at Risk in US Tiff, Beatty Says." *Toronto Star,* 29 March 2003, A1.

Wines, Michael. "Putin Again Rejects US Calls for Support of a War." *New York Times,* 1 March 2003, A8.

Index

Printed and bound in Canada by Friesens

Set in Stone by Artegraphica Design Co. Ltd.

Copy editor: Francis Chow

Proofreader: Amelia Gilliland

ENVIRONMENTAL BENEFITS STATEMENT

UBC Press saved the following resources by printing the pages of this book on chlorine free paper made with 100% post-consumer waste.

TREES	WATER	SOLID WASTE	GREENHOUSE GASES
5	**2,275**	**138**	**472**
FULLY GROWN	GALLONS	POUNDS	POUNDS

Calculations based on research by Environmental Defense and the Paper Task Force.
Manufactured at Friesens Corporation